W9-CGR-634

ENCYCLOPEDIA OF

FAMILY HEALTH

ENCYCLOPEDIA OF

FAMILY HEALTH

CONSULTANT
DAVID B. JACOBY, MD
JOHNS HOPKINS SCHOOL OF MEDICINE

VOLUME
10

OCCUPATIONAL HAZARDS—PERSONALITY

MARSHALL CAVENDISH
NEW YORK · LONDON · TORONTO · SYDNEY

Marshall Cavendish Corporation

99 White Plains Road

Tarrytown, New York 10591-9001

© Marshall Cavendish Corporation, 1998

© Marshall Cavendish Limited 1998, 1991, 1988, 1986, 1983, 1982, 1971

Update by Brown Partworks

The material in this set was first published in the English language by
Marshall Cavendish Limited of 119 Wardour Street, London W1V 3TD, England.

Printed and bound in Italy

Library of Congress Cataloging-in-Publication Data

Encyclopedia of family health
17v. cm.
Includes index
1. Medicine, Popular–Encyclopedias. 2. Health–Encyclopedias. I. Marshall Cavendish Corporation.
RC81.A2M336 1998   96–49537
610'. 3–dc21   CIP
ISBN 0-7614-0625-5 (set)
ISBN 0-7614-0635-2 (v.10)

INTRODUCTION

We Americans live under a constant bombardment of information (and misinformation) about the latest supposed threats to our health. We are taught to believe that disease is the result of not taking care of ourselves. Death becomes optional. Preventive medicine becomes a moral crusade, illness the punishment for the foolish excesses of the American lifestyle. It is not the intent of the authors of this encyclopedia to contribute to this atmosphere. While it is undoubtedly true that Americans could improve their health by smoking less, exercising more, and controlling their weight, this is already widely understood.

As Mencken put it, "It is not the aim of medicine to make men virtuous. The physician should not preach salvation, he should offer absolution." The aims of this encyclopedia are to present a summary of human biology, anatomy, and physiology, to outline the more common diseases, and to discuss, in a general way, the diagnosis and treatment of these diseases. This is not a do-it-yourself book. It will not be possible to treat most conditions based on the information presented here. But it will be possible to understand most diseases and their treatments. Informed in this way, you will be able to discuss your condition and its treatment with your physician. It is also hoped that this will alleviate some of the fears associated with diseases, doctors, and hospitals.

The authors of this encyclopedia have also attempted to present, in an open-minded way, alternative therapies. There is undoubtedly value to some of these. However, when dealing with serious diseases, they should not be viewed as a substitute for conventional treatment. The reason that conventional treatment is accepted is that it has been systematically tested, and because scientific evidence backs it up. It would be a tragedy to miss the opportunity for effective treatment while pursuing an ineffective alternative therapy.

Finally, it should be remembered that the word *doctor* is originally from the Latin word for "teacher." Applied to medicine, this should remind us that the doctor's duty is not only to diagnose and treat disease, but to help the patient to understand. If this encyclopedia can aid in this process, its authors will be gratified.

DAVID B. JACOBY, MD
JOHNS HOPKINS SCHOOL OF MEDICINE

CONTENTS

Occupational hazards	1232	Pacemaker	1300
Occupational therapy	1238	Pain	1302
Ointments	1240	Pain management	1306
Open-heart surgery	1242	Painkillers	1308
Operating room	1245	Palate	1311
Ophthalmology	1248	Pancreas	1314
Optic nerve	1250	Pap smear	1316
Optometrist	1252	Paralysis	1318
Oral contraceptives	1254	Paraplegia	1322
Organ removal	1258	Parasites	1326
Orgasm	1260	Parathyroid glands	1331
Orthodontics	1262	Parkinson's disease	1334
Orthopedics	1267	Pathology	1336
Osteoarthritis	1272	Pediatrics	1340
Osteopathy	1276	Pelvic inflammatory disease	1346
Osteoporosis	1280	Pelvis	1348
Otitis	1282	Penicillin	1353
Outpatients	1284	Penis	1356
Ovaries	1288	Peritoneum	1358
Overdoses	1290	Pernicious anemia	1362
Oxygen	1293	Personality	1364
Ozone layer	1296		

Occupational hazards

Q I read somewhere that inhaling some kinds of dust found at work can be dangerous. Why is this?

A While it is not desirable to have any foreign particles entering the lungs, some dusts are more dangerous than others. A stonecutter who works only with marble and inhales its dust has practically no chance of getting lung disease. However, if he were chipping away at sandstone, the risk of lung disease and death caused by the dust would be great. The reason for these differences is not fully understood. Many dusts, such as asbestos, are a special danger and can cause cancer of the lung and the pleura (lining of the lung), as well as the disabling disease asbestosis. (Note that the use of asbestos in building and industry is now strictly controlled.)

Q Are computer screens harmful to health? I have heard mixed reports about their safety?

A Reports on the risks to health from radiation as a result of using computers are very mixed, but prolonged use of terminals may encourage physical problems such as eyestrain, headaches, pain in the back, neck, arms, and fingers (carpal tunnel syndrome) to more general stress. Many of these ailments are avoided if the terminal is set in a properly designed workstation. Regular breaks should be taken away from the computer screen, with at least 10 minutes' rest every hour.

Q We have a representative in our office who is solely concerned with health and safety. Why do we need one?

A Every year thousands of office staff are injured at work. Half the injuries are caused by falls, such as tripping over trailing wires or carelessly placed objects on stairs. Accidents of this kind can be prevented quite easily, and a safety representative is very helpful in assessing the potential dangers to staff and advising the management accordingly.

Every year, occupational hazards result in disease, injury, and sometimes death. There is a variety of potential problems and many can be prevented.

Health hazards associated with work have existed for centuries. In the last few hundred years, with the development of industrialization, very specific occupational hazards have been recognized. While industry was slow to acknowledge and deal with the problems, safety measures are now regarded as a high priority by many employers and trade unions.

Apart from the personal toll that such occupational disease and injury can bring, there is a heavy economic price to pay. Millions of working days are lost each year in the US through work-related health problems.

Many of the most serious occupational hazards have been brought under control by legislation. However, the risks can never be eliminated completely as new products and working methods are devised and tried.

There is also the reality that accidents with machinery can never be totally eliminated because of human error. However, these accidents can be minimized. Employers should ensure that the safety standards are maintained and members of staff should always adhere to safety regulations.

Zefa

Hazardous materials

Occupational hazards may arise with the use of gases, liquids, or solids. Substances can enter the body through the lungs.

One dangerous metal is lead, a toxic substance that has been used in the manufacture of batteries, rubber, paint, roofing, and soldering material. It can enter the body through the inhalation of small dust particles and fumes or by ingestion (see Lead poisoning).

The earliest symptoms may include fatigue, headache, loss of appetite, constipation and mild abdominal pain. Acute poisoning can result in severe abdominal

Some occupations are more dangerous than others. Mining (left) exposes workers to coal dust and tunnel collapses; construction work (above) can lead to falls.

pain, muscle weakness, kidney damage, convulsions, coma, and death.

Mercury, a silver-colored liquid which has been used in some thermometers, is another hazardous metal. It has been used in the electrical industry to manufacture fluorescent lamps and precision instruments, as well as in dentistry.

Mercury poisoning causes jerky movements starting in the fingers, irritability, and drowsiness. In the final stage, the person becomes disturbed. Other symptoms include sore throat and gums, vomiting, and diarrhea. Compounds from mercury can also be dangerous when they occur in the form of industrial effluents which are absorbed by fish we eat. These can cause blindness, mental deterioration, lack of coordination, birth defects, and even death.

Cadmium, a soft metal that is used for increasing the hardness of copper, and as a protective plating for other metals is particularly dangerous. Once a person has inhaled or ingested a certain amount, there is no known cure. Poisoning can be gradual because the amount of metal in the body builds up slowly. However, at a critical point the lungs and the kidneys will cease to function properly, causing death (see Poisoning).

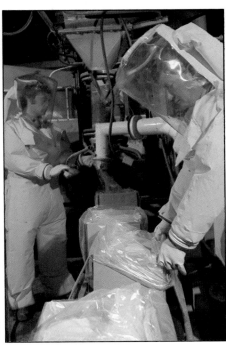

Deep sea diving (above left) can cause the bends. Industries such as smelting (below) and chemical manufacturing (above right) expose workers to very high temperatures as well as poisonous fumes. Numerous laws relating to work safety have been enacted to protect workers and also help prevent serious injuries.

1233

Q I work shifts and often have to work nights. Will this affect my health?

A About 20 percent of people enjoy working nights, while another 20 percent dislike it intensely and have to quit. No studies have shown any difference in causes of death between day and night workers. However, if you have been working during the day and then are put onto a night shift, it can take time for your body to adapt. Problems include digestive disorders, fatigue, and an increase in accidents.

Q I work near a very hot furnace. Am I in danger from very high temperatures?

A Normally the body can adapt to raised temperatures, but if your job also involves physical labor, and if the salt and water lost during sweating are not replaced, you may suffer from heat stroke, or heat syncope, leading to loss of consciousness. Treatment for both conditions involves cooling the body and also rest. If you become used to high temperatures, heat tolerance is likely to be greater and the chance of heat stroke reduced.

Q I am a smoker. Can this increase the risk of getting a work-related disease?

A Yes. There is much evidence now against smoking and it is likely to increase the risk of your developing a number of health problems. One problem is smoking damages the airways, undermining the natural defense of the lungs. This allows harmful substances easier access into your body.

Q Why are substances believed to cause cancer still being used in industry?

A It is not possible to eliminate these substances entirely from many industrial processes. But the Occupational Health and Safety Administration constantly studies these substances to establish safe levels, and safeguards to protect workers. Some companies do not follow these guidelines, but in doing so they risk legal action.

Chromium, a silver-white, hard, brittle metal, is used to make various steels including stainless steel, and high-speed tools. Its compounds are used in chrome plating as well as the production of pigments in paints and inks. It is also used in leather tanning, in timber preservation, and in photography and dyestuffs. The major danger of chromium is that even slight contact with dilute solutions can cause skin ulcers (see Ulcers).

The inhalation of fine droplets or mist containing chromium salts can cause ulcers inside the nose. Although lung cancer has not been associated with chrome plating, it has been linked with the manufacture of chromates. Asthmatic symptoms can occur, as can a chrome sensitivity—a strong reaction to chrome following symptoms of exposure.

Many liquids are classed as solvents, and employees in nearly all occupations are exposed to them. Solvents evaporate very quickly, and the vapors can enter the body by inhalation through the lungs, the skin, and more rarely, through the digestive system. Once they enter the body, they can attack the liver, the heart, the lungs, and the nervous system.

Solvents are found in inks, varnishes, glues, cleaners, dry-cleaning fluids, and many other substances. Some of the most dangerous ones may be pleasant to smell, while others which are foul-smelling can be quite harmless.

Trichlorethylene smells good but it can lead to loss of consciousness and death. Benzene is another pleasant-smelling solvent used in the manufacture of artificial leather, some detergents, pesticides, and paint removers. It can cause dizziness and coma. When poisoning is chronic, leukemia may result.

Because of the dissolving properties of solvents, they can attack the skin and cause the condition called dermatitis (see Dermatitis). Contact with solvents should be strictly limited.

All isocyanates are dangerous. They are used in the manufacture of a variety of polyurethanes that are used to make foams, adhesives, lacquers, and paints. Overexposure to isocyanates that are in the air can lead to painful skin inflammation, eye irritation, and to breathing difficulties including severe asthma. Some people can also develop an isocyanate-sensitivity.

Incidence of accidents at work

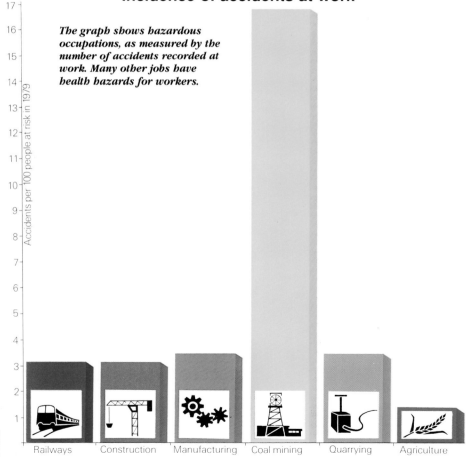

The graph shows hazardous occupations, as measured by the number of accidents recorded at work. Many other jobs have health hazards for workers.

Accidents per 100 people at risk in 1979

Railways Construction Manufacturing Coal mining Quarrying Agriculture

Aziz Khan

Dust is the biggest killer in industry. Some dusts are relatively harmless, while others are deadly. There are four basic categories: the first is nuisance or inert dust such as plaster of paris, starch, and portland cement. These can accumulate in the body without producing a serious reaction. Toxic dusts include lead and chromium compounds. They can have serious effects on specific organs in the body like the kidneys and the nervous system. Dusts that produce allergic reactions, such as some wood dusts and fungus spores from grain, can cause asthma and eczema (see Eczema). There are some dusts, like asbestos and coal dust, that change the lung tissue, making the lungs inefficient. These cause death and serious disability in hundreds of people (see Asbestosis).

The danger of dusts depends not only on the type of dust but on the amount and the time over which it is breathed. Breathing a lot of dust in a short time can be more harmful than breathing a little over a long time.

Healthy lungs can cope with a certain amount of dust and fumes without any ill effects. However, the body's defense mechanisms are unable to cope with the onslaught of dangerous or excessive dusts. This is why elimination of dust in the working atmosphere is so important, and why protective clothing and respiratory equipment must be used (see Lungs and lung diseases).

In many industries, working with deafening noise used to be accepted as part of the job. However, it is now a hazard for which there are controls and preventive measures (see Noise).

Basic preventive measures are to deaden the noise of machinery, and instruct workers to wear earmuffs or plugs that reduce sound levels (see Hearing).

Laboratory accidents which may lead to contamination can be avoided by following safety procedures.

Zefa

Emergency first aid

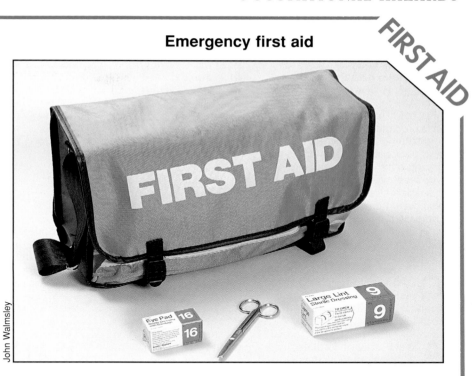

John Walmsley

To give first aid in an emergency, first check if the patient is breathing. If breathing has stopped, start mouth-to-mouth resuscitation at once. Next, check for serious bleeding. Control bleeding by pressing at the site of the wound with a sterilized pad or with your fingers. Raise the injured limb, if possible, to help slow the blood flow. If the patient is unconscious, make sure he or she can breathe and that the throat is not obstructed. Then place the person in the recovery position. Find expert help immediately.

Other injuries	Treatment
Burns and scalds	Cool the area by flushing with plenty of clean, cool water. Then cover with a sterile dressing or clean material. Do not apply any ointment, burst any blisters, or remove any clothing sticking to burns.
Chemical burns	Remove contaminated clothing, taking care you do not contaminate yourself, and dilute the chemical by flushing with plenty of water. Then apply a dry dressing.
Chemical in the eye	Quickly flush the open eye with clean, cool water and continue for at least 10 minutes.
Foreign body in the eye	If the object cannot be removed easily with the corner of a clean piece of material or by flushing with water, send the patient to the hospital.
Broken bones	Unless there is a danger of further injury, do not move the patient until expert help arrives.
Electric shock	Do not touch the patient until the current has been switched off. If breathing has stopped, give mouth-to-mouth resuscitation and call for expert help.
Gas inhalation	Move the patient into fresh air, but wear suitable breathing equipment so that you do not become a victim yourself. If breathing has stopped, give mouth-to-mouth resuscitation.
Amputation of finger	Keep pressure over the stump to prevent arterial bleeding. Wrap the finger in an ice pack. Rush the patient and protected dismembered finger to the hospital.

Q I've heard that if a husband works with dangerous substances his wife can be affected. Is this true?

A Yes. This can occur if proper precautions and personal hygiene are not followed. Cases of lead poisoning have been seen among families of lead workers who went home without changing their work clothes. Employees can also carry home contaminating fibers on their clothing. However, strict regulations normally ensure that such risks are becoming a thing of the past.

Q I work in industry and am planning to have a baby. Are there any health risks that could affect my pregnancy?

A There are laws to protect women from most dangerous hazards, such as lead. Other risks can include waste anesthetic gases to which operating room staff can be exposed that can cause abortions and birth defects. Radiation is a danger, and a fetus is 10 times as vulnerable as an adult. Mercury and its compounds, which can produce mental abnormalities in children, are a potential problem. It should be remembered that the fetus is at risk from all toxic substances that are transferred via the mother. This is why smoking and drinking alcohol in pregnancy are not recommended.

Q I use a pneumatic drill whose noise level is well controlled. Could the vibrations affect my body in any way?

A The major hazard for people using vibration tools is vibration white finger. The blood supply to the fingers is impeded and the fingers appear pale and can tingle and feel numb. At a certain stage, the tissue damage becomes permanent. Employees with poor circulation should not do this sort of job. Others should wear warm clothing and padded gloves when using the tools. Where possible, employees should be in a warm environment to ensure good circulation in the extremities. Hours for this type of work should be strictly limited.

Zefa

It is important to ensure that you are sitting correctly when you are working at a computer screen, and that you take regular breaks to rest your eyes.

Occupational injuries

Every year, some people employed in manufacturing jobs die as a result of an occupational accident or disease. Some jobs have a notoriously high risk of death, such as lumberjacking or working on oil rigs. Other jobs are not dangerous in themselves but involve machinery that can give rise to accidents if misused.

A number of accidents occur through the use of unguarded machinery. Laws declare that all machinery must be safeguarded, but some employers try to cut corners, and do not always ensure that this is done. Moreover, some employees believe that the safeguard is slowing their output and costing them pay. Such people can deliberately remove the safeguards and so risk losing a limb.

Machinery maintenance is especially hazardous because safeguards often have to be removed for access. Unfortunate mistakes, such as failing to switch off the power supply, can be the cause of other serious injuries. Many injuries in factories are caused through the misuse of hand tools. Eye injuries from fragments of metal flying off drills, or chips of stone or metal split off while hammering, are common. Employees do not always like wearing eye protection, but such a basic precaution prevents minor eye injuries.

Certain types of hand tools such as chainsaws can cause an unfortunate condition that is known as vibration white finger. The symptoms are pale or blue tingling fingers. This can progress to pain, or loss of sensation (see Numbness). Unfortunately, there is no known cure for white finger. Because the injury causes a cold-sensitive spasm of the veins, employees who must use vibration tools should wear padded gloves, and keep their hands as warm as possible.

Finally, falls in factories account for another high proportion of occupational injuries. Many of these falls occur on a level floor and are a result of clutter from boxes and various other items left lying around. Spilled liquids and general untidiness can also cause falls. Trailing wires, filing cabinet drawers left open, and poorly lit stairs are other avoidable traps that can predispose to accidents (see Accident prevention).

Preventing injury

Many occupational injuries can be prevented by following commonsense safety regulations. Members of staff should make sure that they wear any safety equipment their employer provides for them. Employees also have a responsibility to encourage better office and factory maintenance. While there will always be some occupational hazards in life, taking a few simple precautions can help to reduce the various risks that people encounter as part of their job.

Occupational hazards

Hazard	Industry	Mode of entry	Symptoms	Treatment	Prevention
AIDS	Doctors, dentists	Needle stick injuries	Fever, fatigue, attacks of shingles or herpes (see AIDS)	Antibiotics but no cure	Safe sex using condoms, not sharing needles
Asbestos	Numerous, including shipbuilding, pipe and boiler lagging, building	Inhalation	Breathlessness, dry cough, cancer of the lung or pleura (lining of thorax and lungs)	Remove from further exposure to inhalation and relieve symptoms (see Asbestosis)	Enclosure of dust producing process, wearing masks and gloves, using substitute materials
Cadmium	Plating on metals, production of alloys, paints, enamel, and pigments	Inhalation or ingestion	Irritation of eyes and nose, breathlessness, vomiting, diarrhea, colic, coughing, headache, kidney damage	Symptomatic only	Enclosure of the process, wearing masks and gloves, monitoring of the environment
Chromium	Auto industry, steel, pigments, leather tanning, photography	Inhalation	Ulcers on skin, especially nasal membranes, asthmatic symptoms	Ointment and local treatment of ulcers	Enclosure of the process, environmental monitoring, wearing masks and gloves
Hepatitis	Laboratory and hospital workers	Contact with infected blood or excreta (see Hepatitis)	Weakness, loss of appetite, malaise, jaundice	No specific treatment Hepatitis A, usually self-limiting disease	Safety clothing and protocols to avoid contamination
Isocyanates	Manufacture of polyurethane, foams, adhesives, synthetic rubbers, paints	Vapor inhalation or contact with skin	Dermatitis, coughing, eye irritation, asthma, and breathlessness	Removal from contact, symptomatic treatment	Exhaust ventilation, wearing masks and gloves
Lead	Batteries, rubber, paint, roofing, and soldering	Ingestion, inhalation (see Lead poisoning)	Headache, constipation, pain in the abdomen, muscle weakness, paleness, kidney damage, convulsions, coma	Removal from exposure, chelating elements that remove lead and change its properties, oral penicillamine	Exhaust ventilation, personal hygiene, environmental monitoring, regular analysis of blood and urine samples
Mercury	Electrical industry, fluorescent lamps, dentistry	Inhalation, ingestion, absorption through skin	Jerky movements, irritability, drowsiness, bleeding gums	Removal from source of contact	Enclosure of process, exhaust ventilation, wearing masks and gloves
Noise	Shipbuilding, drop-forging, boilermaking		Deafness (see Noise)	Remove from further exposure	Reduce noise of machinery, wearing earplugs
Radiation	Medicine, welding checks, atomic energy and weapons, luminous dials	Irradiation through the body, ingestion of contaminated particles	Burns, scaling of skin, loss of hair, cancer, cataracts, dermatitis, genetic damage	Symptomatic; immediate removal from contamination	Screening from source, monitoring, wearing masks, gloves, and protective clothing
Silicosis	Pottery, mining, quarrying, sandblasting	Inhalation	Dry cough, breathlessness, bronchitis, extreme respiratory disablement	Remove from further exposure, treat symptoms	Wearing masks and gloves, damping dust, enclosing process
Solvents	Inks, varnishes, glues, paints, degreasing and dry-cleaning agents	Inhalation, skin contact, ingestion	Numerous due to damage to nervous system, liver, heart, lungs; dermatitis	Various. Remove from exposure	Exhaust ventilation, monitoring environment, wearing masks and gloves
Vibration	Building, welding, forestry	Contact with tool	Pale, numb fingers	Removal from contact	Warm environment, wearing masks, and padded gloves
Wood dust	Furniture, wood polishers, lumberyards	Inhalation and contact with skin	Dermatitis, respiratory irritation, nasal cancer	Symptomatic	Dust extraction, wearing masks and gloves

Occupational therapy

Q Since my wife had a stroke her right arm has become almost useless. She wants to be more independent, but finds cooking and cleaning with only one good hand is frustrating and slow. Can anyone help her?

A Physical therapists can help her rebuild muscle strength. Occupational therapists can teach her how to perform the physical movements she finds difficult, such as showering or dressing. They will also have many special tools she can use to make household tasks easier and they will teach her how to use them.

Q My husband has had major depression. Will he need occupational therapy?

A Depression often happens when there is an inability to cope with stress. Therapy can help people become more resilient. The exercises may involve encouraging more self-confidence and social skills, like talking in front of others. It may mean helping someone who has not worked for a while to work with other people and accept responsibilities again.

Q I am frightened of having a bath because it is difficult to get out of the tub. What kind of help can I get?

A An occupational therapist can be asked to visit you. He or she will analyze the problem and may suggest aids that can help, such as a nonslip mat, a bath seat, and a rail on the wall above the bathtub. He or she can help arrange for you to get these and teach you how to use them.

Q Why did my child need to have occupational therapy in the hospital when she was recovering from pneumonia?

A Any long hospital stay can be boring and demoralizing, especially for a young child. A child who is depressed does not recover as quickly; but a child who is active and happy will find it much easier to readjust to the outside world when he or she is well again.

Occupational therapy involves the use of activities that can help people with some kind of impairment to reach their maximum level of functioning and independence. The therapy can help people cope with all aspects of daily life.

Occupational therapy has a complementary role to physical therapy. Physical therapists work to improve any physical impairment such as mobilizing stiff joints, strengthening weak muscles, and improving coordination. They may use activities such as planing wood to exercise a weak back, a treadmill to exercise the legs, or weights to strengthen arms.

Occupational therapists help patients who are having problems performing everyday tasks. For example, they will teach someone with one arm how to dress him- or herself or cut up his or her food. They may have special tools that they can teach patients to use. Most occupational therapy departments will have a kitchen, bathroom, and bedroom section where patients can try out aids and practice new techniques.

Occupational therapists can also treat people with intellectual impairment or with a psychiatric illness. Therapists use activities like painting and music, that provide opportunities for self-expression (see Psychotherapy). They also use discussion and social activities, to help shy and withdrawn patients express themselves and relate better to others. Shopping, cooking, and work activities help patients cope with daily living.

Occupational therapists can also help people with an impairment to live at home. This can mean arranging for the provision of aids such as extended legs to raise an armchair. They may work with architects to plan major alterations, such as a downstairs bathroom that is suitable for someone who uses a wheelchair.

Therapists also work in centers where patients with physical or intellectual impairment or psychiatric illness go to meet other patients and enjoy a pleasant change in their surroundings.

Benefits of therapy

Patients with a temporary problem, such as a hand injury, will need some physical therapy to get their hand moving again as quickly as possible.

People with a long-term illness, such as arthritis, need occupational therapy such as special exercises or tuition in how to use adapted household tools to help them cope with the practical and psychological problems that they face.

Patients who have been in a psychiatric facility because of depression, anxiety, or schizophrenia will need the support of occupational therapy in the form of "talk out" therapy or social involvement sessions as part of their treatment.

John Greim/Science Photo Library

Older people who tend to sit at home doing very little may begin to lose their ability to do the things they could manage before. These people can also benefit from therapy (see Physical therapy). It can stimulate them into wanting to do more for themselves and show them easier ways of doing tasks around the house.

How therapists work

In the hospital, occupational therapists work as part of a team alongside doctors, nurses, and physical therapists. Therapists may initially see patients in their rooms but usually continue treatment in the hospital occupational therapy unit. The therapists often make home visits with their patients before they are discharged to find out if people will be able to manage. If there are problems, the occupational therapist can arrange for appropriate help to be offered. Some outpatients may be advised to continue occupational therapy at the hospital, or they may have access to treatment at home.

Various forms of treatment are available in special units. Among these are centers where intensive daily treatment is available. There are also children's units, hospitals offering special day treatment for the aged, stroke units, spinal injuries units, and burns units. Occupational therapists are usually part of the teams that offer treatment at all these facilities. Therapists are also beginning to work in special schools that cater specifically for children with physical impairments.

In psychiatric facilities occupational therapists work with both psychiatrists and psychologists. Large outdated hospitals usually rely on a number of occupational therapy departments that can serve different types of patients. In the smaller, modern units that are now attached to regular hospitals, occupational therapists may work either in their own department or on the floors. They may also work in special units that are designed to treat patients with drug and alcohol dependencies.

Alternatively therapists may work outside the hospital in a special community setting. Specific techniques such as behavior modification may be used for patients who need to overcome psychological problems. In hospitals for the intellectually impaired, occupational therapists are especially concerned with helping patients to develop everyday social skills (see Behavior therapy).

In the community, occupational therapists may be part of a team with other types of workers. The therapists usually take a special responsibility for people with impairments. Some occupational therapists either work in, or run, day centers created specially for such people.

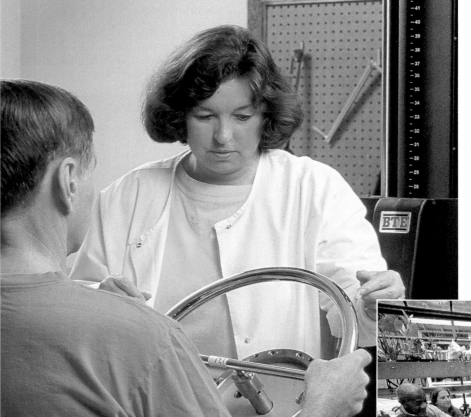

Here are some of the many applications of occupational therapy. Older people (far left) find both companionship and mental stimulation in an art therapy session. A male patient (left) is using a steering wheel in a therapy session to test the strength of his arms.

At a group horticultural therapy session (above) patients practice potting plant cuttings. This activity is designed to improve perceptual and social skills, as well as those relating to coordination and movement.

Ointments

Q Should I apply ointment to a burn?

A After you have cooled the heat of a burn with cold water, put on an appropriately soothing over-the-counter burn cream, such as one containing mafenide acetate or silver sulfadiazine; your pharmacist can suggest one. You should cover it with gauze, or wet dressing, to keep the burned skin moist and protected. At night you may wish to sleep with the bandage off to keep the skin dry and exposed to the air to prevent other complications.

Q What is the difference between using an ointment and a cream?

A Ointments are greasy substances which can absorb water. Creams already have water mixed into them as an emulsion. This means that a cream is usually cooler and easier to spread. Many ingredients will dissolve in oil or water but not both, so creams are the usual vehicle for water-soluble substances. Where either water or oil can be used, ointments work better for thick, tough skin such as psoriasis. Creams, such as those used in cosmetics, are much more suitable for sensitive and soft areas like the face.

Q Is it safe to use ointments while I am pregnant?

A A small amount of the active ingredients of any ointment are absorbed through the skin into the body. If the ointment is being used only in a small area, this is no problem and it is safe to continue throughout a pregnancy. However, it is always safest to ask your gynecologist. If you have to use the ointment on the whole body for a skin disease, an appreciable amount may be absorbed, so you may need different medications to use while you are pregnant. During pregnancy, many skin problems such as eczema and psoriasis may improve or become worse. Special ointments that are recommended for the treatment of stretch marks and itching are completely safe to use, although always check with your doctor.

Whether they soothe or soften, protect or heal, ointments are grease-based preparations that can relieve a vast range of medical conditions and skin discomfort.

An ointment is a greasy preparation for use on the body. It is usually applied to the skin, but special formulations are made for the eyes, mouth, and other specific parts of the body. An ointment can be therapeutic (healing) in itself, working in a protective way. It may also have an active ingredient dissolved in it, in which case it is used as a vehicle for the dissolved medicine.

What are ointments?

There are several different types of ointments, that vary according to the ease with which they mix with water. Non-emulsifying ointments such as paraffin are immiscible (they cannot be mixed with water). These ointments can be used as barriers to prevent the skin from becoming wet or drying out. They are also helpful and soothing, for example, where urine is irritating the skin in an incontinent aged person or a baby. Similarly, if the skin is being regularly exposed to extremes of weather, a non-emulsifying ointment can provide very useful protection.

Some ointments act as a barrier which protects the skin from damage by water and wind. They are grease-based, and help the skin to keep its natural moisture.

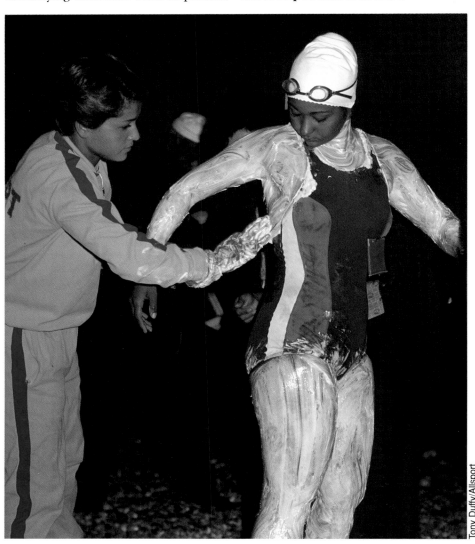

Tony Duffy/Allsport

Emulsifying ointment contains fats which can dissolve in water into tiny globules. So while they retain their greasiness, emulsifying ointments can be mixed with watery ingredients and absorb moisture from the skin. Such ointments can be used as a substitute for soap for people with dry skin which is made drier by using ordinary soap and water (see Skin and skin diseases).

Water-soluble ointments are effective vehicles for drugs that need an oily base, but they can still be removed easily by washing.

Protective ointments

Ointments can be used simply for their protective properties, as happens with long-distance swimmers who cover themselves in grease before setting off. Ointments are also used as a barrier by yachtsmen whose hands and faces become very chapped when exposed to the wind and sea.

People with dry skin conditions such as eczema (see Eczema), and psoriasis (see Psoriasis) use them as well. In these cases dry calloused skin also needs softening. The ointments prevent natural evaporation so that the skin is softened by its own moisture. Barrier ointments can also be used to protect normal skin from other harmful substances such as wart treatments.

The water-resistant properties of ointments make them useful for the eye, mouth, vagina, and rectum (see Diaper rash, and Hemorrhoids). In these moist areas ointments will stay in place better than creams or other preparations and do not have to be reapplied so frequently. However, some difficulty in removing them may be a disadvantage on other parts of the body.

Protective vehicles for drugs

As well as being protective, ointments may be used as vehicles for medicines and other active ingredients. The chemicals are simply dissolved in them in the appropriate concentrations.

They also make good bases because most medicines dissolve easily in oily fats. Since ointments mix well with the skin's own oils, their healing properties go directly to the skin cells. In pastes, which are a variation of ointments, powder is suspended without being dissolved. The ointment mixes into the skin's own greasy layer, taking the active chemicals to the skin cells where they are to act.

Skin diseases have many parallels with diseases that attack the rest of the body, and they can be tackled with the same drug. For example, antibiotic ointment treats skin infections, antihista-

Ointments for the home

Burns:	Most ointments contain antiseptic (aminacrine hydrochloride) and can be used on a minor second-degree burn, a burn which has blistered. If the burn area does not heal quickly, ask your doctor's advice without delay.
Chilblains:	Chilblain ointment may help to increase blood flow to the skin and the act of actually rubbing it on the skin may also help to stimulate circulation. However, the best advice for this condition is to ensure prevention by keeping feet and hands warm.
Eye problems:	Eye ointment should be used exactly as the instructions recommend and only for a very short time. If the symptoms persist for several days, ask your doctor's advice.
Skin disorders:	Calamine ointment soothes uncomfortable, itchy skin. A protective ointment eases the discomfort of skin made dry and sore by sun or wind. It is also a useful treatment for mild diaper rash.
Stings:	Calamine ointment cools and soothes.
Sunburn:	Calamine ointment and zinc ointment are both soothing.

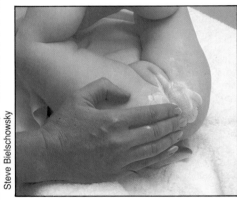

Steve Bielschowsky

Protective ointment has a soothing effect on skin made sore by diaper rash.

mines treat allergic problems, steroids reduce inflammation, and so on.

Because of their medicinal content, these kinds of ointment may require a special prescription, but many others are readily available without prescription from local drugstores. In particular, there are soothing preparations to rub on injuries (for example, hot ice and Ben Gay). Considerable benefit comes from actual rubbing into the skin, which provides a counterstimulus to the nerves transmitting the pain. This stimulation may be intensified by an irritant in the preparation itself which keeps up activity, encouraging blood flow to the area so that it becomes hot (see Irritants).

Antiseptics and cosmetics

Some ointments contain an antiseptic. Unfortunately, some people often think that if they apply this type of ointment

to a wound it will stay free of any infection. They fail to appreciate that this is not the case unless the wound is actually clean to start with. If it is not, the result will be a contaminated wound that has then been covered by a protective layer of ointment. This effectively seals in the bacteria so that a serious infection can then erupt. The wound should always be thoroughly cleaned with soap and water before any ointment is applied to it (see Infection and infectious diseases).

There are large numbers of ointments available for cosmetic purposes. On the whole, these work as barriers, and the other ingredients present are merely perfumes and colorings.

Dangers

It is easy to see if an ointment is problematic. One trouble is the development of a skin infection caused by rubbing an ointment harboring bacteria into the skin.

Always clean the skin before applying any ointment. Sometimes, an allergy may develop to an active ingredient or even to the ointment base. This is particularly likely with antihistamine and antibiotic ointments, which cause a red itchy inflammation of the treated area (see Allergies).

Absorption of drugs through the skin can occur, but the dosage is generally very low. However, problems may occur when large areas of skin have to be treated, such as in the skin conditions of eczema and psoriasis. Never apply ointments any stronger than is necessary to control the skin ailment (see Burns, and Dressings).

Open-heart surgery

Q My son has a hole in the heart but the doctor is not going to operate. Why is this?

A There are many types of holes in the heart, but basically the only ones that need treatment are the large ones that affect the functioning of the heart. A small hole can be of no importance and should not prevent your son from leading a perfectly normal life.

Q My wife has just had open-heart surgery, and she was in the intensive care unit for three days afterward. Does this mean that there were problems?

A No. It is routine for all patients who have had open-heart surgery to spend a few days in the intensive care unit after surgery so that they can have the specialized nursing care that they need.

Q I have been told that I need to have a valve in my heart replaced. Isn't this a rather risky operation?

A In the early days of open-heart surgery, there was a high risk involved, but now the risk is small. If you have been told that you need a valve replacement, the chances of success are much greater.

Q Can you tell me what an artificial heart valve looks like, and how does it work?

A There are various types, but the most common ones fitted by surgeons today are either a ball of plastic about the size of a small marble (that sits inside a metal cage), or like a little trapdoor that opens and shuts a small amount. Both types allow blood to flow in one direction only. Alternatively, specially prepared pig's heart valves may be used instead.

Q What are the most and least common reasons for performing open-heart surgery?

A The most common reason is to replace a heart valve. Heart transplantation is the least frequently performed type of open-heart surgery.

Modern heart surgeons can perform operations that were previously unthinkable—like heart transplants, for example—because the patient's heart can now be stopped during surgery and the blood circulated by a machine.

The term *open-heart surgery* describes surgery on the heart when the chest is opened, the function of the heart is taken over by a machine, and the heart is operated on directly. Before this technique was developed, any heart surgery was performed through a small incision in the chest. Instruments were passed into the heart through the incision, and surgery performed with the heart still beating.

In the 1950s a machine was devised that could pump the blood without damaging the red blood cells too much and at the same time saturate the blood with oxygen. This meant that the patient's heart could be allowed to stop beating temporarily so that surgery could be performed inside it (see Surgery).

Before surgery

Before undergoing open-heart surgery for any type of heart disease, the patient will have had several tests, and the doctors will try to treat the condition with medicines if it is at all possible (see Heart disease). However, if the disease does not respond well to treatment, surgery will be recommended. In the early days of open-heart surgery, the patient was often so ill by the time he or she came to have surgery that the results were poor. Nowadays heart surgery is recommended much earlier in the progress of a disease, when the patient is relatively fit and able to withstand a major operation.

To diagnose the exact nature of the heart disease, patients have a cardiac catheterization. A fine tube 0.04 in (1 mm) in diameter is passed into a blood vessel in the arm or leg and fed into the heart. Pictures can then be taken of the heart, and an exact diagnosis is made by injecting a special kind of dye that is opaque to X rays. The tube can also be used to measure blood pressure and can be passed into the coronary arteries to show up a narrowing or blockage of the arteries.

The operation

The patient is first injected with an anesthetic drug and maintained with gases that are delivered via a mask (see Anesthetics). While the patient is still in the anesthetic room, he or she will be given an IV (an infusion into the vein, see Intravenous infusion), together with needles in an artery and a vein to measure

the arterial and venous pressure both during and after the operation.

The patient is then taken into the operating room and the operation begins (see Operating room). First the skin over the breastbone (sternum) is cut, and then the bone itself is divided using an electric saw. The division is widened with special instruments called retractors, and the heart is then exposed.

Then the patient is transferred onto the bypass machine. This has to be done very carefully, to avoid serious damage to the brain from lack of oxygen (see Brain). At this stage the pressure in the arteries is continuously monitored on a television screen. First a large tube is inserted into the aorta (the main artery leading out of the heart) and large tubes are inserted into the vena cavae (the two main veins that bring blood back to the heart, see Heart). These tubes are connected to the bypass machine, which consists of a pump and an oxygenator. The oxygenator allows oxygen to diffuse across a membrane and into the patient's blood that is being pumped through the machine.

The machine is operated by a trained technician who monitors the pressure of the blood and the speed of flow. The blood passes out of the patient's vena

Specialist nursing care after open-heart surgery includes continuous monitoring of the patient's heart on an electrocardiograph.

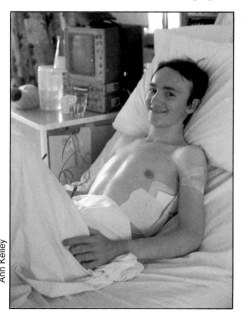

Ann Kelley

The function of the bypass machine

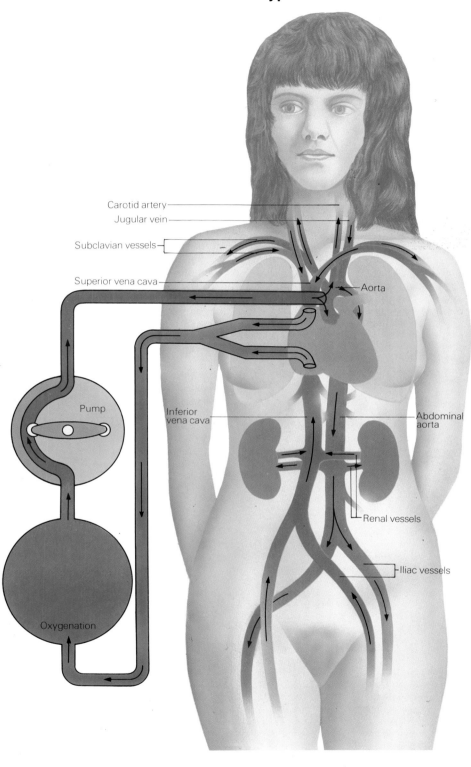

Carotid artery

Jugular vein

Subclavian vessels

Superior vena cava

Aorta

Pump

Inferior
vena cava

Abdominal
aorta

Renal vessels

Iliac vessels

Oxygenation

Venner Artists

cava, travels along a tube to the bypass machine, passes through the machine, then back into the patient via another tube. The patient's heart, which is now empty of blood, usually stops spontaneously; or it can be stopped by an electric shock, special drugs, or cold fluid (cold cardioplegia). The heart can now be operated on since its function has been taken over by the bypass machine.

Types of operations

Hole in the heart: In a hole in the heart operation, a cut is made through the heart muscle to reveal the defect. This is repaired sometimes by sewing the edges of the hole together, or sometimes by sewing a patch of artificial material or a portion of the heart's fibrous covering (the pericardium) over the defect. The cut in the heart muscle is then sewn up.

Valve replacement: There are four valves in the heart that allow blood to flow in one direction only, so that when the heart contracts blood is forced into the arteries, and when the heart relaxes blood enters the heart from the veins. The valves can become faulty either by becoming leaky (insufficiency) or constricted (stenosis), so blood has difficulty in passing through them (see Valves).

In a valve replacement operation, the old valve is cut out and a new one is sewn in position. The replacement valve may be made from metal and plastic, or a specially prepared natural valve from a pig's heart may be used. The valve is sewn in place with many fine stitches to insure that there is no leak between the valve and the heart muscle.

Coronary artery surgery: Coronary arteries can become narrowed, and when they do, the blood supply to a particular part of the heart becomes inadequate. If this happens suddenly the patient has a heart attack, but if it is gradual the patient suffers from angina pectoris (choking, suffocating chest pains). If an X ray of the coronary arteries shows a localized blockage, then surgery may be desirable (see Coronary arteries, and Thrombosis).

Although it is not really open-heart surgery, the most common procedure in coronary artery surgery is a coronary artery bypass graft, in which the blockage is bypassed using a piece of vein (see Grafting). A length of vein is taken from the patient's leg and cut to the right length. Then two small holes are made in the diseased coronary artery: one above and one below the blockage. The vein is sewn onto the holes using tiny stitches, so that one end of the vein is above and one end is below the blockage. Grafts are also frequently used to connect the blocked artery to the root of the aorta. This type of surgery has become more

Open-heart surgery is made feasible by the use of a heart-lung bypass machine, which temporarily takes over the heart's function. Tubes are inserted into the patient: one into the aorta and one into the vena cavae. These are connected to the bypass machine, which takes over the pumping and oxygenating of the blood.

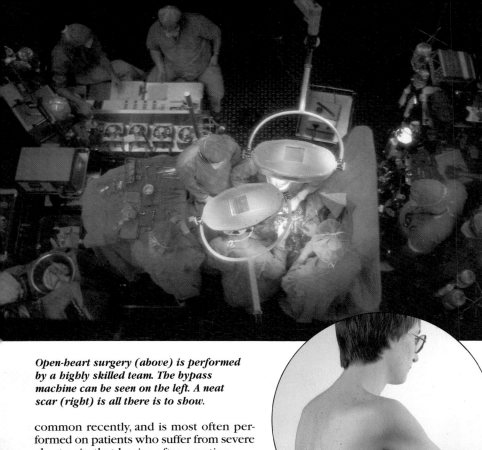

Open-heart surgery (above) is performed by a highly skilled team. The bypass machine can be seen on the left. A neat scar (right) is all there is to show.

common recently, and is most often performed on patients who suffer from severe chest pain that begins after exertion.

After surgery

Once surgery has been completed, the patient is taken off the bypass machine and his or her heart is restarted. This is done by stimulating the heart electrically and gradually phasing out the bypass machine, while carefully monitoring arterial pressure. Sometimes drugs have to be injected directly into the heart to stimulate it to contract forcefully.

A fine wire is placed in the heart muscle, and it is left sticking out through the chest wall, so that if the heart starts beating irregularly in the immediate postoperative period, the wire can be connected to a pacemaker immediately (see Pacemakers). The bypass tubes are removed, and the breastbone is stitched together using wire stitches. Several drainage tubes are generally left in for a few days following surgery, and the arterial and venous pressure monitoring lines are also left in until the patient's condition is considered to be stable.

Recovery time from surgery varies depending on the type of operation and how ill the patient was beforehand. Most people take about three months to convalesce. If a patient has an artificial valve inserted, he or she will be given anticoagulant drugs to prevent blood clotting on the valve (see Valves).

Outlook

The advent of open-heart surgery in the 1950s was a major step forward in the treatment of many heart conditions. Before these operations were available, many people died who could otherwise have survived for years. This applied especially to people with valve disease and to children who were born with various heart defects. In the days before operations for a hole in the heart, if the defect was serious, there was very little chance of many affected children surviving into adulthood. There is also evidence that suggests that coronary artery surgery prolongs life in many cases.

It is probably fair to say that the outlook after surgery depends very much on the medical care given before surgery, assuming that the surgery goes well and that there are no complications. The risks of surgery nowadays have been reduced to such a low level that the outlook may well be determined by how long the patient had the heart disease before he or she sought medical help.

However, if the condition is diagnosed before the disease has progressed too far, and if surgery is performed promptly, the long-term outlook is extremely positive. Many people with artificial valves are able to lead full lives.

With the heart stopped from beating, the surgeon can perform complex and delicate surgery on the tissues.

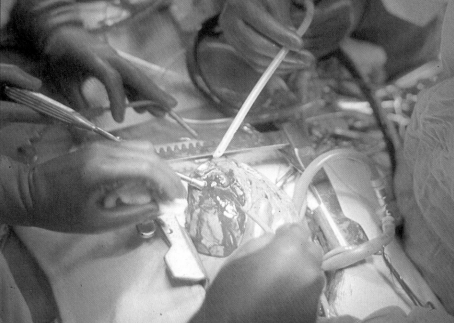

Operating room

Q Who are the people in the surgeon's team who help with the operation?

A The number of people in the surgeon's team varies with the size of the operation to be performed. For a major operation there will be the surgeon, one or two assistants, and the nursing staff. The assistants are usually surgeons, doctors, or medical students. The operating room nurse is responsible for getting all the instruments ready for the operation, and for handing the appropriate ones to the surgeon. The nurse is also responsible for making sure all the instruments are accounted for after surgery.

Q My husband had surgery on his stomach last week, and he was in the operating room for approximately four hours. Does this mean that the operation went wrong or was very difficult?

A Not necessarily. Nowadays the patient is kept in the recovery room after surgery until he or she is awake, before being sent back to his or her room. Once there the patient is attended by staff who are specially trained in postoperative care. Your husband may have taken a while to come around from surgery, but this is all perfectly normal.

Q Is anything done to reduce the possibility of eye fatigue during long procedures?

A The drapes used to cover the area around the operation are usually a restful color, such as gray or green, and this is where the surgeon will occasionally focus his or her attention. Also, the light that is used during an operation does not cast shadows, thus enabling clear vision.

Q Do operation wounds get infected these days?

A No matter what precautions are taken, any surgery carries a slight risk of infection. However, since the advent of sterilization, this risk has been greatly reduced.

The operating room is a high-tech environment where surgical procedures are performed. It is equipped with all the equipment that will be needed for the surgery itself, and for any emergencies that may arise.

An operating room (OR) is the area in a hospital where patients are prepared for an operation. The surgery is carried out, and the patient then recovers before being taken back to his or her room. Within the same complex are scrubbing up and preparation rooms where the surgical team gets ready and where the instruments are laid out on special carts after being sterilized (see Sterilization). Administration of the operating room is carried out in adjoining offices. In a big hospital there may be a dozen operating rooms, each with its own surgery list.

Sterilization
In the last century it was discovered that infection in a surgical wound could be

Modern operating rooms are well equipped and as sterile as possible. Lighting is positioned so that the surgeon and his or her assistants have a clear, well-defined field of vision in which to operate.

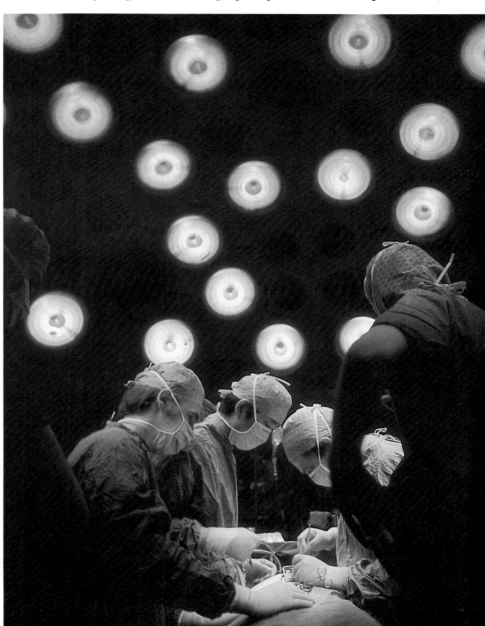

Adam Woolfitt/Susan Griggs

prevented by using certain techniques to destroy bacteria in the air, on the surgeon's hands, and on the instruments. Before this, virtually every wound became infected, and a patient was very likely to die from the infection even if the operation was successful. Modern sterilization methods make wound infection very unusual (see Infection and infectious diseases).

The air in the operating room is cleaned through filters that remove bacteria, and it is then pumped through vents directly into the OR itself. The pressure maintained inside the OR insures that air is then swept out of the various exits. Thus all the air in the OR remains clean, and there is no need for an air-lock system when a person enters or leaves the OR.

All instruments, sutures, and anything that comes in contact with the wound during the operation are sterilized. They may be heated in a device called an autoclave, which is a pressurized chamber capable of delivering super-heated steam. Disposable equipment is usually sterilized by gamma irradiation at the place of manufacture; those instruments that would be damaged by the heating process are chemically disinfected.

Everyone who enters the OR area has to change into special clothes, including shoes. The surgeon and assistants clean their arms and hands with a disinfectant in a process that is called scrubbing-up, and they wear sterile gowns and rubber gloves. All members of the team wear masks to prevent germs from being breathed into the wound (see Hygiene).

The patient's skin in the area of the proposed surgery is disinfected, and once surgery is in progress, nobody except the surgeon and his or her assistants may touch the operating field. The surgeon must not touch anything that has not been sterilized. However, there will be several other assistants in the OR, such as the anesthetist and nurses, who are free to move around provided they do not handle any sterile items.

This operating room is ready for the next operation, with its state-of-the-art operating table and an array of sophisticated equipment and lighting.

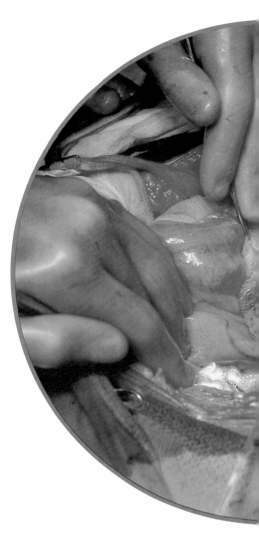

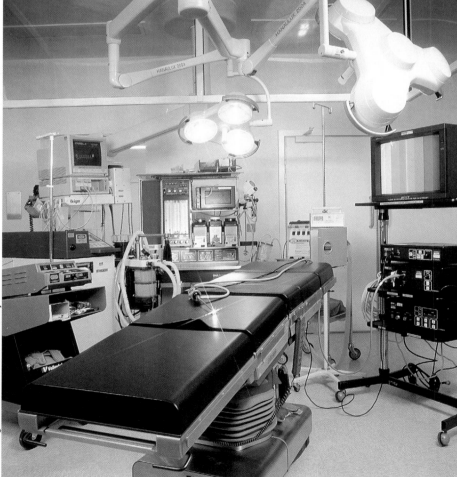

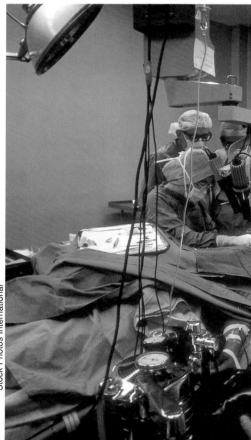

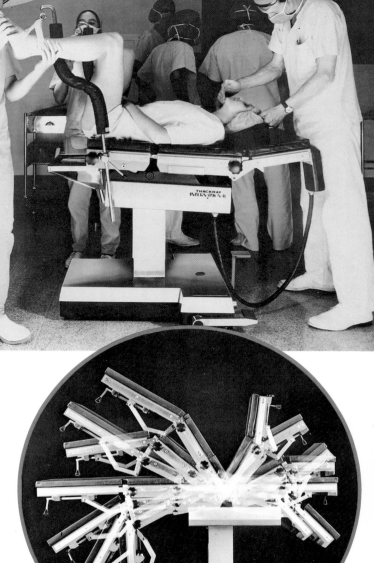

The operating table (above and right) has to be versatile to cope with different surgical positions and to provide support for the patient's body.

Though an operation in progress may look like a crowd scene (left), everyone has specific duties to perform. The only hands that are allowed in the operating field (left, above) are those of the surgeon and his or her assistants.

Charles Thackeray

Anesthesia

Modern anesthesia requires the use of highly sophisticated equipment. A patient who is undergoing major surgery is usually given an intravenous injection of an anesthetic drug that puts him or her to sleep within seconds (see Anesthetics). This takes place in the anesthetic room which is immediately adjoining the OR. The patient is wheeled into the OR and he or she is kept asleep during the operation by gas.

A machine administers the correct amount of gas and oxygen via either a mask or a tube connected to the windpipe (trachea). In many cases a respirator is also used. This acts as a pump, pushing gas and oxygen in and out of the lungs. This may be necessary since the patient may receive a muscle relaxant at the same time as the anesthetic to make it easier for the surgeon to work, and this also tends to affect the muscles of breathing.

Modern developments

Recent innovations include a sophisticated type of sealed unit with air locks, used in the OR, and spacesuits worn by the surgeons which prevent any expired air from reaching the patient. The risk of a patient's wound becoming infected is thereby reduced even further.

Ophthalmology

Q If I need surgery on my eye, will it be done by a general surgeon or by an ophthalmologist?

A In America, all eye surgery is performed by specialist eye surgeons called ophthalmologists. They use special instruments to examine the eyes, and to perform eye operations. Many of these instruments are scaled down versions of the type of general medical instruments used in operating rooms, or in a surgery.

Q At what age should children first have their eyes tested?

A All babies should have their sight tested on a regular basis from the age of six months onward. One of the most important of the child health clinic's functions is to look for squinting, so that it can be treated in the very early stages to avoid the suppression of sight in the affected eye. It is actually quite normal for babies to squint, or to look cross-eyed, soon after birth, but it should disappear by the age of three months. A baby still squinting after this age should be taken to the doctor or child health clinic to be examined. When the child begins school, the school health service will make regular checkups.

Q If you are having an ordinary medical examination, would the doctor check your eyes, or do you have to see an ophthalmologist?

A Most medical examinations include some assessment of your visual acuity (that is, the ability to see objects without blurring). The doctor will also use an ophthalmoscope to examine the back of the eye (retina). This is the only place in the body where blood vessels can be seen clearly. If your doctor suspects that you might need to wear glasses, he or she will send you to see an optometrist. Alternatively, if he or she thinks that you are more than short- or long-sighted, and that you need to be examined by someone with more specialist knowledge, you will be referred to an ophthalmologist.

Doctors who specialize in ophthalmology are equipped to deal with all aspects of eye disease, and they can perform intricate surgery to save a patient's sight.

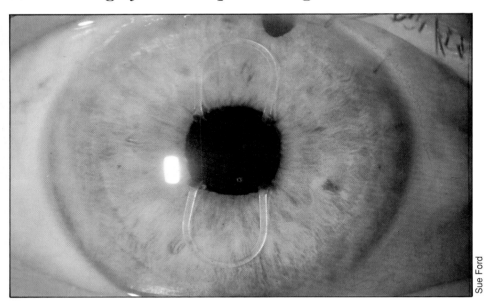

Sue Ford

In order to aid vision, a plastic lens is sometimes implanted into the eye after a cataract has been removed.

Ophthalmology is the study of eye diseases. It is an unusual area of medicine in that nearly all the doctors who specialize in it are experts in two fields: not only are they eye specialists, but they are also highly skilled surgeons.

The ophthalmologist performs complicated tests on the eye, detects problems, and prescribes treatment; as a surgeon, he or she performs intricate and delicate surgery to improve, and often save, eyesight (see Eyes and eyesight).

Treating eye problems

Most of us have had our eyes tested, either because we think we need glasses or as part of a general medical checkup. But only people with more serious problems need to see an ophthalmologist.

If you go to your doctor with some deterioration in your vision, he or she will examine your eyes. If the problem is a refractive error (an inability to focus properly), your doctor will advise you to have your eyes tested for glasses by an optometrist. If you need specialized corrective treatment, you may be sent to an ophthalmic practitioner (a doctor who specializes in eye problems but does not do any surgery). Fortunately, only a few people actually have symptoms like the clouding of vision caused by cataracts (see Cataracts), that would make referral to an ophthalmologist necessary.

Ophthalmologists also deal with cases of trauma (accidental damage) to the eyes. Despite the eye's vulnerability to certain types of injury, many people fail to wear protective goggles when working with industrial equipment, such as grinding wheels or jackhammers, or even when they are riding on motorcycles (see Accident prevention). As a result ophthalmologists often have to perform quite intricate surgery to remove chips and splinters that have penetrated the cornea (the transparent front to the eye) and have lodged in front of the pupil.

Ophthalmic equipment

One of the basic tools of the ophthalmic trade is the ophthalmoscope, which is used by all doctors and optometrists, not just eye specialists. The ophthalmoscope shines a thin pencil of light into the eye and enables the doctor to look along the beam at the retina, the light-sensitive surface at the back of the eye. The ophthalmoscope has a number of lenses so that other parts of the eye can be examined.

When a more detailed look at the front of the cornea, the anterior chamber, or the iris is needed, an instrument called a slit lamp ophthalmoscope is used (see Cornea). The ophthalmologist may put drops of a fluorescent dye into the eye to make scratches or abrasions on the cornea show up more clearly. The slit lamp is also used in conjunction with a tenometer to measure the pressure in the eye. Raised pressure is indication of glaucoma (see Glaucoma).

Eye surgery

Although the ophthalmologist spends much of his or her time in the eye clinic testing different aspects of people's vision, perhaps the most exciting part of the job is in the OR. All of the many surgical procedures that are performed on the eye require great skill and precision. The size of the structures involved is often so very small that the surgeon uses a special surgical microscope.

One of the most common procedures is the removal of a cataract. The diseased lens can be replaced by a plastic intraocular lens or by glasses, both of which help to aid vision. Surgical treatment may also be necessary to prevent loss of sight due to glaucoma. By operating on the iris and allowing fluid to drain from the anterior chamber of the eye, the ophthalmologist can relieve the high pressure in the eyeball that is causing poor vision.

When damage to the cornea results in scar formation, it may become opaque, making the eye effectively blind. Surgery can help by cutting out the whole cornea and replacing it with a corneal transplant (see Donors).

Laser surgery can help with some of the complications caused by diabetes by

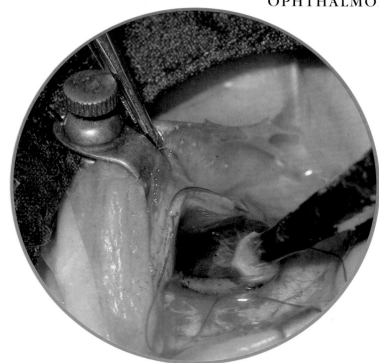

destroying abnormal blood vessels in the retina (see Lasers). Ophthalmologists can also reattach a detached retina.

Surgery can be performed on the structures surrounding the eye, to adjust the eye muscles to correct a squint, or clear the tear ducts that drain into the nose to treat very watery eyes.

Most cataracts affect the entire lens and need surgery. One method used involves the use of a cyroprobe (above), which is a probe with a frozen tip (see Freezing).

A slit lamp ophthalmoscope (below) is often used by the ophthalmologist if a more detailed look at the eye is needed.

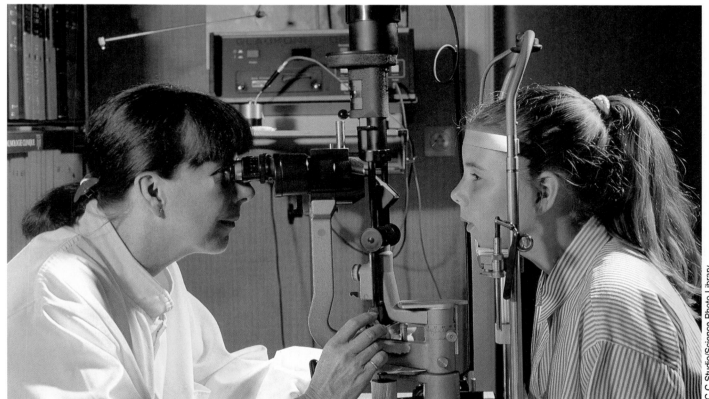

Optic nerve

Q What is the doctor looking for when he shines a flashlight in my eye?

A He is looking at the light reflex. Damage to the optic nerve interrupts the pathway of messages going down the nerve and back up to the pupils. An early sign of damage to the optic nerve is a failure of the pupils to constrict when a light is shone on them. Other problems in the brain or eye can also interfere with this reflex.

Q A friend of mine sleeps with his eyes open. Does the optic nerve still channel information to the brain and do pictures register in the brain?

A Your friend must be an extremely unusual person, but assuming that he does manage to sleep with his eyes open, one must presume that information from the eyes does reach the brain. Whether the pictures register or not would be a difficult matter to prove.

Q I'm told we all have a natural blind spot in the eye. Can you explain what it is and what effect it has on sight?

A The blind spot is the point at which the optic nerve enters the eye. There are no rods or cones here, which are the cells that enable us to see movement and color. It doesn't affect our sight at all, because the point at which the lens concentrates light is slightly to one side of the blind spot.

Q As the optic nerves from the two eyes cross, does this mean that if one of the nerves is damaged the other can still channel all the necessary information?

A Not quite, because not all the information from one eye passes across to the other side; only half of it does. However, the point that does most of the visual interpretation and the point at which the lens concentrates light is represented on both sides. So even with loss of vision over half the visual field, such as after a stroke, the patient is still able to read.

The optic nerve is a bundle of nerve fibers that carries impulses from the retina—the light-sensitive lining of the eye—to the base of the brain.

The back of the eye behind the lens is called the retina, and it is made up of a layer of light-sensitive cells. Every one of these cells is connected by a nerve to the brain, where vital information about pattern, colors, and shapes is computed (see Nervous system). All the nerve fibers collect together at the back of the eye to form one main cable, which is known as the optic nerve. This runs back from the eyeball through a bony tunnel in the skull to emerge inside the skull bone just beneath the brain, in the region of the pituitary gland; here it is joined by its fellow optic nerve from the other eye (see Eyes and eyesight).

The nerves from the two sides then cross over so that some information from the left eye is passed to the right side of the brain and vice versa. Nerves from the temporal (side) part of each retina do not cross over and so stay on the same side of the brain, whereas those fibers from the central part of the eye, the part that does most of the seeing, run to either side of the brain (see Brain).

The optic nerve
The optic nerve is a bundle of nerve fibers carrying minute electrical impulses down tiny cables, each of which is insulated from the next by a fatty layer called myelin. At the center of the main cable, and running its entire length, is a large artery called the central retinal artery. It emerges at the back of the eye and the vessels from it spread over the surface of the retina. There is a corresponding vein that runs back down the optic nerve alongside the central retinal artery and that drains the retina.

Location
Nerves emerging from the retina are sensory. Unlike nerves that supply muscle (motor neurons), which only have one connection on their way to the brain, optic neurons make more than one connection. The first of these lies just behind the point where the sensory information from each eye is swapped. This crossover point is called the optic chiasma and it lies very close to the pituitary gland. Immediately behind this crossover is the first connection or cell station, called the lateral geniculate body. Here information from the left and right eyes is swapped again across the midline. The function of

this connection is linked with the reflexes of the pupils (see Reflexes).

From the lateral geniculate body the nerves fan out on each side around the temporal (side) part of the brain forming the optic radiation. They turn slightly and collect to pass through the main exchange, the internal capsule, where all the motor and sensory information that supply the body is concentrated. From there the nerves pass to the back of the brain to the visual cortex.

What the optic nerve does
There are two types of light-sensitive cells in the retina, the rods and the cones, and just like photoelectric cells they convert light energy into electricity. The rods are used principally to detect objects in the dark. They are very sensitive to movement, so they notice objects coming in from the extremes of the visual field in dim light. The cones are responsible for sharp color vision and they are most plentiful at the fovea, the point where the lens focuses light. However, there are no

A vertical section through a human eye that shows the optic nerve (below). Close-up of the blind spot, the retinal area covered by the optic nerve (bottom).

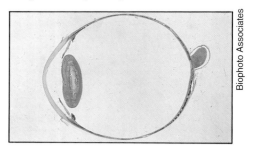

Biophoto Associates

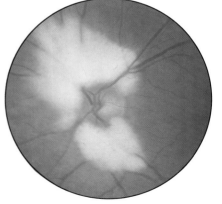

Sue Ford

The mechanics of seeing

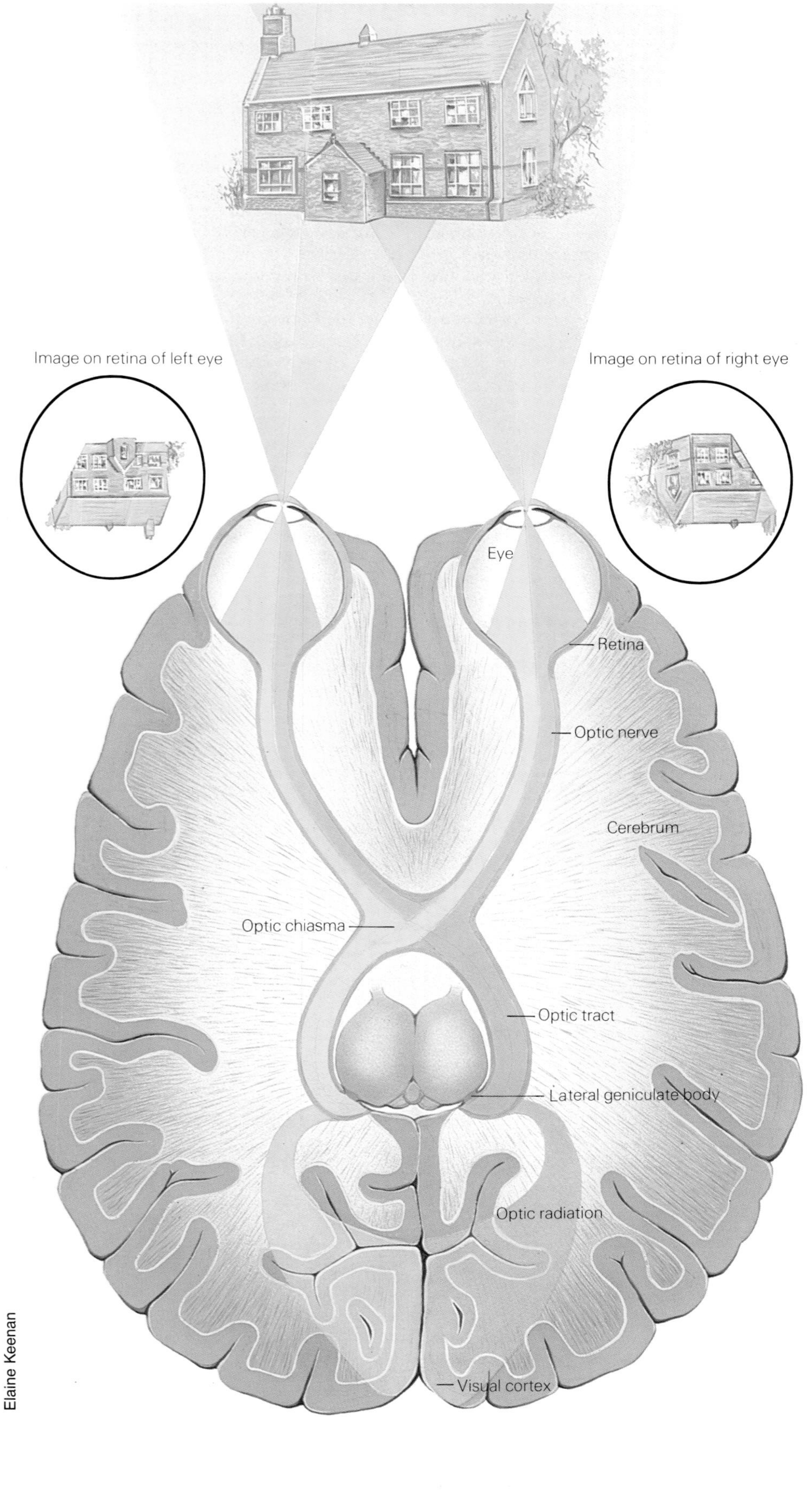

Image on retina of left eye

Image on retina of right eye

Eye

Retina

Optic nerve

Cerebrum

Optic chiasma

Optic tract

Lateral geniculate body

Optic radiation

Visual cortex

Elaine Keenan

rods or cones at the point where the optic nerve enters the eye. This is known as the blind spot because light focused here is not perceived.

The diameter of the pupils is controlled in the same way as the aperture in a camera. Light falling on the retina sends impulses up the optic nerve to the cell station just behind the optic chiasma and then back to a motor nerve that supplies the muscle of the pupil. The brighter the light, the tighter the pupil constricts.

What can go wrong

Obstruction of the central retinal artery leads to sudden total blindness. Although this is rare, it may occur if the nerve swells in its bony tunnel through the skull and presses on the artery. The blood vessels running over the top of the retina may rupture and bleed over the surface, thereby cutting out the light (see Diabetes). Some toxins can affect the retina and optic nerve. The most common is methanol (wood alcohol), which can cause blindness (see Poisoning).

Inflammation of the optic nerve itself is not uncommon in multiple sclerosis (see Multiple sclerosis). This causes visual loss as a blind spot develops in another part of the retina called a scotoma. If the optic nerve is sufficiently inflamed, it turns pink and sticks out like the head of a thumbtack from the back of the eye, called papilledema. Tumors of the pituitary gland may press on the chiasm, producing various visual abnormalities depending on which fibers it constricts.

It is common for a stroke to interfere with the blood supply to the nerves that pass through the internal capsule, the main exchange center of the brain (see Stroke). Damage to this area results in a complete loss of movement and sensation on one side of the body and an inability to see objects moving in from that side. Sight, movement, and sensation are quite normal on the opposite side. This condition is called hemiplegia. Damage to the visual cortex at the back of the brain, for example as a result of a blow to the back of the head, may cause total blindness.

The right and left eyes have slightly different fields of vision. Each visual field is split into a right and left side. When light rays reach the retinas, they are transposed and inverted. These rays travel down the optic nerves to the optic chiasma, where a crossover takes place. All the information from the left side of each eye travels down the optic tract through the lateral geniculate body and the optic radiation to the right visual cortex and vice versa. Later the images are combined and interpreted by the brain.

Optometrist

Q I've started having severe headaches. People say this can be caused by defective eyesight. Should I have my eyes tested by an optometrist, or is it a medical problem?

A Of all the thousands of people who go to their doctors each year complaining of headaches, only a tiny minority are found to be suffering from defective eyesight. It is much more likely that you are having tension headaches, or that you are getting migraines, a particularly severe type of headache. However, if you also notice symptoms such as the blurring of objects in the distance, or if you have difficulty reading or feel that your eyes are tired and strained at the end of the day, it is worth having your vision tested. If defective sight is the cause of your headaches, glasses will probably cure them.

Q Is it true that you can ruin your sight by wearing someone else's glasses, even if they do seem to improve your vision?

A Babies and young children, can be seriously affected by wearing the wrong glasses. An adult may strain his or her eyes or begin to get headaches if they are trying to use someone else's glasses. Therefore, you should never wear glasses that are not your own. If you do have defective sight, an optometrist can give you the proper glasses in order to correct it completely.

Q My mother, who is in her seventies, is having more and more difficulty with her eyesight. Even her new glasses don't seem to help. What could be the problem?

A Not all problems with the eyesight can be corrected by an optometrist. Cataracts, the clouding of the eye lens, require surgery and not glasses. Equally, the retina, the light-sensitive area at the back of the eye on which the image forms, can degenerate in old age. This is something neither glasses nor surgery will help.

Testing eyes and prescribing glasses when necessary is the work of the optometrist, who cannot perform surgery or prescribe drugs but is trained to diagnose eye defects.

There are three types of eye problems that require the specialist services of an optometrist. The first is myopia (near-sightedness), which makes it difficult to see objects in the distance. The second is hypermetropia (farsightedness). Here distant objects are usually quite well defined, but there is difficulty in reading small print and in focusing close up. Finally, there is presbyopia, which people develop as a natural consequence of aging.

Focusing close up becomes increasingly difficult, even if there has been no previous hypermetropia (see Aging).

Any of these problems can be complicated by the condition known as astigmatism, in which the eye is unable to

A child who wears glasses need not refrain from playing active games and sports. However, he or she will have to be a little more careful than other children.

focus equally well on vertical and horizontal objects (see Astigmatism).

Vision

Sight depends on light, and light should be thought of as individual rays traveling in straight lines. These can only change direction if they pass through certain materials, like the glass of a camera lens or the transparent tissue of the eye. This bending of light rays is called refraction.

By refraction, rays of light are concentrated into the chamber of the eye so that they cast an image on the light-sensitive area at the back known as the retina. (The structure of the eye is described in Eyes and eyesight.)

Most of the refraction takes place at the front of the eye in the cornea, the eye's transparent window. There is further

Ron Sutherland

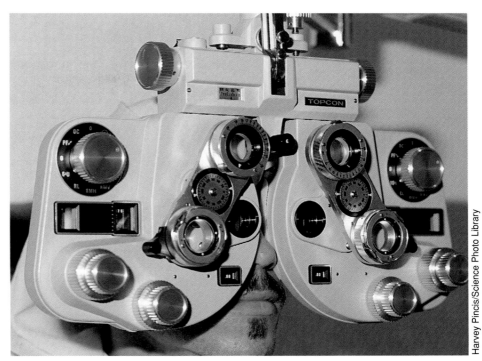

Harvey Pincis/Science Photo Library

Machines such as this one can help an optometrist gauge the type and the strength of lens you may need to correct your sight.

refraction as light passes through to the lens at the center of the eye, but the main function of the lens is fine focusing. This is achieved by the circular ciliary, a muscle that surrounds the lens (see Cornea).

The basic reason for poor eyesight, or imperfect refractive capacity, is not a fault in the lens's focusing power but a fault in the shape of the eyeball. Its ideal shape is more or less spherical. If it is too long and thin, the cornea tends to be too rounded. The rounder (stronger) the cornea, the more sharply it bends light rays with the result that the image is focused in front of the retina in space, leaving a blur on the retina itself. This is nearsightedness.

If the eyeball is too short the cornea will be too flat. It will not bend the rays sharply enough, and the image will fall behind the retina, causing farsightedness. In both near- and farsightedness the ciliary muscle tries, but fails, to compensate for the defect.

Astigmatism is caused by an imperfectly curved cornea. Myopia, hypermetropia, and astigmatism are all congenital (present at birth) and hereditary.

Visiting the optometrist

An optometrist particularly looks out for disorders of focusing. The basic item of equipment that all optometrists use is the test chart, which is usually positioned 20 ft (6 m) away from the patient.

The letter that is at the top of the chart is of a size that can be read easily at 197 ft (60 m) by someone with normal sight. The next row down can be read at 118 ft (36 m) and each successive one

at 80, 60, 40, 30, 20, and 16.5 ft (24, 18, 12, 9, 6, and 5 m) respectively. If you can read the seventh row at 20 ft (6 m), your sight is considered to be normal. This is called 20/20 vision. The first number refers to your distance from the chart and the second number refers to the distance of the row you can read.

The optometrist will ask you to wear a special frame while you are looking at the chart. He or she will fit a combination of lenses into this and ask you how clearly you can read the appropriate row of letters. This will enable him or her to determine the strength of the lens that is required to give you 20/20 vision.

At the same time the optometrist will peer into each eye through a retinascope. This enables him or her to see whether you are near- or farsighted. It also shows when the correct strength or combination of lenses has been put into the frame. This is usually different for each eye.

If both tests show the same strength of lens, the optometrist has confirmation of your requirement and can prescribe glasses. The retinascope is also needed to test for astigmatism. If you have this defect, the glasses prescribed will be designed to correct it.

Finally your optometrist will advise on whether you can wear contact lenses instead of ordinary glasses (see Contact lenses), and when you should return to have your sight retested.

Oral contraceptives

Oral contraceptives, commonly called the Pill, are the most reliable reversible method of birth control available today, and one of the most widely used.

Q Can the Pill cause a loss of interest in sex?

A Some women do find that their interest in sex is decreased when they go on the Pill (see Libido). However, this can often be corrected by a change of Pill. If you have this problem, and are concerned, it is worth seeing your doctor and getting a prescription for a Pill that contains a different balance of hormones.

Q I have varicose veins and I have heard that the Pill can make them worse. Is this true?

A If your varicose veins are minor, and if you are not in a high-risk category for any other reason (e.g., your medical history or if you smoke), you will probably be able to take the Pill without any complication. Talk to your doctor before the Pill is prescribed.

Q Should I regularly take a break from the Pill in order to allow my body to get back into its normal menstrual cycle?

A There is no need to do this frequently, as was once considered necessary. Nor is there any indication that women who have irregular periods when they are off the Pill need to have extra breaks from it. It is now generally thought that, provided you are fit and healthy, the Pill can be taken continuously without a break. You should, however, have a regular medical checkup.

Q Should I tell any doctor I see that I'm on the Pill, even if the consultation is about something entirely different?

A Yes. A doctor knows which drugs interfere with each other, and can avoid prescribing those that will reduce the effectiveness of the Pill. He or she needs to be aware that you are taking it, because it can affect the results of any laboratory tests that you may have to have. It is also very important for a doctor to know what Pill a woman is taking in the event that she has to undergo any type of surgery.

Oral contraceptives are taken by mouth in pill form to prevent pregnancy (see Pregnancy). They are made of synthetic hormones that are similar to those that naturally occur in a woman's body. Hormones are the body's chemical messengers that influence or control body cell activity. They are produced mainly by organs known as endocrine glands. When hormones are released into the bloodstream, they seek out particular cells and slowly stimulate or suppress their activity. There are hormones which govern sexuality and fertility: oral contraceptives contain synthetic versions of sex hormones that are specifically designed to prevent conception (see Hormones).

The idea of chemically altering the body's environment to prevent pregnancy is not new. Many cultures, such as the ancient Egyptians and Native American tribes chewed certain leaves to increase or decrease their likelihood of fertility. The availability of oral contraceptives became widespread in the 1960s, and has become linked with women's liberation, and the ability of women to control the functioning of their own bodies.

Some oral contraceptives work by stopping ovulation (see Menstruation), others make it difficult for sperm to reach the egg, or for a fertilized egg to implant in the wall of the uterus.

The combination Pill is made up of estrogen and progesterone. It is taken daily for 21 days. This is followed by seven, or in some cases, six Pill-free days during which withdrawal bleeding takes place. The progesterone-only Pill (known as the mini-Pill, but not commonly used in the United States) is taken every day. The triphasic Pill is a type of combination Pill that contains different amounts of the two synthetic hormones for different times in the month.

How oral contraceptives work

Different types of oral contraceptives work in different ways. The combined Pill contains hormones very much like those produced by the body during pregnancy. This means that the pituitary gland, which normally sends a message to the ovaries to produce a monthly egg, acts as if the body is already pregnant. It does not send its egg-stimulating hormone to the ovaries, and therefore ovulation does not take place (see Pituitary gland).

The progesterone-only Pill (the mini-Pill) does not always prevent ovulation. It makes fertilization by the sperm more difficult by thickening the mucus in the cervical canal (the passage that leads from the vagina to the uterus), and it inhibits the formation of the uterine lining (in which the fertilized egg must implant itself). As a result, implantation and pregnancy do not take place.

The different types of Pill

A number of pharmaceutical companies make contraceptive Pills. Although there are versions of the Pill that have different brand names, they are all made from the same hormones: the combination Pill with estrogen and progesterone, and the progesterone-only Pill as named. However, different brands offer different synthesized versions of progesterone.

Triphasic Pills contain the same two hormones found in the combination Pill, but in a different amount for each week of the cycle, and are said to mimic the menstrual cycle more effectively.

Some women prefer to take a Pill every day, so there are some 21-day combination Pills that include seven dummy pills to be taken throughout the fourth week. If you think you will find these Pills easier to remember, it is worth asking your doctor for them.

The progesterone-only Pill must be taken every day, and it can cause changes in a woman's periods while she is taking it. Some women do not have any bleeding for several months, others have frequent breakthrough bleeding during the month. However, most women do not have any problems of this kind. Bleeding does not mean that the Pill is not working properly, but if you find irregular bleeding troublesome, ask your doctor for advice. If your period is more than two weeks overdue you are probably not pregnant, but you should see your doctor. The type of Pill you take will be up to you and your doctor. The progesterone-only Pill is thought to involve less risk of circulatory problems, so it is often the Pill of choice for those who may be at risk from this kind of disease. Estrogen can cause blood clots in the veins, hypertension, and high blood pressure (see Estrogen).

There are many positive effects of the Pill, not least the protection from unwanted pregnancy. The reliability of

Facts about the Pill

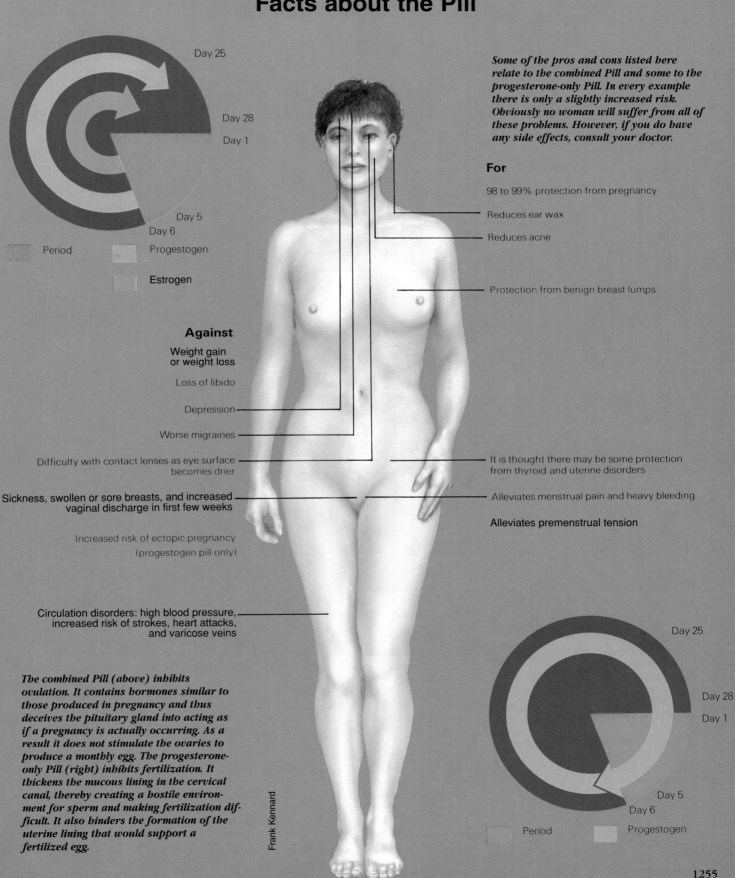

Day 25

Day 28
Day 1

Day 5
Day 6

Period Progestogen

Estrogen

Some of the pros and cons listed here relate to the combined Pill and some to the progesterone-only Pill. In every example there is only a slightly increased risk. Obviously no woman will suffer from all of these problems. However, if you do have any side effects, consult your doctor.

For

98 to 99% protection from pregnancy

Reduces ear wax

Reduces acne

Protection from benign breast lumps

Against

Weight gain
or weight loss

Loss of libido

Depression

Worse migraines

Difficulty with contact lenses as eye surface
becomes drier

Sickness, swollen or sore breasts, and increased
vaginal discharge in first few weeks

Increased risk of ectopic pregnancy
(progestogen pill only)

It is thought there may be some protection
from thyroid and uterine disorders

Alleviates menstrual pain and heavy bleeding

Alleviates premenstrual tension

Circulation disorders: high blood pressure,
increased risk of strokes, heart attacks,
and varicose veins

The combined Pill (above) inhibits ovulation. It contains hormones similar to those produced in pregnancy and thus deceives the pituitary gland into acting as if a pregnancy is actually occurring. As a result it does not stimulate the ovaries to produce a monthly egg. The progesterone-only Pill (right) inhibits fertilization. It thickens the mucous lining in the cervical canal, thereby creating a hostile environment for sperm and making fertilization difficult. It also hinders the formation of the uterine lining that would support a fertilized egg.

Frank Kennard

Day 25

Day 28
Day 1

Day 5
Day 6

Period Progestogen

1255

Q I have been on the Pill for five years and I now want to become pregnant. When should I stop using the Pill?

A It is worth coming off the Pill right away to give your body time to resume its normal menstrual cycle. You may find that there is a delay before regular periods return. You should use another method of contraception until you have had two periods, after which time you can try to become pregnant. The delay that sometimes happens between stopping the Pill and the hoped-for pregnancy may not be due to the Pill at all, or it may be that the body needs a little more time before ovulation begins again. If you have tried for a year or more to become pregnant without success, a fertility clinic may be able to help you.

Q I became pregnant when I forgot to take two Pills, but I continued taking them for a while because I didn't know I was pregnant. Can this have harmed the baby in any way?

A Taking the Pill during the early weeks of pregnancy has not been shown to harm the developing fetus, but research into this area is continuing. Doctors advise any woman who suspects that she may be pregnant to stop taking the Pill and use another method of contraception until it has been confirmed whether or not she really is pregnant.

Q How often should I have a medical checkup when I'm on the Pill?

A You should see your doctor after the first three months on the Pill, and thereafter have a checkup every six months. Your blood pressure should be checked, and if it is high, the doctor may prescribe a different type of Pill.

Q Will I gain weight if I go on the Pill?

A Not necessarily: on first taking the Pill, approximately one-third of women gain weight, one-third lose weight, and one-third stay the same weight.

Taking the Pill

- Taking the combination Pill at the same time as part of a routine makes it easier to remember
- If you miss a day, take two Pills the next day then continue with the rest of the pack as normal
- If you miss two days, double up the dose for the next two days, and use additional contraception until your next period
- If you miss three days, throw out the pack and use alternative contraception until your next period. Then, start a new pack, but follow the same procedure that your doctor advised when you first started taking the Pill
- After your first month on the Pill, if troublesome side effects do not disappear, contact your doctor

the combined Pill is 99 percent and of the progesterone-only Pill 98 percent. The Pill can also actively protect women from certain disorders, such as the formation of benign breast lumps. Since the body is no longer going through the menstrual cycle many of the problems associated with periods (premenstrual tension, pain, and heavy bleeding) can be alleviated (see Premenstrual syndrome). Research also suggests that it may offer some protection against uterine cancer, but this has not yet been confirmed.

Side effects
Troublesome side effects may occur at the beginning of a course of Pills. Some women find that when they first start taking the Pill they feel nauseous, gain weight, get—or are cured from—acne, or their breasts become swollen and sore. Some women who suffer from migraines may find that their condition is made worse by the Pill, although others find that their condition improves (see Migraine). The Pill can also affect a woman's ability to wear contact lenses, since the amount of fluid on the surface of the eye may be reduced.

The combination Pill can also cause depression and loss of libido (sex drive). If you suffer from these symptoms when you are on the Pill, discuss them with your doctor so that an alternative type of Pill can be considered (see Depression).

The most dangerous side effect of the combination Pill is the increased likelihood of circulatory disorders such as high blood pressure, thrombosis, heart attacks, and strokes (see Blood pressure, Heart disease, Stroke, and Thrombosis). For this reason, your doctor will check your blood pressure while you are on the Pill. In rare cases a blood clot in the veins may be fatal if a bit of the clot breaks off and goes to the lungs. Fortunately circulatory problems affect only a tiny minority of women on the Pill, and the risk has been greatly reduced by the introduction of Pills containing lower doses of hormones. However, because the Pill does increase the likelihood of these disorders, prospective Pill-users must be screened to see if they are at risk. Your own medical history and that of your family will need to be studied by your doctor (see Circulatory system).

Smoking, being overweight, and being over 35 years of age all increase the risk of these disorders, so women in any of these categories are often advised not to use the combination Pill (see Smoking, and Obesity). For some Pill users, there is also an increased risk of gallbladder disease (see Gallbladder and stones).

The progesterone-only Pill does not seem to carry such risks, and it is the one most often prescribed for older women.

The progesterone-only Pill is not quite as effective in preventing pregnancy as the combined Pill. Because the progesterone-only Pill does not actually prevent ovulation, there is a small chance that an egg will be fertilized. If this happens there is a tiny risk that the egg will implant itself outside the uterus, since the uterine lining is not soft or spongy enough to receive it. This is called an ectopic pregnancy, and it can take place in one of the fallopian tubes (see Ectopic pregnancy). The risk of ectopic pregnan-

Ron Sutherland

cy is small, but it is a dangerous condition, and needs immediate treatment. Any persistent pain in the lower abdomen should be reported to the doctor.

When a woman stops taking the Pill, the return of her menstrual cycle may be delayed, but it is now thought that this does not affect fertility in the long term (see Endocrine system). The initial choice of Pill will be made by your doctor or gynecologist. Most women start with a

A woman taking the pill is able to lead a full and satisfying life, free of anxiety about unwanted pregnancy and of many of the discomforts that can accompany periods.

low-dose combination Pill. Your doctor will advise you to start taking the combination Pill on day one of your next period. The combination Pill should be taken at the same time every day, at whatever time of day is best for you. Many women find that taking it before bedtime is easy to remember. If you forget to take a Pill one day, double up the dose on the next day. If you miss two days, double the dose for the next two days. However, you will need to use additional contraceptive precautions (see Contraception).

The effectiveness of both types of Pill may be affected by a stomach upset (either vomiting or diarrhea), because it could mean that the chemicals in the Pill have not had time to be absorbed into the body before the contents of the stomach are emptied (see Vomiting, and Diarrhea). Other medication, including some antibiotics, drugs for epilepsy, and certain sedatives and painkillers can also reduce the effectiveness of the Pill. Check with your doctor to make sure that there is no risk of this happening.

Coming off the Pill
Most women can remain on the Pill until they reach menopause (see Menopause). However, because there is an increased risk of clotting, if you are likely to be bedridden for several weeks or months your doctor or gynecologist may suggest that you stop taking the Pill temporarily as a safety measure.

Common problems and solutions

Missed one combination Pill	Take two pills at the usual time, and continue with the rest of the packet as normal
Missed two combination Pills	Double the dose for the next two days, and then take the rest of the packet as normal. Protection may have stopped so use an additional form of contraception until the end of the month
Diarrhea or vomiting	Continue to take pills as normal if you are keeping them down
No period in the Pill-free week	Check with your doctor to see if you are pregnant and therefore whether or not to start the next packet of pills. Until you see your doctor, use a diaphragm or condom (both with spermicide)
Unpleasant side effects at the beginning of a course of Pills such as depression, nausea, weight gain or loss, headaches, and swollen breasts	Wait to see if these symptoms gradually disappear over the first month, if they do not, go back to your doctor to discuss alternative Pills or methods of contraception

Organ removal

Q If one of my lungs is removed, will the space that it leaves make my chest collapse?

A No. Your remaining lung will soon spread out to fill some of the cavity. In doing so it will increase in size, which means that its air spaces will grow too. This in turn means that more oxygen will come into contact with the blood pumping through it.

Q I have been told that after having one of my breasts removed I could have a silicone implant, but are these safe?

A In addition to saline-filled breast implants, silicone implants have been used. However, concerns about possible health risks when silicone is used has led to many lawsuits, and the bankruptcy of one manufacturer. No scientific study has yet demonstrated a clear health risk, but silicone implants are no longer used, partly because of ongoing concern about possible health risks, but partly because of the legal liabilities that are involved (see Mastectomy).

Q I am having one of my ovaries removed. Will I still be able to get pregnant?

A In most cases, yes. Normally each of the two ovaries releases an egg on alternate months. Therefore after one ovary has been removed, you may find it takes a little longer to become pregnant. Some women ovulate more from one ovary than from the other, in which case the chance of conception depends on which ovary is removed.

Q My husband is having his prostate gland removed. Will it affect our sex life?

A The prostate does not secrete sex hormones, so the gland's absence will not affect your husband's performance. However, depending on the type of operation that is used to remove the prostate, damage to the nerves can lead to impotence.

There are few better examples of the human body's astonishing adaptability than its capacity to survive, in good working order, after an organ has been removed.

It is common knowledge, even common sense, that a human being can survive with only one eye. Less obvious is that we can do well without one of our two lungs, kidneys, testicles, or ovaries.

In addition to this the stomach, which is not duplicated, can be removed entirely, and provided that appropriate surgery is performed, the patient will be capable of normal digestion in the intestine (see Digestion). Likewise the larynx (the voice box) can be removed, and the patient can learn to talk by burping air up the esophagus (see Larynx and laryngitis).

Some organs, especially the liver, do not have a twin but instead consist of several units, one of which can be removed completely without endangering the whole because of its powers of regeneration (see Liver and liver disease).

Why remove an organ?
The obvious, but of course not the only, reason for removing an organ is because it has become so diseased that it is a danger to the rest of the body. For example, a breast in which a cancerous tumor has developed must be removed, wholly or partially, as early as possible before the cancer spreads (see Tumors).

Accidents, particularly auto accidents, account for a significant number of organ removals. Ruptured spleens or kidneys that cause internal bleeding are the typical result of being thrown violently against the steering wheel.

What can and cannot be removed
Humans can survive the removal of any organ that is one of a pair, provided that the remaining organ is in good condition. But we can also manage without an appendix, tonsils, adenoids, gallbladder, or spleen. These are not paired organs, but their function does not need to be maintained, because tens of thousands of years of changing living and eating habits, have made them partially or wholly unnecessary to the survival of the individual. In the same way the womb is essential for reproduction but not for the individual's survival (see Uterus).

The decision to remove an organ
In spite of the body's ability to adapt, the decision to remove an organ is never taken lightly. One of the major considerations before deciding to carry out surgery

will be whether to perform a partial or full removal. Whenever it is possible, the surgeon will opt for removal of only the unhealthy part, and will go to great lengths to preserve even the smallest area of healthy tissue.

The thyroid is an example of an organ that is seldom removed completely. It controls growth and metabolism, and for various reasons it can become overactive, with resulting ill effects on, for example,

Organ removal often leaves an almost invisible scar, as with this woman's appendectomy. The surgeon was able to make the incision along a skin crease.

the heart. The surgeon's aim is to remove enough of the thyroid to put its hormone production back in balance (see Thyroid). The same applies to the ovaries: the surgeon tries to leave behind enough healthy tissue for them to continue to secrete hormones (see Ovaries).

Another consideration is how much additional surgery will be required. Considerable plumbing difficulties occur when removing some organs, quite aside from the obvious necessity of joining or tying up blood vessels. Take away someone's stomach, for example, and it becomes necessary to join the esophagus (down which food travels toward the stomach) to the intestine.

The heart and liver present more serious dilemmas. A diseased heart can be removed and replaced with a donor heart, but the candidate for such a transplant needs to be psychologically, and physically, capable of undertaking the strict regimen of medication that follows (see Transplants). This is a lot to ask of someone who has been living for some time with serious heart disease (see Heart transplants).

Obviously a surgeon wants to avoid an organ transplant if possible (see Donors). They can be very successful, but the risk of rejection is unavoidable (see Immunosuppressive drugs). In the case of a diseased liver, a transplant is sometimes possible, but the crucial question is how much of the organ has been affected for example by malignant (spreading) cancer (see Cancer).

After surgery

Most of the problems associated with organ removal disappear as the body adapts to the loss. People who have a lung removed are breathless at first, but later recover some of their breathing capacity. Minor adjustments to the diet are necessary after stomach removal. Some discomfort under the arm is felt after a breast removal, but it usually disappears with appropriate exercise.

If a hormone-secreting organ, such as an ovary or the thyroid, is removed completely, it will be necessary to find an alternative way of controlling the hormone level. Usually this means that the patient must take hormones orally for the rest of his or her life (see Hormones).

Probably the biggest problem is psychological. Your doctor should explain that one of the chief marvels of the human body is the ability to survive a loss. In some cases the experience of organ removal can have positive advantages, after the removal of the uterus a woman's sex life can actually improve because she is no longer bothered by the pain and bleeding of uterine disorders. In addition, it is surprising how many relationships have actually been improved by the rethinking of life's purpose, and the challenge that goes hand-in-hand with facing surgery of this kind.

Organs that may be removed

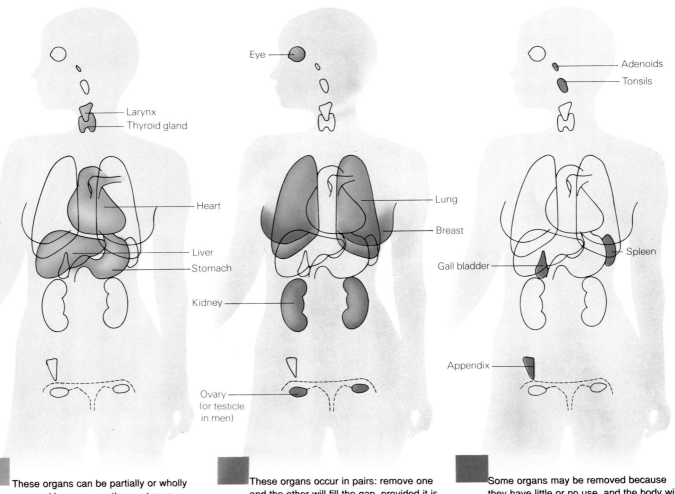

Venner Artists

These organs can be partially or wholly removed because another part, or a replacement, can take over their function.

These organs occur in pairs: remove one and the other will fill the gap, provided it is working properly.

Some organs may be removed because they have little or no use, and the body will function quite well without them.

Orgasm

Q My friend says that she regularly has multiple orgasms. Can this be true, and can any woman have them?

A It may well be true, but not everyone has this experience, nor is it that common. Each woman has a different threshold of sexual response, and this can vary during a lifetime. Some women may have one very intense orgasm at a time, others may have a series of orgasms of varying intensity. If you are satisfied with the orgasms that you have, relax and enjoy them.

Q I am having prostate surgery. Will this affect my ability to have orgasms?

A No. If the surgery and subsequent recovery are without problems, you should experience no difficulties. However, as there is a high incidence of impotence following certain types of prostate surgery you may wish to discuss this issue with your doctor.

Q I have heard that there are two types of female orgasms: vaginal and clitoral. Is this really true?

A No. All female orgasms depend on clitoral stimulation. This is achieved either indirectly or directly. Sexual intercourse provides indirect stimulation of the clitoris, since the movement of the penis inside the vagina results in friction on the vaginal lips, which are connected to the clitoral hood. Direct stimulation of the clitoris takes place when the clitoris is stimulated manually or during oral sex. Some women climax easily from indirect stimulation and others need direct stimulation.

Q I think my wife is faking orgasms, but she always denies this. What should I do?

A Try telling her that your doubts are making you feel insecure, and that your questioning is a reflection of this. What you want to establish is more trust and less pressure. Once you both relax, the situation may improve.

Orgasm, the climax of sexual arousal, has been called the most exquisite of all physical sensations. What happens to the body during an orgasm, and how strongly does the mind govern human sexual response?

An orgasm is simply a reflex response to sexual stimulation. But even though physical stimulation is essential, the mind also plays a vital role. A lack of sexual attraction or emotional involvement, worries about sex, or tension in other areas of life can all affect the ability to reach orgasm (see Stress). Frank, open discussion can help to overcome any difficulties (see Intercourse).

Male orgasmic problems

Most men find that reaching orgasm is relatively easy. However, problems can stem from the inability to maintain the plateau phase, the second stage in the orgasmic cycle when the penis is erect (see Erection and ejaculation). This can result in either premature ejaculation (when a climax takes place very quickly after arousal has begun) or the loss of erection. In rare cases there is a physical reason for this, though in some cases other factors such as drugs for treating depression or high blood pressure, or overindulgence in alcohol, can all make arousal or orgasm difficult; diabetes medications can cause impotence. A man experiencing problems should consult his doctor to rule out physical causes.

The most common reason for difficulty with orgasm is psychological. A man may find it easy to maintain an erection and have a satisfying climax by masturbating, but fail to do so when he is with a partner. Some men worry about their performance and fear failure; others find that lovemaking makes them feel so nervous and overexcited that they climax before sexual intercourse begins. Both these problems can begin after an unsatisfactory experience, which leads to anxiety from then on.

Discussion with a partner is helpful so that the man does not feel under so much pressure to perform. Sex therapy

Male orgasm

During the male orgasm, the prostate gland forces the sperm mixed with seminal fluid into the urethra. The muscles around the urethra give rapid involuntary contractions, which forces the semen out of the penis at high pressure. Three or four major bursts of semen are followed by weaker, more irregular contractions.

Female orgasm

A female orgasm starts as a buildup of sensation around the genitals. Before orgasm there is a feeling of tension, when the pelvic muscles surrounding the vagina and uterus contract. The orgasm is felt as a series of rhythmic muscular contractions, first around the outer third of the vagina, then spreading upward to the uterus.

can be very successful also as it often gives the man an opportunity to learn more about his sexuality and helps him to feel more relaxed about it (see Sex).

Female orgasmic problems

Women often find it more difficult to have orgasms. Some women may have physical problems, such as an unusually overdeveloped hymen, an inflammation of the vagina or bladder, or a shrinkage of the vaginal lining after menopause, all of which can produce pain during intercourse (dyspareunia). In other cases the sex drive (see Libido) can be affected by drugs the woman is taking, including the contraceptive Pill. Women who are

experiencing such difficulties should consult their doctor.

Many women are able to have orgasms through masturbation on their own, but find it impossible to climax when they are with their partners. This may simply be a question of technique; the woman may need direct clitoral stimulation but her partner may only be willing to have intercourse and nothing else.

Other women find it difficult to ask for what they want, so their partners are unaware that different techniques are needed. An unvarying pattern of cursory foreplay followed by intercourse can also cause difficulties, since what a man may consider to be merely the prelimi-

naries to real sex, i.e., intercourse, may be what the woman finds most pleasurable and stimulating. She may be just about to reach climax, but because direct clitoral stimulation ceases, she is unable to do so. To overcome this problem, either the woman or her partner should continue to stimulate the clitoris manually during intercourse.

Some women have never had an orgasm, either alone or with a partner. The reasons for this are various and include simple lack of knowledge and a fear of insisting that their partner help to satisfy them. Therapists advise women who have never had an orgasm to explore their bodies and find out about their sexual response through masturbation, either manually or by using a vibrator (see Masturbation). Once they begin to have orgasms, they can communicate their desires and appropriate techniques to their partners.

Almost every couple can achieve a satisfactory sex life once they have relaxed about it, whether through therapy or just by talking about it.

Orthodontics

Uneven or protruding teeth need not be a cause of lifelong embarrassment. In most cases they can be corrected fully by orthodontic treatment.

Q I am 28 years old and have overlapping front teeth. Am I too old now to have them fixed?

A No. Orthodontic treatment can be carried out on adults. However, it does tend to take longer than when it is done in childhood, but provided you can accept the idea of wearing an appliance, it may be still possible for your teeth to be corrected. Very severe discrepancies of tooth position are sometimes beyond the scope of orthodontics, even in childhood, and occasionally it may be necessary to give surgical treatment.

Q My daughter's teeth are very crooked and unsightly. However, the dentist tells me that he cannot consider giving her any orthodontic treatment until she improves her oral hygiene. What should I do?

A You should insist that your daughter cleans her teeth properly. Your dentist is quite right in refusing treatment without satisfactory oral hygiene. Unless your daughter cleans her teeth and gums thoroughly every time she brushes them she will probably lose her teeth when she is an adult. Also, wearing orthodontic appliances without cleaning the teeth properly can result in gum disease and tooth decay. This is because the presence of an appliance may make ordinary dental care more difficult, and thus an existing oral hygiene problem could be made much worse.

Q Is there any danger that wearing an orthodontic appliance might actually damage my teeth?

A Provided that you clean your teeth thoroughly to prevent any plaque from accumulating, the presence of bands or wires in the mouth will not cause any damage. However, if the appliance is not cleaned and therefore becomes a reservoir of bacterial plaque, tooth decay will be the inevitable result.

Orthodontics is a branch of dentistry. It is concerned with correcting the position of irregular teeth and correcting any fault in the way the upper and lower teeth come together, or bite. Appliances such as braces, which move the teeth into their correct position, are usually needed in orthodontic treatment. Where the teeth are too crowded, some of them may have to be extracted to provide the space they need to grow normally.

The normal position of teeth

Ideally, the upper and lower rows of teeth—the dental arches—should be symmetrical, with the teeth in even positions. There should be no overlapping (crowding) and no spaces. The upper arch should be slightly larger than the lower one, so that when the teeth bite, the upper teeth all fit just outside the lower ones.

This perfect arrangement of teeth is not found very often. Just as people vary

Normal bite

Normal bite: the upper and lower rows of teeth should be symmetrical, with the teeth in even positions, not overlapping. The upper teeth should fit just around the lower teeth, with the upper arch slightly larger than the lower arch. Such an ideal rarely exists. Incorrect bite: malocclusion occurs when the front teeth grossly overlap or protrude over the bottom row. Teeth may be spaced or overcrowded. Treatment for malocclusion is by a fixed appliance.

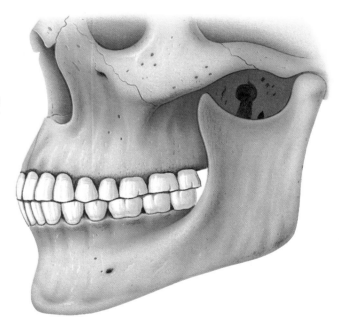

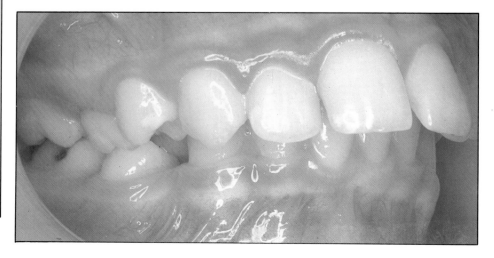

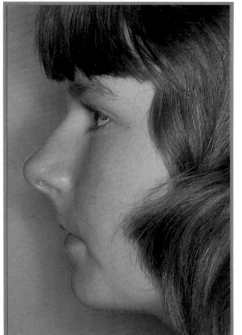

in their height and in other physical characteristics, so they vary in the position of their teeth and the structure of their jaws. Slight variations from the ideal pattern do not affect the health of the teeth or a person's appearance. In fact, many people would consider a minor degree of tooth irregularity attractive (see Teeth and teething).

Orthodontic treatment is needed when the teeth are so uneven that they spoil the individual's appearance, cause dental problems, or when they do not give a proper bite, known as malocclusion.

Causes of irregularities

Most of the factors that actually determine the size and position of the teeth, as well as the size of the jaw, are inherited. Characteristics inherited from both parents affect how the teeth will grow. For example, a child who has a father with large teeth and a mother with small jaws may have a combination of teeth and jaws that do not match, and may have very overcrowded teeth (see Genetics).

In some cases, environmental factors influence how teeth develop. Persistent thumb-sucking, for example, will change the position of the incisors (the four central teeth in both the upper and lower jaws). Tooth position may also be affected by diseases of the jaw, but this is rare.

People who have significant irregularities of their teeth or jaws may develop additional problems. For example, teeth that overlap are more difficult to clean, and this may result in gum disease and tooth decay.

An incorrect bite, where the lower incisor teeth bite against the roof of the mouth instead of against the upper teeth, may cause inflammation in the palate. In some people, when the teeth come together they bite on the wrong side of the teeth in the opposite jaw. This may damage the jaw joints because the patient has to bite to one side to avoid teeth that are in the way. Such misalignment can cause arthritis.

Incorrect bite: malocclusion

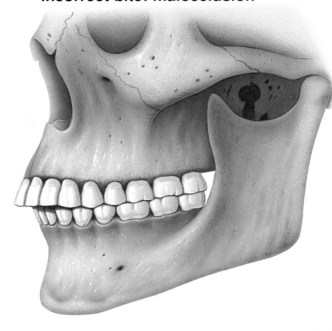

The photographs above show a child before and after orthodontic treatment. Note the striking changes in her profile. The photographs below show the same child's teeth in their original state, and during and after treatment. The teeth were irregularly spaced, protruding, and maloccluded. A fixed orthodontic appliance was used to correct these irregularities and was worn for three years. After treatment, her bite became regular, with the teeth correctly positioned.

Mike Courteney

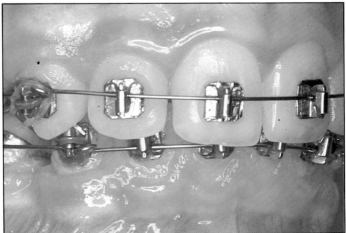

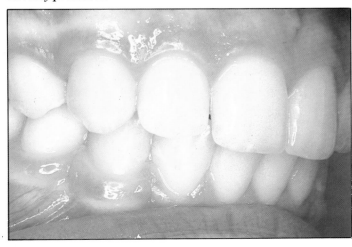

Charles Day

ORTHODONTICS

Grossly irregular or spaced teeth may cause problems with speech, although this is unusual. However, a person may feel embarrassed by irregular teeth and seek treatment to correct the irregularity.

Treatment

The age at which treatment is given depends on the development of the teeth. Sometimes treatment can begin before all the baby teeth have fallen out, but it is often necessary to wait for the premolars (the teeth in front of the molars) and permanent canine teeth (those next to the incisors) to come through, which is usually between the ages of 11 and 12.

Any treatment needed is then discussed with the patient, and in the case of a child, with the parents. The orthodontist takes impressions of the teeth, and makes plaster models from these. X rays confirm the presence of, and locate, any teeth that have not yet grown, and assess the shape of the jaw (see X rays). The orthodontist may photograph the patient's face and teeth to assess what to do. This also serves as a record to show the patient how much was done when treatment is completed.

Why extractions are necessary

Crowding of the teeth usually occurs when the tooth size is so large that there is not enough space in the jaw for them all to grow normally and evenly spaced.

Where there is only a slight degree of overcrowding, patients may be advised to accept the situation. However, where it is more severe, treatment is needed, usually before all the permanent teeth have come through, to prevent other problems developing, such as difficulty in cleaning the teeth (see Growth).

At one time it was thought that overcrowded teeth could be aligned simply by enlarging the dental arches. Although this treatment helps in the short term, it has been shown that overcrowding will eventually recur. In most cases, the only treatment that is successful in the long term is to extract some of the teeth already in place. This provides enough space for the rest of the teeth to come in and develop normally.

The orthodontist will carefully consider which teeth to extract. When all the teeth are in good condition, it is usually

Children who persist in thumb-sucking once their permanent teeth come through may require orthodontic treatment (below).

Ron Sutherland

Removable orthodontic appliances

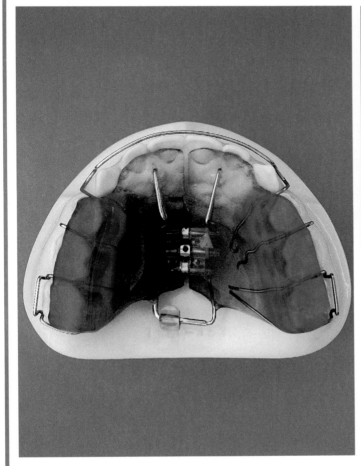

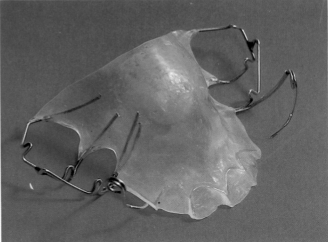

The photo (left) shows one of the new designer orthodontic appliances made for adolescents. It is made of acrylic and is designed to hold crooked teeth in place until they settle into a more even pattern. This type of retainer comes in a range of designs, including a ladybug, zebra, tiger, frog, the American flag, and a rainbow. Glitter and sparkles can also be added.

The purpose behind these very individual appliances is to involve the young patient more in the care of his or teeth. Many young people, particularly teenagers, are very resistant to the idea of wearing such a visible appliance. By redesigning retainers and adding brightly colored, fashionable designs, it is hoped that young people will wear them as often as they should.

There are various types of removable orthodontic appliances, the most common of which is shown top right.

Teenagers often find this very visible type of orthodontic treatment embarrassing. A solution is designer appliances (above left).

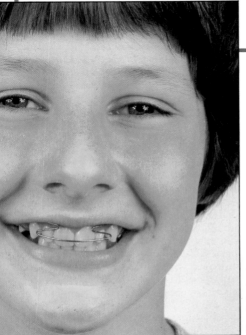

Ron Sutherland

the first premolars that are removed. However, if certain teeth are very heavily filled or badly positioned, for example, these teeth will be extracted instead of the first premolars.

Once the teeth have been extracted there is often a spontaneous improvement in the positions of the adjacent teeth, which tend to move into the spaces that have been created. Because, the improvement is not usually enough to fully correct the irregularity of the teeth, an appliance is also needed.

Orthodontic appliances

There are two main types of orthodontic appliances: functional and mechanical. Both types move the teeth into the correct position and hold them there until they can maintain the position unaided. Functional appliances improve the way the upper and lower teeth meet, or bite. They move the entire dental arch as one unit, unlike fixed and removable appliances, which move individual teeth. Functional appliances are therefore only effective when a child is growing rapidly. For example, if all the upper teeth are too far forward, a functional appliance fitted at the right age can mold the upper arch back as it grows, insuring a better contact with the lower arch when biting.

Mechanical appliances do not necessarily need growth to be effective, but they do the job more rapidly during a phase of growing. The two main types of mechanical appliance are removable appliances (which the patient can take out) and fixed appliances (which are bonded to the teeth). Fixed appliances exert a greater degree of control on the teeth and can produce movement in any

Q Is wearing an orthodontic appliance painful?

A It depends on the appliance and the extent of the dental work that must be done.

Q What special precautions are required while wearing an orthodontic appliance?

A The most essential one is to maintain good oral hygiene. Removable appliances should be taken out at least twice a day, and the teeth thoroughly cleaned with a toothbrush and dental floss. The appliance should also be scrubbed using a toothbrush and toothpaste. This should keep it free from any bacteria. Fixed appliances are more difficult and time-consuming to clean. The most effective way of cleaning around them is to use a very small toothbrush. If the gums begin to bleed on contact with the toothbrush, they may be inflamed, and even more thorough brushing is required. This may make the gum bleed at the time, but if thorough brushing is maintained, the gum will become firmer and will no longer bleed when brushed. If you continue to have problems with your gums, see your dentist.

Q I have heard that badly misplaced teeth can be transplanted. Is this true?

A It is possible to transplant completely buried teeth, but there must be adequate space for them. This method of treatment is used mainly in cases where upper canine teeth have failed to erupt. This occurs in about two percent of people, and the teeth concerned remain below the surface, usually in the palate. Such a tooth can be removed surgically and then immediately inserted into a specially prepared socket in the right place. After the transplant it is necessary to hold the tooth in place with a splint while the healing process takes place (this usually takes about three weeks). While most teeth that have been transplanted remain in good condition, a small number have to be removed subsequently, either because of infection or because the root has been destroyed.

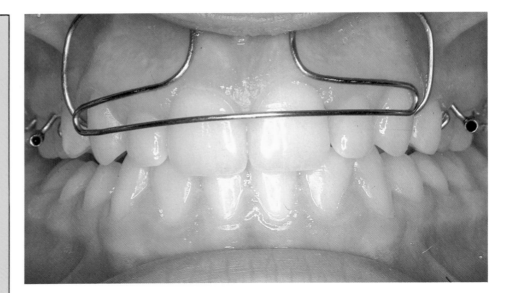

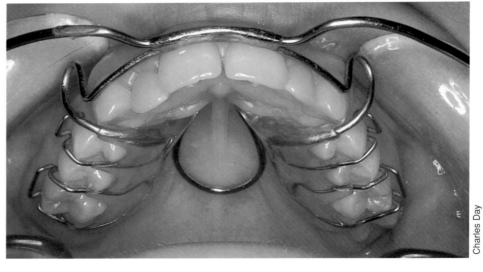

Charles Day

This shows the front view of a removable orthodontic appliance in place (top), and a view of the mouth when extra-oral traction is fixed permanently to it (bottom). The whole appliance is worn 14 hours a day.

direction. Removable appliances can only produce a tilting action on the teeth.

In general, fixed appliances are used in the more complex cases, where teeth need to be rotated or moved. Removable appliances are used in cases where the teeth can simply be tilted back to their correct position.

Removable appliances usually need to be worn both day and night if they are to move the teeth effectively. The appliance is regularly adjusted by the orthodontist, but there may be auxiliary components, such as elastic bands, that the patient has to change.

Extra oral traction (force applied to the teeth from a source outside the mouth) is sometimes applied to removable or fixed appliances to move teeth back further.

Orthodontic appliances must be adjusted monthly, and treatment usually lasts between 18 months and two years, depending on the problem. Although many patients experience some initial discom-

fort, after an orthodontic appointment, this usually disappears after a few days.

Outlook

Malocclusion can be treated successfully because the bone that supports the teeth responds to light pressure, allowing the teeth to be pushed into place. Irregular teeth can be made even and the bite of the teeth can be corrected to a considerable extent. However, it is doubtful if the shape of the jaws themselves can be improved by orthodontic appliances. Patients with very severe discrepancies of the jaw position usually need surgical treatment. In most cases there will need to be some preliminary orthodontic realignment of the teeth.

Orthopedics

Q My son has been put into a whole body cast after an accident. Since he won't be able to wash, will his skin suffer?

A The skin can manage even when it is covered by a plaster cast. When the plaster is finally removed, the dirty skin will have the appearance of sandpaper. This is because it has continued to grow and has shed scales. This unpleasant texture is not a long-term problem and should certainly improve within a few weeks.

Q Is it best to have a bone graft, or set in a pin?

A It is always better to let things heal naturally whenever it is possible. A pin, plate, or other piece of metal is used in the join only if the orthopedic surgeon believes the fracture will not unite firmly without it. A pin holds two bones together, while a graft adds bone pieces that are missing. The cast keeps the injury immobile while it heals.

Q I am having a replacement knee joint. Will this offer the same strength and movement as a real knee?

A A mechanical replacement can't offer the range of movement of a normal knee joint. There will be some limitation of movement in the twisting action that ordinary knees perform, but which the hinge of the replacement joint cannot do. Although it is limited, the range of motion with a replacement will be better than your current knee.

Q After I had my broken leg mended, I found that it was a little shorter than the other. Can an orthopedic surgeon do anything about this?

A Your leg is shorter now because you suffered a severe fracture and have lost a few bone fragments as a result. If you are experiencing any difficulty in walking, it would be a good idea to visit an occupational therapist, who might be able to fit a lift into your shoe.

Orthopedics is the surgical specialty treating diseases and injuries to bones and soft tissues. Orthopedic surgeons deal with a wide range of problems, from fixing sprains and fractures to replacing entire joints.

A broken bone that is left on its own will usually heal, or *unite* as called in medical terminology (see Bones). The orthopedic surgeon tries to make sure that the fracture unites in a good position so that the limb will function well afterward. He or she also insures that no complications develop (see Fractures).

Treatment of fractures

A limb fracture is usually diagnosed in the hospital emergency room. Any simple fracture can be set there, and a cast may be applied, often under anesthetic. The patient will not usually see the orthopedic consultant until he or she has visited the outpatient unit to have the cast inspected and X rays taken (see X rays). This check ensures that the bone ends are fitting and the splint is holding up to everyday wear.

The orthopedist will decide when the cast should come off, and if a new one is required. Most simple fractures of the arm stay in a cast for four to six weeks. Leg fractures are likely to take twice as long because the limb is weight-bearing.

A plaster cast is the most common way to treat fractures, but it has its limitations. Some areas of the body, such as the shoulder and hip, are difficult to hold in place (see Hip). The use of plaster as a cover may cause problems, since the skin itself may have suffered injury and need watching. A cast also stops joints from moving and they may become stiff (see Joints).

A cervical collar provides support for the back of the neck and the lower part of the head. Such support is necessary in cases of whiplash or similar types of injury.

Tom Stewart/Zefa

Reduction and internal fixation

The orthopedic surgeon may decide that a fracture needs an operation. This may be necessary when the bones cannot be brought into a satisfactory position by other means, or when the fracture would confine the patient to bed for an inconveniently long time (see Surgery).

In this type of operation, an incision is made in the skin along the length of the bone, and the surrounding muscles are then pulled back. The periosteum, a layer of tissue that coats the bone, is peeled back from the fracture. Ends of the bones are carefully cleaned and fitted together, or reduced. The ends are joined with a piece of metal using a technique called an internal fixation. A strip of metal is usually screwed along the length of the bone, which crosses the fracture site in a

A fractured leg in traction. The purpose of traction is to pull the bone ends apart and then align them properly.

Putting a leg in traction

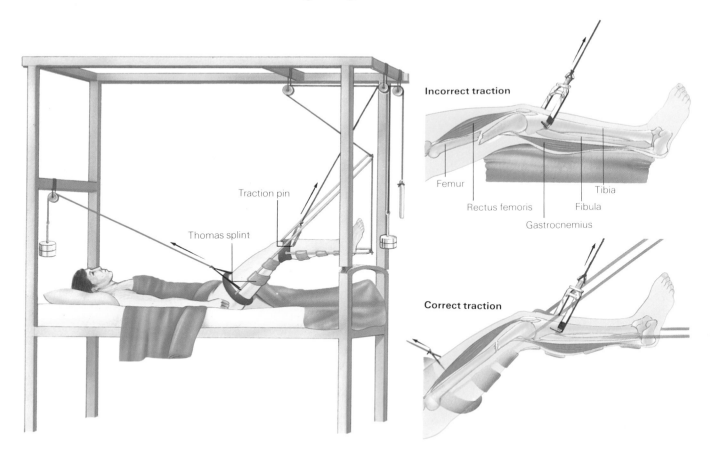

Traction pin

Thomas splint

Incorrect traction

Femur

Rectus femoris

Gastrocnemius

Tibia

Fibula

Correct traction

Aziz Khan

The shaft of the femur has been fractured and traction must be applied parallel to the fracture to exactly align the fractured bone ends. The calculations are complicated, because many different forces have to be counterbalanced to achieve the correct alignment. One factor is the pressure that is exerted by the leg muscles. The leg must be held in exactly the right position so it can counteract and then compensate for the pull of the muscles. The wrong position is shown in the top diagram; however, it has been corrected above. Once the relevant forces have been considered, the correct alignment can be achieved.

procedure called plating. In some cases a long nail is used to hold the bone ends in position, and this is driven up through the hollow shaft of the bone through its entire length.

Pin and plate operation

When the head of the thighbone is fixed, a pin is driven in from the side of the femur and up the center of the broken neck. This insures that the pin stops just short of the joint. It is held in place with a metal plate screwed to the side of the femur. Such a procedure is called a pin and plate operation.

The advantage of fixation by pinning or screwing is that the patient can walk around within days of the operation and a plaster cast is usually unnecessary. The pin and plate surgery is particularly suitable for elderly people who fall and fracture their hips. The metal used is inert and can stay in the body without causing trouble or discomfort to patients.

Traction for fractures

Traction is used almost exclusively for fractures of the leg. After such an injury the muscles tighten up and pull the bone ends past each other, so that the lower fragment rides up to lie alongside the upper fragment. Unless the bone ends are pulled apart and correctly aligned, this will result in union of the fracture with some shortening of the limb.

Traction is applied to the lower bone fragment by means of a weight hung from a steel pin that is driven through the shinbone or heel. The weights are usually hung from an arrangement of pulleys placed at the end of the bed. A 200 lb (91 kg) man needs heavier weights than a six-year-old child. To prevent the weights from pulling the patient out of bed, the foot end is sometimes placed on blocks. The advantage of traction is that it leaves the joints free to move, and skin wounds can be monitored (see Traction).

Bone grafting

Some fractures, particularly those located in the tibia, may fail to unite. In such cases, pieces of bone can be taken from another part of the patient's own skeleton and grafted (see Grafting).

A favored site for the donor bone is the pelvis, which is high up on the hip (see Donors). A strip of bone up to 4 in (10 cm) long can be cut from this bone without damaging the rest of the skeleton. The fracture is first cleaned thoroughly and small pieces of bone graft are placed inside, causing the body to form strong new bone around the bone graft. After this operation is performed, a sound union of the fracture gradually takes place over the next few weeks.

Compound fractures

A compound fracture, with broken bone ends that penetrate the overlying skin, has a high risk of infection and must be treated carefully. This involves cleaning the wound thoroughly. Dead muscle and skin is cut away, removing the possibility of infection with bacteria that can cause gangrene (see Gangrene). After the wound is cleaned, the bone ends can be brought together and the skin sewn into place.

This X ray shows a femur fracture repaired by pin and plate. The use of metal causes no discomfort to the patient.

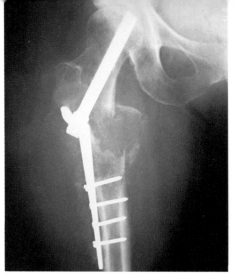

C. James Webb

Pin and plate

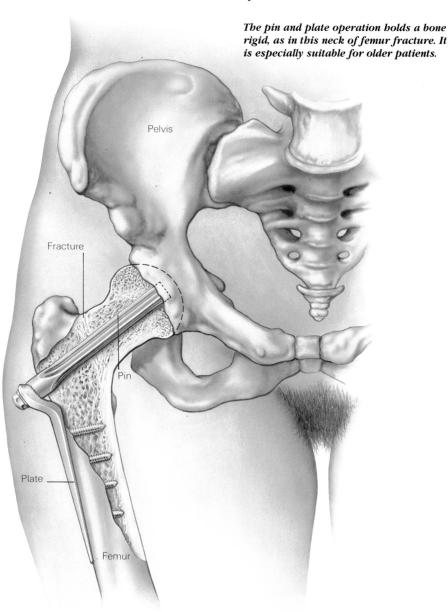

The pin and plate operation holds a bone rigid, as in this neck of femur fracture. It is especially suitable for older patients.

Pelvis

Fracture

Pin

Plate

Femur

Frank Kennard

Q My little girl has spina bifida and uses braces on her legs to help her walk. Will she ever be able to do without such prominent supports?

A Spina bifida sometimes affects the nerves going to the muscles of the legs, resulting in partial paralysis. There is nothing wrong with the bone. Your little girl may wear braces because she has partially paralyzed legs. As she grows older, however, more sophisticated and less noticeable supports can be used.

Q I've heard of football players who have had knee cartilage removed. Why is this?

A The knee is unique among the joints of the body in that it has two triangular wedges of cartilage that lie within the joint cavity. These act as shock absorbers and take the wear and tear of twisting and running. They are attached firmly to the capsule of the joint (around the edges) and to the bone of the knee joint (at the center). Unnatural twisting movements, such as those that occur in sports, separate these two points and can tear the cartilage. Once this happens, because no blood supplies the cartilage, it can never heal. It then gets in the way of normal joint movement and must be removed. This does not make a lot of difference to the use of the knee joint afterward, but it may lead to osteoarthritis over time.

Q Is it possible to transplant whole bone from one patient to another?

A In theory, it would be feasible to transfer whole bone, but there are reasons why such whole bone transplants are unnecessary. There is abundant bony material in a patient's own skeleton, and an artificial bone will have been created using synthetic base material. When this artificial bone is inserted in the body, it becomes invaded by bone-making cells and is gradually adopted by the patient's body. Marrow from bone is transplanted successfully from one person to another.

Internal fixation is usually avoided, because this makes the possibility of a serious infection more likely. If the skin wound cannot be closed with stitches, skin grafting may become necessary.

Ruptured tendon
A rupture of the Achilles tendon at the back of the heel is a common injury. The patient experiences sudden pain at the time of the injury and suffers considerable discomfort afterward. This may be treated by stitching the tendon together, or by putting the ankle in a cast.

Tendons can take six weeks to join together, and during this time they may come apart again or become stuck to the surrounding tissue. This is particularly unfortunate when tendons that lead to the fingers are involved. Very delicate and

In sports like football, sudden movements make strenuous demands on the body. Players are likely to suffer such common injuries as torn cartilage.

complicated surgery may be necessary to restore movement (see Tendons).

Repeated dislocation
Reduction of dislocation is usually simple when the patient is fully relaxed under anesthetic. However, problems can arise when a repeated dislocation occurs.

An example of this would be after a shoulder injury when the first dislocation has weakened the surrounding tissue. In such a case, surgical reconstruction of the joint capsule is required. Since joint injuries often result in some stiffening, it may become necessary to employ physical therapy. This can greatly improve movement and also strengthen muscles (see Sports medicine).

Treating disease
Orthopedic surgeons also treat a variety of different conditions that are not actually the result of any injury. These include such serious problems as birth defects and deformities in young chil-

dren, arthritic conditions, bone cancers, and disorders of the spine.

Orthopedic surgeons and specialists also treat defects such as a congenital dislocation of the hip, which may run in families (see Genetics). With this condition, the ball of the baby's hip joint either fits poorly in its socket, or it does not lie in the socket at all. This is usually detected in the first few weeks of life. When it is, the baby is put in a splint or cast to hold the legs apart so that the hip fits firmly in its socket. The hip usually develops normally if treatment is started early enough. If the baby is more than a few months old, surgery may be necessary.

Joint replacement surgery

In recent years, better wearing materials such as titanium and polyethelene have made it possible to replace entire joints (see Joint replacement). The most common surgery is hip joint replacement. This is where a metal ball and plastic socket are cemented into the thighbone

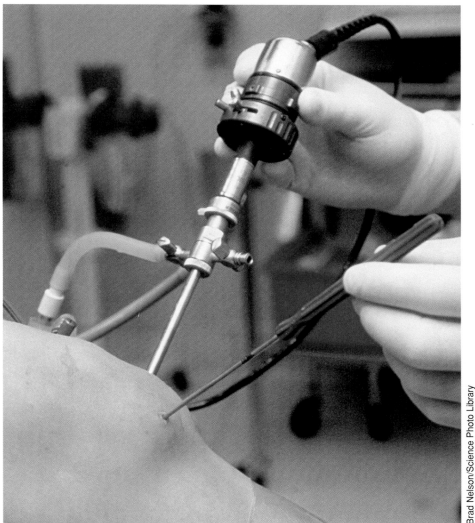

Brad Nelson/Science Photo Library

and hip socket with acrylic cement. This treatment is successful in relieving the pain and stiffness of wear-and-tear arthritis but it is not yet certain how long the artificial hip joint will continue to work before it wears out or loosens. As a result many surgeons are cautious of performing this operation on people under 60 (see Arthritis).

The knee, elbow, shoulder, and knuckle joints can be replaced in a similar way.

Recent advances

Many orthopedic surgeons now use an instrument called an arthroscope for looking inside a knee joint. This instrument is like a small telescope that the surgeon can insert into the joint through a small puncture wound (see Endoscopy). He or she can then judge the condition of the joint and cartilages and even perform some surgery without actually having to open the joint. Advances in this field are improving the surgical treatment of many knee injuries.

This arthroscope allows the surgeon access to remove or reshape any damaged cartilage on a patient's knee joint by remote manipulation. This type of surgery is known as minimally invasive keyhole surgery.

Some orthopedic surgeons now perform microsurgery using extremely fine stitches to join together severed nerves and blood vessels that are no bigger than a matchstick. This type of surgery is performed under a large microscope with the use of very delicate surgical instruments. A number of highly publicized operations have shown that even whole severed limbs can be reattached successfully (see Microsurgery).

In addition, there have also been many developments in the design of artificial replacements, called prostheses (see Prostheses), for missing parts of the body, including artificial valves for the heart. Technical developments that improve artificial limbs have given many amputees hope for a better quality of life.

Osteoarthritis

Q I have suffered from osteoarthritis for many years. Will my daughter inherit this condition?

A Osteoarthritis cannot be inherited. However, there is often a tendency for people in the same family to develop osteoarthritis of the hands. This might reflect the fact that members of the same family often have similar interests, and thus may subject their hands to the same types of stresses.

Q I've read that professional football players often suffer from osteoarthritis, but I thought that exercise was good for you. Are some sports considered unhealthy?

A Aerobic movement that works your large muscle groups (e.g., your legs), is very good for you (see Exercise); repeated stresses and shocks to your joints are not. Gymnasts and ballet dancers land on their bare feet countless times. They land incorrectly when they are learning, and they land hard as they leap higher and swing faster in the air. This repeated shock wears away the cushiony cartilage between the joints.

Particular sports tend to lead to specific complaints. Bicyclists often get knee problems and football players often experience a form of arthritis in the middle bones of the foot. This is probably due to the fact that these parts of the body suffer from repeated small injuries.

Exercise itself is good for you, but repeated injuries are not, and these may cause osteoarthritis.

Q Does cold, damp weather tend to make the condition of osteoarthritis worse?

A This is such a common report from patients that it seems very likely to be true. However, there is no logical medical reason to suggest why a cold, damp climate should make the disease more severe. It may be that people are simply more aware of the pain that is caused by osteoarthritis when the weather becomes dreary, damp, and cold.

Many people regard aching and painful joints as an inevitable part of aging. The cause may be a condition called osteoarthritis. Drugs can relieve pain, and in severe cases surgery can offer dramatic improvement.

Alain Dex, Publiphoto Diffusion/Science Photo Library

People who have stiff and deformed osteoarthritic fingers can still be active. Mechanical devices can help.

Osteoarthritis is one of the most common forms of arthritis. Half of the population over the age of 50 has some signs of the disease, which can also affect people in their 30s and 40s. Although it is possible to get osteoarthritis in almost any joint in the body, there are some joints where it is more likely to occur. These include the hips, the knees, the hands, the back, and the neck.

Osteoarthritis is very painful and can be crippling. The condition reduces the amount of movement in severely affected joints. Treatment is with aspirin or other painkillers, and in serious cases surgery can be performed. It is now possible to replace some of the joints that are most likely to be affected (see Arthritis).

Causes

A great deal is now known about how osteoarthritis develops once it actually occurs, but the causes of the disease remain obscure. Joints between bones are lined with a membrane called the synovial membrane. This forms a bag that surrounds the joint; the bag is filled with synovial fluid. Parts of the joint where the bones come in contact with each other are lined with cartilage. It is the action of the two cartilage surfaces coming into direct contact with each other that bears the weight of the joint.

Cartilage itself consists of a hard network of fibers that contains the cartilage-producing cells and fluid. This cartilage provides an excellent lubricated surface for the moving parts of the joint (see Cartilage). Osteoarthritis is a disease that results from the alteration in the structure of this cartilage (see Joints).

In the first stage of osteoarthritis, a number of small clefts appear on the surface of the cartilage. There is also an increase in the number of cells producing cartilage. At this stage the patient may not notice any symptoms, or they may only experience slight pain and stiffness.

In the next stage the cartilage caps on the bone ends wear thin. Finally, there is no cartilage left and the bone ends bear directly onto one another. There may be considerable destruction of the bone as it is worn away by movements of the joint and also a thickening of the capsule of the synovial membrane that surrounds the joints.

Unlike cartilage, bone is able to repair itself as it gets eaten away. However, the way in which bone manages this around an osteoarthritic joint is disorganized. This can lead to the appearance of rough deposits that result in more harm than good to the joint (see Bones).

The cause of osteoarthritis seems to be the continual stress on the joint, which accounts for the name *wear-and-tear arthritis*. However, this theory does not explain why joints that bear the same amount of weight are not always equally affected. For example, while the hip and knee are likely to be involved, the ankle is not (see Knee).

Some factors may predispose a patient to develop osteoarthritis. For example, a history of repeated small injuries may be a causative factor. People who engage

Homecraft Supplies

The thick molded handles on these utensils can help osteoarthritis sufferers perform daily tasks such as cooking food.

regularly in sports such as professional football may be more likely to experience osteoarthritis, particularly in the feet (see Sports medicine).

Deformity of the limb or a joint may be another contributory factor. This can lead to severe stresses on the joint, such as a repeated injury.

Another factor making osteoarthritis more likely is when the nerve supply to a particular joint is interrupted due to

Treating osteoarthritis

Site	Symptoms	Treatment
Hands	Usually affects the joints between the bones of the fingers, producing characteristic lumps on either side of the furthest joint (Heberden's nodes). The thumb is often involved. Joints are painful on movement	Aspirin and related drugs. Immobilizing the thumb in a cast may be helpful
Feet	Pain on walking, most commonly found in the joint at the base of the big toe	Aspirin and related drugs. Surgical shoes or surgery may help
Ankles	Very rare, unless there is some bone deformity	—
Knees	Affects more women than men. Sometimes very little pain. Knock-knees can result	Basic treatment is with drugs, but very painful or deformed joints can be treated surgically
Hips	Pain particularly on walking. Can lead to a limp or a waddle if both hips are involved	Initial treatment is with aspirin or a related drug. A walking stick may be helpful. Surgery such as joint replacement may be used in more severe cases
Spine	Most common in the neck. Causes pain and limitation of movement. Neck involvement can lead to blackouts or weakness in arms and legs	Aspirin and other pain-relieving drugs. A neck collar worn at night may be helpful
Shoulder	Rare, unless there has been some injury. Immobility and stiffness are usually more of a problem than pain	Exercises combined with painkilling drugs may help to ease shoulder movement
Elbow	Rare. Pain is the main problem and it may occur at rest, but there may also be numbness in the arm and hand and loss of muscle power	Aspirin and related drugs are used for the pain. Pinched nerves may have to be freed by surgery

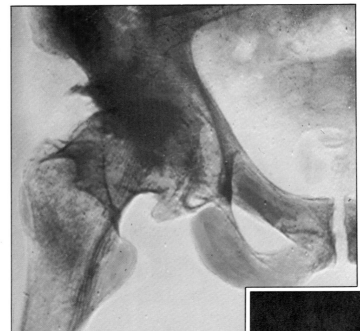

Q I have had both cartilages removed from my left knee. Am I likely to get osteoarthritis as a result?

A There is no certainty you will get the disease, but people who have had their cartilages removed have more osteoarthritis of the knee than people who haven't. And the chances of this occurring increase if you get a knee injury when a cartilage is torn. This may lead to some abnormalities in knee function, and this may cause osteoarthritis. To avoid repeated injury to your knee, you should give up contact sports (if you play them).

If this sounds a bit depressing, remember that many people over 50 years old will develop some osteoarthritic symptoms.

Q I have osteoarthritis and find that my joints tend to stiffen if I sit down for an hour. Is this a common experience for people with the disease?

A Yes. People with arthritis tend to feel stiff after they have not moved their joints for a while. In rheumatoid arthritis, which is also common, affected patients often feel stiff in the mornings. This also happens with osteoarthritis.

The stiffness only lasts about 15 minutes in osteoarthritis, whereas patients with rheumatoid arthritis experience this symptom for a much longer period of time.

Q Are men or women more likely to experience osteoarthritis, and does it affect the sexes differently?

A Osteoarthritis is a disease that particularly affects the elderly. Since women live to a greater age (in general) than men, it would appear that more women suffer from the condition. However, with younger age groups, men and women are almost equally affected. The condition may be even slightly more common in younger men.

Also, the two sexes tend to get the disease in different joints. In men it is more common for the hips to be involved, and in women the hands, knees, and the base of the thumb are affected.

These X rays of an osteoarthritic hip (left) and knee (below) show how the disease has affected the joints. Normally bones are lined with cartilage, causing joints to be protected. Here the cartilage caps have worn down and the bone ends bear directly onto each other. They, too, are worn down by movement. Pain and stiffness will result.

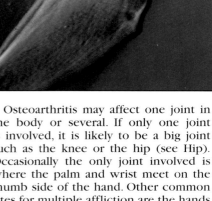

CNRI/Vision International

some problem in the nervous system (see Nervous system). Since the sensation of pain is interrupted, the patient may injure a joint repeatedly and not be aware of it (see Numbness).

However, in the majority of patients showing signs of osteoarthritic disease, there is no obvious cause.

Symptoms

The main symptom of osteoarthritis is pain. This can vary from a simple dull ache in an affected joint to excruciating pain on movement that may make patients practically immobile.

Usually the pain from an osteoarthritic joint is more severe during movement. But there may also be a duller aching pain when the joint is at rest. This pain is thought to result from the disorganization of the way that the veins drain blood from the joint. Pain during rest may be due to the joint being congested with blood (see Pain).

The pain tends to become steadily worse, but not always in the affected joint. It is very common for osteoarthritis of the hip to cause pain in the knee on the same side, or in the back.

Osteoarthritis also causes stiffness. This is usually worse in the morning, but it tends to become better within a few minutes. The affected joints may also swell in some cases.

As the disease progresses, there may be considerable deformity in the joints. When badly affected hips and knees creak, doctors call this crepitus. The range of movement may decrease until the joint is almost fixed.

Osteoarthritis may affect one joint in the body or several. If only one joint is involved, it is likely to be a big joint such as the knee or the hip (see Hip). Occasionally the only joint involved is where the palm and wrist meet on the thumb side of the hand. Other common sites for multiple affliction are the hands and the spine.

Dangers

Although very unpleasant, osteoarthritis is not a dangerous condition. Serious problems are most likely to arise when the disease affects the spine in the neck, causing pain and stiffness. This is called cervical spondylosis.

Three problems can arise from this, the first being a pain and stiffness of the neck. The second and third, which are serious but rare, arise from attempts of the bone to repair itself, leading to bone overgrowth. Pressure on blood vessels to the lower part of the brain will cut off the blood supply, leading to blackouts and dizziness when a person looks upward or around to the side. Pressure on the spinal cord or the nerves will lead to weakness in both the arms and legs.

Treatment

Non-steroidal antiinflammatory drugs (NSAIDs) and aspirin are the preferred treatment because not only do they stop pain, but they also reduce inflammation; acetaminophen (Tylenol) reduces pain only (see Painkillers). However, in some cases, injecting corticosteroids into the affected joint markedly reduces both the pain and debilitating effects. A walking stick can help osteoarthritis of the knee and hip (see Pain management).

Joint replacement surgery is performed in severely affected cases. This can lessen pain and improve joint movement. The most successful operation is on the hip joint, although there has been progress in knee joint replacements as well (see Joint replacement).

Apart from joint replacement, there is an operation called an osteotomy where the bones on either side of a joint are remodeled. This can be of great value to improve the way the joint carries weight. This operation tends to be used in younger patients. No one is certain how long replaced joints last, but there is always the option of replacing the joint at some later stage.

Finally, the joint can be completely fused so that it cannot move and cause pain. Although this sounds drastic, it can

be extremely successful in some patients. It may offer tremendous pain relief, often without much loss of function in the affected limb, which probably was fairly stiff in the first place.

Outlook

Once osteoarthritis occurs, it does not disappear. By the age of 65, about 80 percent of the population has X-ray evidence of the disorder. However, only a quarter of these show symptoms of the disease. The symptoms can be greatly relieved by drugs in most cases.

Surgical treatment has advanced greatly in recent decades, bringing tremendous relief to many sufferers, especially those affected in the hip. In other joints, surgical treatment is generally regarded as a last resort.

Hip replacement

The head of the femur is removed, holes are drilled, and plastic cement is pushed in.

A prosthetic ball and stem is inserted into the femur and held in place by the cement.

Stem and head are rejoined, and traction is used to maintain the position of the leg.

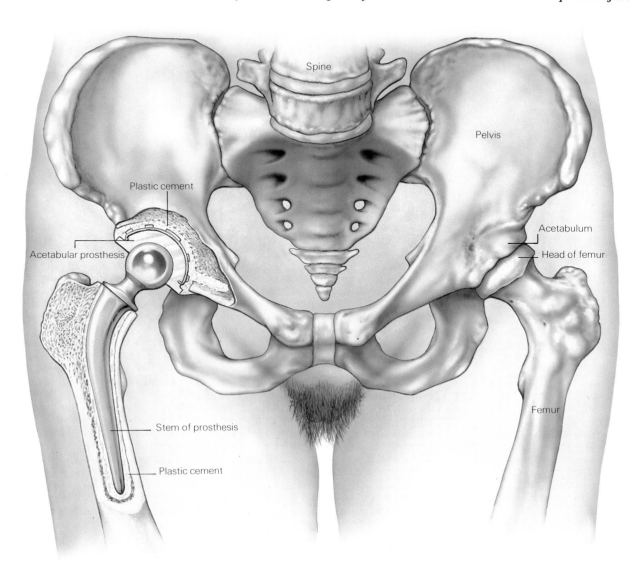

Frank Kennard

1275

Osteopathy

Q Are chiropractors and osteopaths the same?

A No. Chiropractors are limited to doing musculoskeletal manipulations. In the United States, osteopaths may do some manipulation, but they are fully trained and qualified physicians. Osteopaths are qualified to prescribe medicines, whereas chiropractors are not.

Q How can I find an osteopath if my doctor is unable to recommend one to me?

A If your doctor cannot help you to find a suitable osteopath, you might consult one of the professional osteopathic associations. Their services can be found in traditional hospitals or in specialized osteopathic clinics.

Q Are all osteopaths medically qualified?

A Usually, yes. Practitioners who have completed their formal medical training will be identified by the letters D.O. after their names. This is often followed by those letters that signify their membership of a professional organization.

Q My doctor says that my lower-back pain is being caused by a slipped disk. Could osteopathy help my condition?

A There are many different causes of pain in the lower back, and a herniated (slipped) disk is sometimes responsible. A genuine herniated disk will probably require a sustained period of complete bed rest in order to allow natural healing to occur. Skillful manipulation may be helpful, but it is very risky if you have a slipped disk. In cases that are not herniated disks, for example simple strains or sprains of the muscles, ligaments, or joint capsules of the spine, osteopathic treatment, physical therapy, or chiropracty may go a long way to help relieve the symptoms.

The art of manipulation and massage (osteopathy) has been practiced since ancient times. Today it is becoming more accepted as a treatment that can achieve success when conventional medicine seems to fail.

Colorsport

Osteopathy is a system of medicine that diagnoses and treats disorders of the bones, muscles, ligaments, and joints. It is also a therapy that recognizes all parts of the body and takes into account people's health, lifestyle, environment, diet, and stress factors.

The osteopath is a highly trained practitioner who uses his or her hands to treat the body when illness arises. He or she works to restore body control mechanisms, to relieve pain and discomfort, and to improve joint mobility.

Although massage and manipulation have existed since ancient times, the art and science of osteopathy actually originated in the US in the late 19th century. The founder, Andrew Taylor Still, had qualified as a doctor, but like many of his contemporaries, he was skeptical of

The most common strains and sprains that are treated by osteopaths are sports injuries, particularly those that arise in contact sports.

many of the methods then used. He had developed a consuming interest in the structure of the body during his childhood and he chose osteopathy (bone disease) as the name for his system of healing to underline the principle that structure governs function. Although this was doubted by the medical profession of his day, modern research has proved him right. The self-regulating activities that keep numerous body functions within proper limits (homeostasis) are closely related to the structural components by different reflexes of the nervous system. By normalizing the relationships of joints (especially of the spine), muscles, ligaments, and connective tissue, the osteopath can affect the whole body (see Massage, and Manipulation).

Scope of osteopathy

Most people who consult an osteopath do so because they have pain and restricted movement somewhere (often in the lower back, the neck, or the shoulder). These injuries arise for a variety of different reasons that range from accidents to rheumatism (see Rheumatism). However, an osteopath can often resolve these problems faster and more completely than rest in bed or drugs.

Some scientists believe that massage can speed healing by softening the scar tissue, and improving the metabolism and blood flow, but this is not proven.

Osteopaths may also use ultrasound (see Ultrasound), or heat therapies (see Heat treatment).

Medicine divides diseases into the principal categories of organic and functional. Organic illnesses are those in which destruction or permanent alteration of some body tissue or system occurs, for example, tuberculosis, cancer, bone diseases, cirrhosis of the liver, and coronary artery disease. Functional illnesses occur when the body is not working properly, either because of infections, changes in blood pressure, or by recurring symptoms of migraines or asthma, for example. Many illnesses called psychosomatic are given this label because no obvious medical reason can be found for the disorder (see Psychosomatic problems). Anxiety, stress, and emotional

or personality problems often accompany these disorders with the resulting symptoms of muscular tension, disturbed circulation, and altered nerve and hormonal supply (see Anxiety). Osteopathy, by treating these associated symptoms manually, has a constructive and powerful role to play in the healing process.

Osteopathic treatment is actually suitable for people of all ages, whether male or female. It is especially suitable for growing children, since if potential disorders are detected and treated at this early stage, future disabilities can be prevented. Strains, sprains, falls, and other minor injuries generally are only painful for a short time; but the long-term effects that are caused by muscular and ligamentous shortening, fibrosis, and minor derangements in the joints are very common

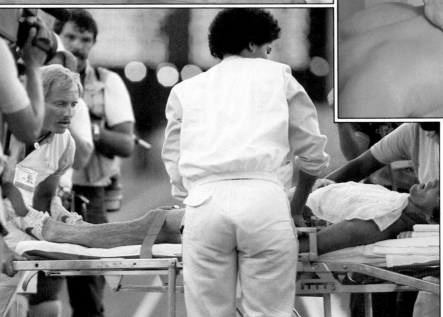

Amateur marathon runners (top left) and thoroughly fit and trained Olympic athletes (left) seem equally prone to muscular injuries that can benefit from the healing manipulation of an osteopath (above). Leg injuries usually heal very quickly. More troublesome are back strains; these may require a lengthy course of treatment before they heal.

Q **What causes the pop sound when the osteopath adjusts my spine?**

A Each vertebra in the spine has four bony projections that form joints with adjacent vertebrae. Each of these joints is enclosed by a fibrous capsule with synovial fluid inside as a lubricant. When the spine is manipulated, the joint surfaces are forced apart, which disturbs the pressure equilibrium inside the joint capsule. The resulting pop is similar in principle to cracking the knuckles. The sound is louder because it goes along the bones of the spine.

Q **My 14-year-old brother has developed a curvature of the spine. Can osteopathic treatment help him?**

A It depends on the reason for the curvature. If it is caused by an accident or poor posture, then a complete cure can be expected. However, a few children develop a more severe curvature (scoliosis), which is hereditary. Regular osteopathic treatment during the growing phase can usually reduce the degree of curvature, but surgical splinting of the spine may be the only answer.

Q **The osteopath I consulted for lower-back pain has advised me to have all my shoes fitted with a higher heel on one foot. Why is this?**

A It may be that you have a primary short leg, which means that the bones in one leg are shorter than the other. This is fairly common, due to either an earlier fracture, or the bones growing at different rates. A primary short leg unbalances the pelvis, forcing the spine to bend to one side or the other, and to form curves in compensation. The unequal pressures and muscular tensions of this posture can cause strains and consequent backaches. Although most human spines are flexible enough to adapt to a small difference in leg lengths, a heel insert or a specially modified shoe may be necessary to level off the pelvis, and so correct the imbalance and spinal pressure.

(see Sprains). Eventually lack of exercise, obesity, increasing age, or a subsequent injury can reveal these weaknesses. If they are left untreated, an increased susceptibility to injury or the onset of arthritis can occur (see Arthritis).

Osteopathic diagnosis and treatment are certainly not a substitute for medicine or surgery in diseases where these methods are clearly more effective. But it can help treat most muscle and bone disorders, functional illnesses, and chronic diseases that can seriously affect the structure of the body.

Training

Osteopaths study a number of medical disciplines including anatomy, physiology, pathology, biochemistry, and neurology, as well as osteopathic diagnosis and treatment. The distinctive feature of the training is the development of great sensitivity of the hands, an essential requirement for proper diagnosis, and the corresponding artistry and subtlety

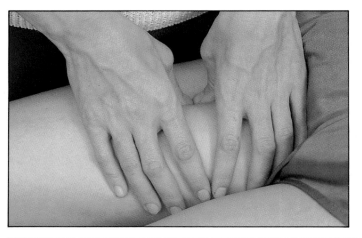

in the application of treatment to the body. Diagnosis of a problem can involve initial X rays, blood and urine tests, and also referral to specialists, in addition to manual techniques (see X rays).

Theory and practice

All the various bodily systems function normally by very sophisticated processes of communication and control. The role of the muscles and bones is actually much greater than simply providing support and a framework for the body. The muscles, for example, besides enabling physical work and self-expression, also affect bone structure and posture, circulation, metabolism, and hormonal balance (see Muscles).

Osteopathy is specifically concerned with how disturbances and injuries of a mechanical nature can negatively influence other bodily processes and contribute to poor health. A central part of this theory has been called the osteopathic lesion. In medical terms a lesion is

Massage often forms part of manipulative therapy. It can revitalize tired muscles as well as more serious problems. Stress can manifest itself in neck strain caused by tensed muscles. Gentle manipulation of the face, head, and neck will loosen those muscles and so relieve pain.

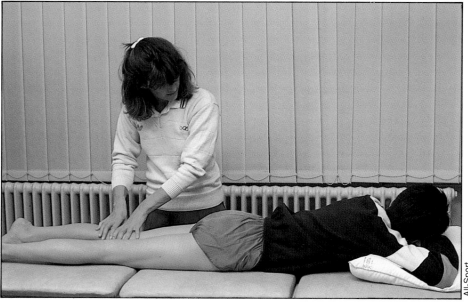

All-Sport

a disturbance of the structure or function of the body, such as a wound, tumor, or chemical abnormality. In osteopathic practice, a lesion is a more complex and subtle disturbance that may appear as a source of pain or discomfort, yet be unnoticed by the patient, or by a routine medical examination.

The osteopathic lesion, discovered by careful touch examination and specific tests, may be an area of contracted muscle or a shortened ligament anywhere in the body. It frequently occurs as a change in normal joint movement in the spinal column.

The vertebrae themselves are passive structures that are pushed or pulled around by the forces of gravity, trauma, and muscular or ligamentous action. The distinctive contribution of osteopathic medicine is to seek out and to then correct these disturbances by manual methods, supplemented when necessary by other therapies, especially change in the diet and the environment. By resolving these disturbances, local pain or discomfort from muscle spasm or irritation of the nerve roots is gradually relieved and altered circulation is achieved, along with the beneficial effects for the overall health of the person.

From the osteopathic point of view, the spinal lesion is generally the largest single contributing factor in this vicious circle of functional and organic disorder. The correcting influences of manipulation are therefore applied to restore the natural defenses and at the same time to encourage the tendency of the body to restore body controls, thereby restoring the patient's good health and his or her general well-being.

Treatment

A typical session with an osteopath generally lasts for between 20 and 30 minutes. Once the cause of the pain or illness has been determined, the osteopath will then decide if manipulation is safe and desirable, and if so, what type of treatment to apply.

Frequently any specific spinal manipulation is preceded by soft tissue work, for example, massage, stretching, and putting the joints through their full ranges of movement. Some osteopaths practice a specialized form of manipulation that is applied to the head and upper neck. This is known as cranial osteopathy, and it is a very gentle treatment that is particularly useful for treating young children, and for treating functional disorders such as migraines, sinusitis, and visual disturbances (see Sinusitis, and Migraines).

The number of osteopathy sessions that are needed for a particular condition will vary widely among individuals, but most osteopaths prefer not only to resolve the main problem, but also to improve the patient's general mobility and health, in order to prevent problems occurring in the future.

Dangers

There are a considerable number of diseases and conditions for which manipulation is undesirable or even dangerous. The practitioner's skill and experience should determine whether or not they try to treat spinal disk herniation, osteoarthritis, or severe sciatica.

However, tuberculosis, malignancy, fractures, acute arthritis, various bone diseases, and severe cases of herniated disks that cause neurological symptoms should not be manipulated under any circumstances. A qualified osteopath can detect these conditions and then make appropriate referrals. This is the major advantage that an osteopath has over a chiropractor (see Chiropractic).

Massage therapy (below) may be intensified by specialized manipulation (left).

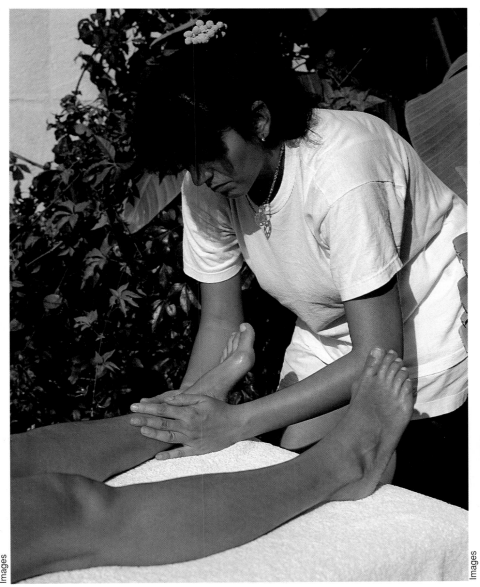

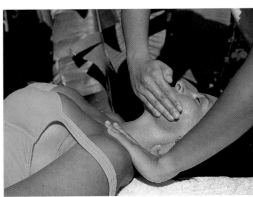

Osteoporosis

Q My grandmother has a humped back. It seems to have occurred gradually since her 70th birthday. She calls it her dowager's hump, and says that it's not worth worrying about because it doesn't hurt. Is she right? And what caused it?

A A dowager's hump is the result of osteoporosis, a condition in which the bones become smaller, lighter, and less robust than normal. Over the years this has meant that some of the bones in your grandmother's spine have become squashed and that others have collapsed into a wedge shape, so that the spine has bent into the hump shape you describe. Your grandmother is right not to worry about it; it is not life-threatening and severe cases are rare. It often causes no pain.

Q I've heard that I can avoid osteoporosis if I drink plenty of milk. Is this true?

A Although some of the constituents of milk are essential for the growth of bones, milk cannot prevent osteoporosis, which is a condition of old age and its accompanying changes in the balance of the body's hormones or chemical messengers. So by all means drink plenty of milk, but don't expect it to work wonders.

Q Is it true that women on hormone replacement therapy do not develop osteoporosis, and if so, why?

A Hormone replacement therapy (HRT) is given to many women who suffer from severe problems associated with menopause. One of these problems is the failure of the ovaries to produce the hormone estrogen, and it is thought that a lack of estrogen is a cause of osteoporosis. Evidence suggests that HRT does seem to prevent or reverse the condition to some extent. Today's HRT usually consists of both estrogen and progesterone hormones. This combination therapy helps to reduce the risk of cancer of the uterus.

This condition of unusually light and fragile bones causes 150,000 hip fractures in US women each year. Yet it is preventable.

The bones in the body are not dead, as some people imagine. They are living material that is constantly changing. When such changes involve a loss of bone, the condition is called osteoporosis.

Causes

The most common cause of osteoporosis is aging. From middle age onward everyone's bones become lighter. This change is generally more marked in women after they have been through the menopause. But it is only when an excessive amount of bone is lost that the symptoms of osteoporosis arise (see Bones).

There are other, more complicated causes of osteoporosis, most of which are rare. In such cases the loss of bone is usually a result of drastic changes in the body that have been brought about by another illness. In these instances the osteoporosis is described as secondary, since it is an effect of the initial (primary) illness and will disappear if the primary illness is cured. Many of these rare causes are diseases of the hormonal system (see Endocrine system).

There is one relatively common secondary cause that is generally described as immobilization, meaning simply that the patient must stay in bed for some reason. Thus osteoporosis is often seen in the bones of a single limb, which cannot be moved because of pain, paralysis, or a broken (fractured) bone.

Symptoms

The condition may cause no symptoms at all, or it may give rise to bone pain and backaches. In advanced cases there may be deformities such as loss of height or a bent spine. The bones tend to break easily from minor accidents or trivial strains (see Lower-back pain).

The most commonly caused fracture is the collapse of one of the spinal vertebrae (small bones). This may not hurt, or it may cause severe pain over that bone, which tends to improve without treatment over the next two or three months. In the long run, several of these fractures may occur, and cause the spine to shorten and bend (see Fractures).

The other common fracture site is the hip, which is particularly vulnerable in older people, whose poor balance and

Elderly people are prone to osteoporosis. The weakened bones can cause minor deformities, falls, and fractures.

How osteoporosis affects the spine

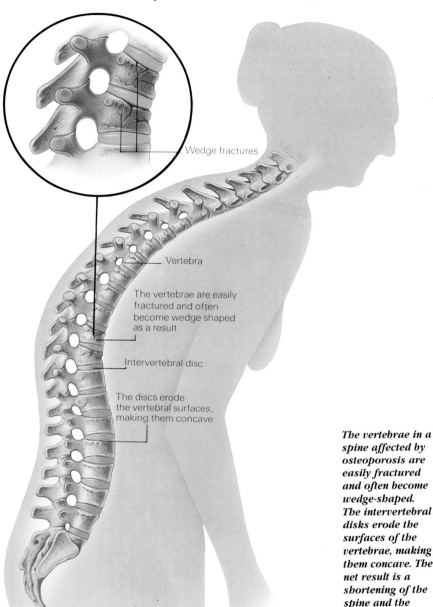

Wedge fractures

Vertebra

The vertebrae are easily fractured and often become wedge shaped as a result

Intervertebral disc

The discs erode the vertebral surfaces, making them concave

Mike Courteney

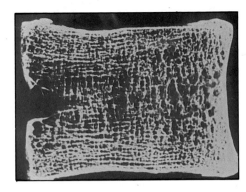

This X ray of a normal vertebra shows bone with both a normal calcium content and a regular structure.

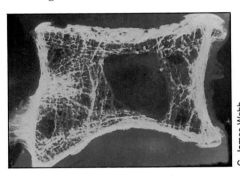

C. James Webb

Osteoporosis in this vertebra shows up clearly. The affected areas look blacker than normal bone would.

The vertebrae in a spine affected by osteoporosis are easily fractured and often become wedge-shaped. The intervertebral disks erode the surfaces of the vertebrae, making them concave. The net result is a shortening of the spine and the characteristic bumped look.

general stiffness make them likely to fall. If an elderly patient has osteoporosis, a relatively minor trauma will often be enough to break the hipbone (see Hip).

Diagnosis
The diagnosis of osteoporosis is confirmed with X rays and bone densitometry nuclear scans, which can measure bone density and predict future risks of osteoporotic fractures. Women generally have these tests done when they reach menopause (see Menopause). Blood tests may be used in order to rule out another

disease that has similar symptoms or whether there is a disease present that can cause secondary osteoporosis, such an overactive thyroid (see Thyroid).

Dangers
Left untreated, osteoporosis can seriously restrict mobility and cause disability. Repeated fractures may confine a sufferer to a wheelchair. Hip and other fractures that cause immobilization have a high death rate in elderly patients.

The associated back troubles may also affect the nerves leading from the spine

to the limbs, causing considerable pain and weakness. In the most advanced cases, the back can become bent almost double, and breathing may become very difficult (see Back and backache).

Treatment
The patient should become as mobile as possible. Regular exercise promotes strong bones and also prevents their deterioration. Following a fracture, the patient is encouraged to get moving at the earliest possible opportunity.

To give the bones the best conditions for growth, a calcium-rich diet is advised (see Calcium). Hormone replacement treatment (HRT) which together with estrogen can help retard further bone loss (see Estrogen, and Hormone replacement therapy). Alendronate is a new drug that can build bone and prevent fractures, although its optimal use has not yet been found.

Outlook
Although aging, lack of exercise, and a calcium-poor diet can all aggravate osteoporosis, the disease can be prevented with regular exercise, calcium supplements, and HRT. New drugs can cure it, so no one should needlessly have to suffer this debilitating disease.

Otitis

Q My husband has had otitis but needs to travel by airplane. Is this dangerous?

A No. However, because the air pressure in the cabin of the aircraft does vary during takeoff and landing, this may be very uncomfortable for your husband if he cannot equalize the air pressure on either side of his eardrum. He should try swallowing, chewing gum, or holding his nose while gently blowing through his nose.

Q My sister loves swimming in the local pool, but one of her friends had to stop going because she was told swimming caused otitis. Is this true?

A Swimming and diving are fine when you have healthy ears. The trouble starts when an avid swimmer ignores the inflammation that is the first sign of otitis, which would then be aggravated by swimming. Occasionally otitis is an adverse reaction to swimming itself, and anyone who knows that they have this tendency should protect their ears with earplugs or a swimming cap.

Q What should I do if my little brother inadvertently puts something in his ear that cannot be removed easily?

A Any foreign material in the ear can and should be removed by a doctor or nurse as soon as possible. Do-it-yourself exploration can damage the eardrum and you should not use Q-Tips in the ears. Similarly, too much wax should be medically treated. It can be softened with mineral oil before being syringed by a trained nurse or a doctor.

Q Is it true that people suffering from otitis will sometimes need urgent hospital treatment?

A The ear lies very close to the brain, so if infection is not controlled there may be a risk of meningitis, which must be treated by a specialist. However, this should not happen if otitis is treated early.

Thanks to antibiotics, otitis (an infection of the ears) should not be dangerous these days. However, it is still important to seek early treatment to help prevent the recurrence of ear problems.

Parts of the ear

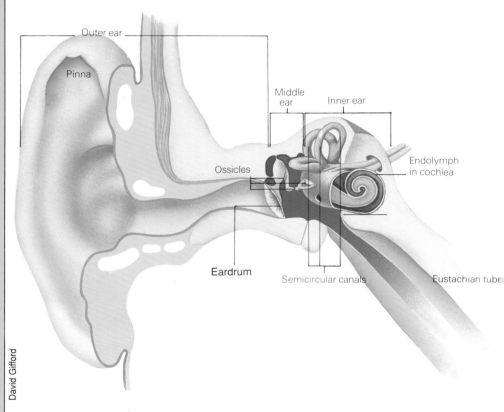

David Gifford

Each ear consists of three parts, which combine to make it the organ of both hearing and balance. The outer ear, or visible part, receives sound waves, which are transmitted via the eardrum to the middle ear. Here the waves are amplified by three bones (the ossicles) before they pass through another membrane and into the inner ear. In this compartment sound vibrations are converted into electrical impulses, which travel along a pair of nerves to the brain which interprets them as sound (see Hearing).

There are membranes between the three parts of the ear. These membranes help to prevent infection, particularly to the sensitive inner ear. However, the process of transmitting information in the form of sound can be interrupted by infection. There are three types of infection: otitis externa, otitis media, and otitis interna, which relate directly to the outer, middle, and inner ear respectively.

Otitis externa

Otitis externa is inflammation of the skin of the outer ear caused by bacteria or fungi. The condition usually arises if the ear is not dried properly after getting wet (for example, after swimming), or if the skin is very sensitive and has a tendency to eczema. The canal leading to the middle ear may also become affected if the wax in it becomes irritated (see Wax in ear). This may occur if the ear is explored with a sharp instrument, such as a matchstick or a pencil.

The ear may become red and itchy, sometimes there is a watery discharge. Drops and ointments are good for clearing up mild cases of inflammation. But if the infection is very severe and painful, antibiotics are usually given orally, particularly because it may not be just the outer ear that is affected. It is always important to remember that any unskilled treatment of the ears is extremely unwise.

Zefa

skull cavity, which was a serious complication of otitis media (see Mastoiditis).

Otitis media is a common condition in babies and young children who may not even complain of an earache but may feel ill and possibly have a temperature. For this reason doctors always examine the ears of young children who have a fever. *Hemophilus,* a bacterium often found in the respiratory tract, is a common cause of otitis. Since it also causes meningitis (see Meningitis), children are immunized against *Hemophilus.*

Chronic otitis media
Occasionally the problem recurs when infection enters the middle ear through the discharging hole in the eardrum. The earache persists, and there may be a slight discharge of pus. Impaired or painful hearing may follow as the eardrum and ossicles become scarred, so prompt treatment is important to prevent this.

With careful cleansing the infection can be controlled. But when the bone is affected, surgery may be needed. Serious defects in the eardrum may be repaired by grafting.

Otitis interna
Otitis interna is now very rare but may occur if a middle ear infection has been allowed to spread, resulting in deafness and giddiness (see Deafness). Treatment should be given immediately, before any permanent damage can be done.

It is best to avoid swimming when there is an ear infection. A simple ear examination (below) will reveal any reduction in hearing due to fluid in the middle ear.

Otitis media
Otitis media is usually the result of a bacterial or viral infection of the nose and throat. The infection reaches the ear along the eustachian tube, the passage leading from the back of the nose to the middle ear. Such complications are very common in children, and may follow an illness like measles, tonsillitis, or a common cold.

Acute otitis media can cause a violent earache and fever together with muffled hearing. This is due to a buildup of fluid in the middle ear, which normally contains only air. When a bacterial infection is suspected, antibiotics are given. Occasionally, the eardrum perforates to discharge the pus (see Pus). Sometimes the eardrum has to be drained surgically to get rid of the pus; however, once the infection has cleared up, the drum heals and there should be no further trouble.

A doctor should be consulted immediately if a middle ear infection is suspected. Sulfonamides and other antibiotics can now prevent mastoiditis, the spread of infection to the mastoid cells or the

Blair Seitz/Science Photo Library

Outpatients

Q My mother has just spent some time in the hospital following a heart attack. Will she have to continue visiting the outpatient clinic when she gets better?

A That depends on her health coverage. Many people in the United States have private health coverage and each case will be followed up by the specialist concerned in his or her office, rather than the patient having to go to an outpatient clinic.

Q I have difficulty getting around, and I cannot afford a taxi. How will I get to the hospital?

A If there is no one in your family who can take you, perhaps there is a neighbor you can ask. Your doctor may be able to put you in touch with a charitable organization that offers such a service. Alternatively, your local church may be able to help. If none of these is possible, money may be provided by your insurance for a taxi.

Q Can I take a friend to the hospital with me?

A Certainly you can. The specialist may allow you to bring your friend in with you when you have your appointment, but you should always ask first.

Q If I am late for an appointment at the hospital, will the specialist still see me, or will I have to wait for another appointment?

A That depends on how late you are. Most specialists see several patients in a morning or afternoon session, so that if you arrive before the end of your appointed session you will probably still be seen. However, if you are very late, the specialist is unlikely to be able to see you, since most specialists have a very tight schedule that is not very flexible. You can always call the hospital if you think you are going to be late, and the staff will advise you about the best thing to do.

When we think of going to a hospital, most of us imagine wards with long corridors of bedrooms. Most of the day-to-day work of a modern district general hospital is generally carried out in the outpatient clinic.

When your doctor feels that you should have the benefit of the advice and treatment of a hospital specialist, he or she will usually recommend that you see one in the part of the hospital outpatient clinic where that particular specialist holds his or her practice. You will need to take a letter from your doctor to the specialist; this will detail the condition that needs to be investigated and treated.

The specialist has all the resources of the hospital to enable him or her to investigate your case and to treat you once a clear diagnosis has been made. Many cases can be handled without the

When you visit the outpatient clinic you will have to wait your turn. Some hospitals provide toys to entertain young children, and magazines for adults to read.

Will & Deni McIntyre/Science Photo Library

patient needing to stay in the hospital, although people who are referred to one of the surgeons at the hospital may need to be admitted for surgery at some point.

Use of outpatient clinics

There has been a great expansion in the use of outpatient facilities in hospitals in recent years, and every effort is made to avoid admitting people unless it is necessary. This is better for the patients and less expensive, and better for the hospital because keeping people in the hospital means that services have to be provided on a 24-hour, seven-day-a-week basis.

Some people need complicated tests even though they are not ill enough to require the level of nursing care that the staff of a surgical or medical unit provide. In view of this, many hospitals have created special wards that are halfway between a ward and an outpatient clinic. These may vary from an investigation unit that takes in patients for tests first thing in the morning and then closes at 5:00 P.M. or 6:00 P.M. every night to five-day wards that are open 24-hours a day during the week but cut the cost to the hospital by closing on the weekends.

The type of tests that these types of investigation wards carry out include all forms of endoscopy (see Endoscopy). The benefit of endoscopies in general is that they only require sedation (where the patients feel sleepy and can breathe on

Most large hospitals have a physical therapy department and outpatients who are convalescing at home can attend. This is a vital postoperative service.

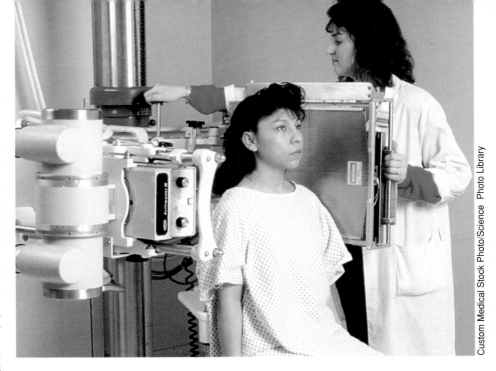

their own, see Sedatives) not a full-scale general anesthetic (where the patient is unconscious and requires artificial ventilation to breathe, see Anesthetics), so a patient can go home the same evening.

In other cases a whole series of blood tests can be carried out—for example, investigating the control of the level of blood sugar in a diabetic by measuring the level every few hours during an entire day (see Diabetes).

Outpatient investigations

Almost all of the tests that are performed on patients in the ward can also be carried out in an outpatient clinic. Because so

An outpatient is being prepared for a neck X ray. An X ray in this region is useful to detect fracture, whiplash, and curvature.

many cases are sent for blood tests from ordinary general hospitals, there is nearly always a special area, often near the outpatient clinic, where specially trained technicians take all the blood specimens. From here the specimens are sent to the pathology laboratory for analysis.

Tests can also be carried out on urine samples that are supplied by a patient who is staying in the hospital. Alternatively the patient may be asked to bring in a specimen, such as sputum from patients with a cough or feces from those with intestinal disorders.

Just as the laboratory performs tests on outpatients, so too does the X-ray department. If you are sent to see a specialist, you may be asked to go to the X-ray department as a result of your visit. Many of the more simple X rays can be carried out there and then and you may go straight back to the specialist with the X rays for him or her to examine. (There are even some hospitals where, for example, you have a chest X ray before you even see the specialist, since it is such a basic investigation in heart and chest disease.) Some X rays, on the other hand, can only be performed on an appointments basis, and you may have to wait to have these done. Barium swallows (see Barium liquids), enemas, and IVPs (kidney X rays) are examples of X ray that you might have to wait for (see X rays).

Aside from X rays and blood tests, there are many other tests that are performed on an outpatient basis. Many of the patients passing through an outpatient clinic are likely to have an electrical

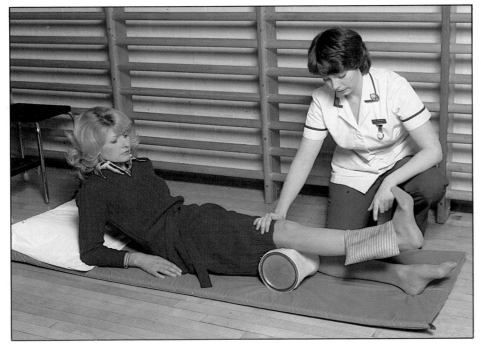

Q If I feel sick at work, can I go to the nearest hospital outpatient clinic?

A No. You should telephone your family doctor. Hospital outpatient clinics are for people receiving short-term or continuous treatment from particular specialists. If you have an urgent problem, you can go to the emergency room (ER) of the nearest hospital. However, you should not do this unless it is a genuine accident or emergency. These departments are always very busy. You must also remember that the doctors and nurses decide on the order in which patients are seen on the basis of the severity of the medical condition, not on a first-come-first-serve basis, so you might have to wait a long time.

All in all, the best thing to do is to see your own family doctor unless you have a really urgent problem such as a badly bleeding wound.

Q I have been to the outpatient clinic at my local hospital three times now, and I have seen a different doctor each time. Why does this happen?

A There are many possible reasons for this. The staff there will usually consist of a specialist doctor and junior colleagues. In many cases it is usual for the specialist to see a new case and then to hand the patient over to another doctor. In addition, junior doctors tend to change positions fairly frequently and move to a new job every six months. However, you can soon expect to see the same doctor more or less regularly.

Q If I am too ill to go to the outpatient clinic but my doctor doesn't think I need to be admitted to the hospital, is there any other way that he can get a specialist's opinion?

A In some cases a specialist may be willing to visit you at home. However, it might be impossible for him or her to come within a reasonable time, or he or she may feel, after discussing the problem with your doctor, that you have to be admitted to a hospital.

John Greim/Science Photo Library

Both occupational and physical therapists help patients in hospitals. Here a physical therapist shows an outpatient exercises.

recording of the heartbeat (an EEG, see Electrocardiogram). Heart patients may also have ultrasound studies done on the heart, just as pregnant mothers attending the prenatal clinic may have a routine ultrasound scan of their babies (see Ultrasound).

Like ultrasound scans, radioactive isotope scanning techniques have added a great deal to the investigation of various problems. Radioactive isotopes are used for diagnosis, and many large hospitals boast a large nuclear medicine department where these tests are performed; here again, many of the patients involved are outpatients (see Scans).

Outpatient treatment

One of the largest hospital departments is likely to be the pharmacy, from which all the drugs are dispensed for both the outpatients and the inpatients. The pharmacy of a large hospital is likely to contain the widest possible range of drugs and because it buys them in bulk, it should obtain them from the drug companies at a cheaper rate than an ordinary drugstore could. The pharmacy may only deal with drugs in the form of medicines, pills, ointments, and so on. The specialists may also ask for all sorts of other medical items such as surgical boots, surgical corsets, elastic stockings, etc., all of which are obtainable from the surgical appliance department.

Outpatients may also need other hospital services. One of the departments that has a large number of outpatients attending it is the physical therapy department. People who require remedial treatment for all kinds of problems usually go there.

A patient there could have recently left a hospital bed after a stroke, for example, or he or she might have attended the outpatient clinic directly with a complaint like a frozen shoulder.

In the same way that you can have therapy as an outpatient, you can also have speech therapy, osteopathy, hearing aids fitted, and counseling from the hospital social work department.

An increasing number of surgical procedures are also being performed in outpatient clinics. It has always been the case that minor operations, such as the removal of sebaceous cysts (see Cyst) or the freezing of warts (see Freezing), were done under local anesthetic as an outpatient. Many hospitals have an operating room in their outpatient clinics especially for this purpose. There has also been an increase in the use of mini D & Cs (see Dilatation and curettage) in which the uterus (see Uterus) is scraped clear of unwanted material. Surgeons now frequently perform in their own offices procedures that involve, for example, injections to treat hemorrhoids or varicose veins.

Radiotherapy (X-ray treatment, usually for cancer; see Radiotherapy) can certainly be carried out on outpatients. The only difficulty with this is that the treatment itself can make people feel ill, so that outpatient radiotherapy has to be reserved for those patients who are not badly affected by their underlying disease. Since this treatment is often given daily, patients need to live within easy reach of the hospital that they are visiting.

One of the most striking growths in outpatient care has been the innovation of day hospitals. A large general hospital might not only have a geriatric day hospital for the elderly, but also a psychiatric day hospital for those recovering from a psychiatric illness.

These institutions provide a place for people in both geriatric and psychiatric groups who have difficulty in coping completely by themselves in the community but who are able to cope if they are given the support provided by a visit once, twice, or even five times a week to the day hospital (see Geriatrics). This type of hospital may also be an appropriate place for active treatment in the form of therapy (see Physical therapy).

The outpatient clinic is now much more than a place where you go to be given pills by a doctor or to be advised to have an operation by a surgeon. There is such a wide range of medical procedures that can be performed in an outpatient clinic that today, hospital admission is reserved for those who really need it.

In larger hospitals, the pharmacy will be able to offer you a wider range of drugs than your local drugstore.

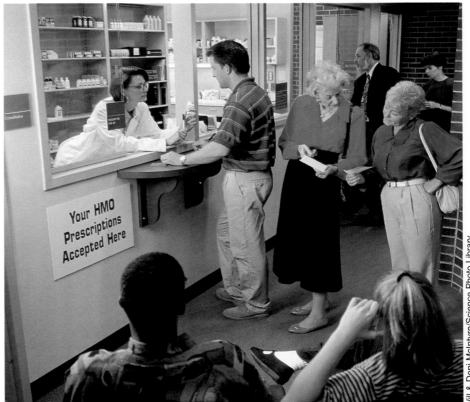

Will & Deni McIntyre/Science Photo Library

Hints for when you attend the outpatient clinic

- Beforehand, ask if you'll need to bring a urine sample or fast
- Let the receptionist know when you first arrive, or if you need to leave the waiting area
- Take a favorite toy or book if you need to bring a young child
- Allow time after your first visit; the doctor may need to send you for tests in other departments
- Bring all your medicines in their original pharmacy bottles
- Be prepared to give a urine specimen when you arrive, some hospitals ask you to bring one from home
- Expect to be examined all over on your first visit
- Do not wear too many tight-fitting clothes that are difficult to take off
- Write down any questions that you want to ask the doctor beforehand
- Don't be frightened to ask anything that you may want to know
- Take a relative or friend if you think you may get confused or flustered

Science Photo Library

Ovaries

The ovaries do more than produce and release eggs that are ready for fertilization. Their other vital role is to produce hormones that maintain the menstrual cycle and give a woman's body its feminine shape.

The ovaries are the parts of the female reproductive system that are designed to make and release mature ova (egg cells). When an ovum is fertilized by a sperm, it marks the start of a new human life. From the first menstrual period to menopause one egg is released monthly, alternately from the left and right ovaries. The ovaries are also essential parts of the hormonal system (see Endocrine system).

Location and structure

The ovaries are two gray-pink almond-shaped structures each measuring about 1.2 in (3 cm) long and about 0.4 in (1 cm) thick. They are found in the pelvis, the body cavity bounded by the hip or pelvic bones, and lie one on each side of the uterus (see Uterus). Each ovary is held in place by strong elastic ligaments. Just above each ovary is the feathery

Site, structure, and function of the ovaries

The ovaries are covered by a layer of cells. The cells that are destined to become eggs pass into the substance of the ovaries, where they are surrounded by a follicle membrane. Each month a single follicle matures, bursts on the surface of one of the two ovaries, and is released. The corpus luteum then develops at the site of the egg's follicle. If the egg is fertilized, the corpus luteum grows and secretes the hormones that maintain pregnancy.

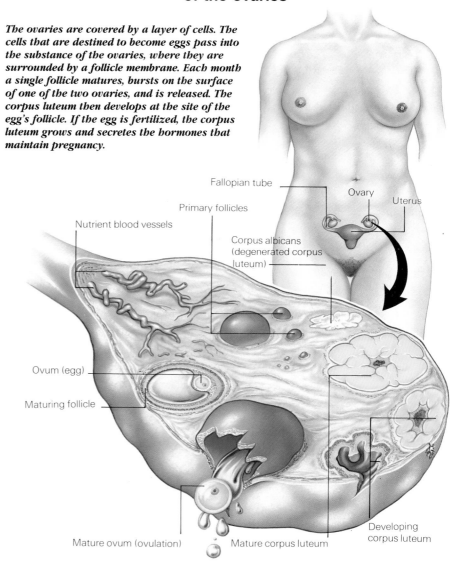

Fallopian tube

Primary follicles

Nutrient blood vessels

Ovary

Uterus

Corpus albicans (degenerated corpus luteum)

Ovum (egg)

Maturing follicle

Mature ovum (ovulation)

Mature corpus luteum

Developing corpus luteum

Frank Kennard

opening of the fallopian tube, which leads to the uterus. Although they are very close together, there is no direct connection between the ovary and the tube opening.

In a mature woman the ovaries have a rather lumpy appearance. The reason for this can be seen by looking at the internal structure under a microscope. Covering the ovary is a layer of cells called the germinal epithelium. It is from these cells that the eggs or ova form; thousands of immature eggs, each in a round casing or follicle (the egg sac), can be seen clustered near the ovary edge.

Much more noticeable are the follicles that contain eggs in various stages of maturation. As these follicles enlarge, and after their eggs have been released, they produce the characteristic bumps on the ovary surface. The center of the ovary is filled with elastic fibrous tissue that supports the follicle-containing outer layer.

Ovulation

Under a microscope the maturing follicles of the ovary can be seen as tiny balls enclosing a small mound of cells. In the center of the mound is the egg cell in its final stages of maturation. When the follicle is ripe and the ovum is mature, the cells at the follicle edge allow the ovum to leave. Exactly how this happens is still a mystery. The ovum is then wafted by the feathery ends (fimbria) of the fallopian tubes into the tube openings.

In their role as egg producers, the ovaries also act as endocrine glands (see Hormones). The ovaries function under the control of the pituitary gland at the base of the brain (see Pituitary gland). The pituitary first makes a hormone called follicle stimulating hormone (FSH), which travels in the bloodstream to the ovaries. FSH stimulates the follicles and causes the ova to mature, and the secretion of the hormone estrogen (see Estrogen). Under the influence of estrogen the lining of the uterus thickens in preparation for receiving a fertilized egg. Estrogen also stimulates the buildup of body proteins and leads to fluid retention.

After a follicle has ripened and burst, another pituitary hormone, luteinizing hormone (LH), goes into action and brings about the development of the corpus luteum in the empty follicle. The corpus luteum helps to establish a pregnancy. In turn the corpus luteum makes and releases its own hormone, progesterone. If the egg is not fertilized within 14 days, the corpus luteum shrinks, progesterone

Though eggs usually are not released during breast-feeding, it is not a reliable method of contraception, so precautions should be taken.

production is shut off, and the lining of the uterus is shed as the monthly menstrual period (see Menstruation). FSH production then begins again and the whole cycle is repeated. If, however, the egg has been fertilized (see Conception), the corpus luteum continues working until the placenta is established, and there is no menstrual bleeding.

Ovary development

Ovary development is largely complete by the time the female fetus is in the third month of life in the uterus, and few major changes will take place until puberty. By the time a baby girl is born, her two ovaries contain a total of between 40,000 and 300,000 primary follicles, each containing an immature egg. At most only 500 of these eggs will be released and probably no more than six will develop into new human beings.

When the ovaries first start making estrogen, they are not yet capable of releasing mature eggs, but this early estrogen stimulates the physical changes of puberty (see Menarche), such as the growth of the breasts, the widening of the hips, and the growth of pubic hair. This happens at least a year before a girl has her first period, and it is a signal that the estrogens have stimulated the release of mature eggs.

What can go wrong

Aside from the normal failure of the ovaries at menopause (see Menopause), the most common problem is the formation of ovarian cysts. These growths, which are usually benign, can grow very large, making a woman's abdomen swell as if she were pregnant. Many small ovarian cysts disappear of their own accord, and cysts usually do not cause pain unless they become twisted within the ovary (see Cyst).

Ovarian cancer is another common, and very dangerous, condition. Treatment with a drug called Taxol has been effective in some cases, and an early diagnosis improves the outlook (see Cancer).

Examining the ovaries

From outside the body the only way a doctor can examine the ovaries is by feeling, or palpating, them.

For a more thorough internal examination a technique called laparoscopy (see Laparoscopy) is used. Carbon dioxide gas is injected into the pelvic cavity under a general anesthetic. The gas shifts the position of the intestines so that they no longer obscure the ovaries. The laparoscope is then inserted through an incision near the navel, and this allows the surgeon to look directly at the ovaries and to take a tissue sample (see Biopsy) if it is required.

Bard Martin/The Image Bank

Overdoses

Q If I take a couple of aspirins for a headache and they have no effect, how long should I wait before taking any more?

A Most medication is meant to be taken three or four times a day, with usually four hours as the shortest safe interval between doses. This applies to aspirin, and so it would be safe to take another two in four hours. If your headache was really persistent, you could make it every three hours. However, if your headache is still giving you trouble in two days' time you must go to a doctor, rather than take any more aspirin.

Q Is it safe to take medicine that you can buy over the counter as often as you want?

A No. Never take medicine that you can buy over the counter as often as you want. The fact that some medicines are available without a doctor's prescription does not mean that there is no risk of getting the dosage wrong. It is vital to follow the manufacturer's instructions carefully when taking even the mildest medication.

Q I have been taking iron tablets for a year. Is there a danger of their effect building up to an overdose?

A No, because the body gets rid of what it cannot absorb. The excess iron passes out of the body in urine and feces. However, an overdose can occur if a substance is given in sufficiently large amounts to do immediate harm.

Q If I were accidentally to give my one-year-old too much junior aspirin, how would I know that he had been given an overdose?

A If you were to give him one tablet too many, there would probably be no unusual signs. However, you must be extremely careful when giving medication to children: their small body size makes them more vulnerable to overdose. Also, never give aspirin to children with flulike symptoms. Consult your family doctor first.

Many people think of an overdose purely in terms of attempted suicide, but accidents with medications are just as common as deliberate misuse.

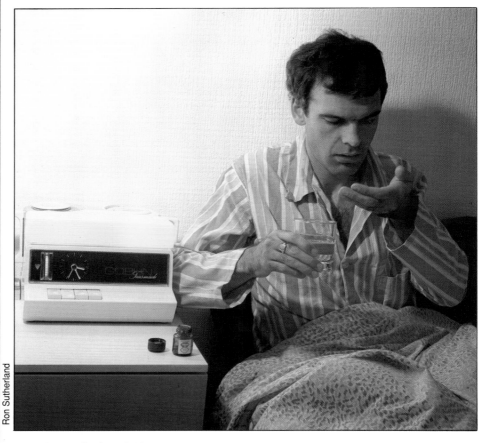

Ron Sutherland

Overdose, whether deliberate or accidental, has become a subject of major concern among doctors. It is something that everyone should know about because almost always a tragedy can be avoided by following a few simple rules about when and how to take medication.

Rarely does overdose happen because a doctor or a pharmacist makes a mistake in prescribing, making up, or labeling a medication. However, the majority of cases arise out of the user's carelessness.

Care should be taken with all medications, not just the ones that are obviously potent. Even commonplace medications, such as acetaminophen, are killers if taken in large quantities, as are many household chemicals.

Children and overdose

Children are the most likely victims of accidental overdose. They are much more seriously affected than adults, partly because of their small body size and partly because medications intended for adults are exact-

Carelessness about the number and mixture of medications taken can result in overdose. A typical overdose scenario can begin by a person taking sleeping pills at night, painkillers in the morning for a headache, and tranquilizers to cope with stress at work. The possible result, when combined with alcohol, is an accidental overdose.

ly that: they can harm a child even if a tiny amount is given. Most medications for children are specially prepared with children in mind, to be given in one teaspoonful (5 ml) doses. Children should not be given medications other than those that are meant for them.

It is possible for medication taken by a pregnant woman to affect the fetus. So no medication should be taken during pregnancy without first consulting a doctor (see Pregnancy).

Medications can also be passed on from a mother to her baby while she is breast-feeding. Again, the simple and necessary precaution is to consult a doctor.

Most overdoses among children occur because they get hold of and swallow their parents' medications out of curiosity. It is common sense to store medications where children cannot get at them. Remember that children can always climb or crawl further than you realize.

To children, tablets look just like candy, so to stop them making such potentially fatal comparisons, do not let them see you taking them. Another good reason for taking your medications out of sight of your child is that young children love to copy grown-ups. If it is good for mommy and daddy, it must be good for them too.

Adults and overdose
Forgetting whether or not you have had a particular pill, or medication, and taking another just to be sure, is the greatest risk. If this happens two or three times a day, or just once with a potent medication, an overdose may occur.

Taking another dose just to be sure is most likely when the patient has to take several different medications each day. To avoid mistakes, put the whole of the day's pills in a small container, checking each time by carefully reading the label, that the pills really are what you think they are. Also, check the instructions, however familiar you think you may be with them. Doctors and nurses do this every time they give a patient medication, so why should you be less careful?

Never take medication from a container that does not have a label, or from one where the label has become unreadable, even if you are sure you can recognize the contents (see Medicines). There are literally thousands of medications available today, and not enough combinations of color, size, and shape for them all to look completely different, so mistakes can be made in identification.

Even doctors and nurses can sometimes be in doubt about the identity of a pill or capsule, and will have to refer to a complicated chart; so again, why be less careful yourself? The checking process only takes a minute.

Q I am terrified that my four-year-old son will accidentally take one of my contraceptive Pills. What would happen if he did?

A If your son were to take one of your Pills, it would probably not do him much harm. However, there is the danger that he would eat the whole lot, and this might cause vomiting. Therefore, if you think that your child has swallowed any drugs, you should take him to the hospital immediately for a checkup. More to the point, why leave pills where your son can get hold of them? If you take more care to hide them, then you'll have no need to worry.

Q What do I do if I find that a member of the family has overdosed on drugs? Should I try to make him or her vomit?

A If you do suspect that a member of your family has overdosed on drugs, either accidentally or on purpose, the first thing you should do is call the Poison Control Center or 911. Immediate hospital treatment is vital in all cases of suspected overdose. Whether or not you should make the patient vomit depends on how long it has been since the overdose was taken, and whether or not the patient is unconscious. If he or she is unconscious, check for breathing or a pulse. If they have neither, and you are trained, you should call 911 and then carry out CPR. If the patient is unconscious, never try to induce vomiting. The overdose will have already entered the body's system, and when someone is senseless there is a real danger that vomit will enter their lungs and cause death.

If you are confronted by someone who tells you they have swallowed a bottle of sleeping pills within the last 30 minutes, you can save his or her life by inducing vomiting. Use ipecac syrup, or talk them into making themselves vomit. Wait for the ambulance. When it arrives, give the paramedics the bottle of whatever medication has been taken, even if it is empty. This is vital for diagnostic purposes when the patient reaches hospital.

Safety with drugs

Ron Sutherland

- Keep all medications in a lockable, dark cupboard, out of the reach of children. Use childproof containers. Don't let children handle medications, or see you taking them.
- Do not keep medications longer than a year. In any case don't keep them longer than their expiration date. Destroy completely what is left of a medication after you have finished taking it, but don't throw it in the wastebasket, or onto a fire, simply flush it down the toilet.
- If a doctor has prescribed a course of medication, complete the course. If in doubt, ask a doctor or a pharmacist.
- Tell your doctor of any side effect experienced from a medication.
- If you are advised not to drink, drive, or operate machinery while taking a medication, don't: it can be dangerous.
- Always read the directions on the label; always take exactly the recommended dose.
- Never treat any problem yourself for longer than a week without consulting your doctor.
- If a medication you have used according to the instructions fails to have the right effect, consult your doctor.
- Only give young children medications that are described on the package as being suitable for them.
- Do not take any medication during pregnancy, or while breast-feeding, without the advice of your doctor.
- If you are taking medication prescribed by a doctor, you should mention this if you consult another doctor.

Doubting the medicine

Sometimes a medication does not have the expected or desired effect, and the patient starts to doubt it. This is potentially dangerous too, because the patient may be tempted to increase the dose slightly, or to take it at shorter intervals. This may pretty obviously seem the wrong thing to do; however, this situation happens surprisingly often, sometimes with tragic results.

Another temptation that is especially strong for those who are already unwell and cannot spare the time to get to the doctor, is to take medication that has been prescribed for someone else in the household on the assumption that it sounds as if it might help. This too can prove fatal.

Similarly, it is unwise to take additional medications, even those bought over-the-counter at a drugstore, while you are already on a course of specific medication. The old and new medications could combine with each other and clash, causing side effects, or they can potentiate each other (exaggerating each other's effects). You should, therefore, always consult your doctor before taking any medication while already taking one that has been prescribed by him or her for your particular complaint.

Symptoms of overdose

These vary according to the medication involved and the amount taken. However, indications of mild overdose (which should still be reported to a doctor) include dizziness, faintness, blurring of the vision, drowsiness, difficulty in concentration, and a mild degree of mental confusion. There may also be some disorientation since overdose victims may not know where they are or how they came to be there. Patients with a more serious overdose may collapse, be difficult to awaken from a deep sleep, or may finally slip into coma (see Coma).

Outlook

Provided the patient is found and transported to the hospital in time, the outlook is generally good. Inevitably, it is the hospital that plays the major role in any treatment. There are three things that the doctor can do: resuscitation in the intensive care unit, gastric lavage (called stomach pumping), and giving chemical antidotes. Very effective antidotes are available for narcotic and acetaminophen overdoses (see Drug abuse). If treatment is given early enough, the patient usually recovers with no ill effects. The important point about overdoses is that prevention makes more sense than cure.

Oxygen

Q **How can you tell if a person is short of oxygen?**

A If a patient has blueness around the lips, it means that the level of oxygen in his or her blood is lower than it should be.

Q **My husband is in the hospital and must have oxygen. Will he always need this extra supply?**

A No, he is most unlikely to need extra oxygen when he comes out of the hospital. The usual reason why people are given oxygen in the hospital is because they have an acute heart problem or an infection in the chest when they already suffer from a long-term chest ailment. The extra oxygen is necessary only to help them with the immediate difficulty, and it is controlled very carefully.

Q **What is an oxygen debt?**

A If you walk or run a long distance, your muscles use most of the oxygen in the bloodstream and your heart and lungs work hard to keep the level as high as possible; but the system still remains in balance. However, if you do something that requires a lot of energy over a short time—like running fast for a block (200 m)—your muscles use up more oxygen than the heart can provide. The muscles can do this because they draw on an oxygen store in a compound called myoglobin. Once the stored oxygen is used up it needs to be replaced; this is the oxygen debt.

Q **I often feel very tired and lethargic. Is this because I am running short of oxygen?**

A No, almost certainly not. Everybody feels tired sometimes. However, oxygen shortage is hardly ever the cause. Some heart or lung conditions can make a person breathless with any sort of exercise. Anemia, however, can cause a person to become tired and listless, and it does involve a low oxygen level. Consult your doctor if you are worried.

We cannot live for more than a few minutes if our oxygen supply is cut off. It is the single most important substance on which human life depends.

Oxygen is an odorless, tasteless, and colorless gas. Its main source on Earth is from living green plants. Oxygen also makes up about one-fifth of the air that we breathe, and the work of the lungs, the heart, and the blood vessels is primarily concerned with carrying oxygen from the air to the body's cells, where it is needed to produce the energy that the tissues need to stay alive.

What oxygen does

Oxygen is essential for the production of energy in the body. Just as an automobile burns gasoline with oxygen, and a log fire uses both wood and the oxygen in a room to produce heat, the body's cells use oxygen in exactly the same way; they burn up their fuel—usually in the form of sugar—with oxygen to produce energy. The waste products of this chemical reaction are the same both in the body's cells and in the waste products created by automobiles—carbon dioxide and water. However, although some of the body's cells are able to function for a short while without oxygen, the brain cannot.

Oxygen from the air is inhaled, then absorbed by the lungs and carried in the blood to all the body tissues. When the amount of oxygen needed for a particular physical task is greater than can be supplied at the time, the result is what is known as an oxygen debt. A person makes up the shortfall in oxygen supply by panting and breathing in very deeply, so as to take in as much oxygen as possible—for example, immediately after a period of strenuous physical exertion (see Breathing).

Oxygen-enriched air in a mask is given to this athlete after an accident during a marathon.

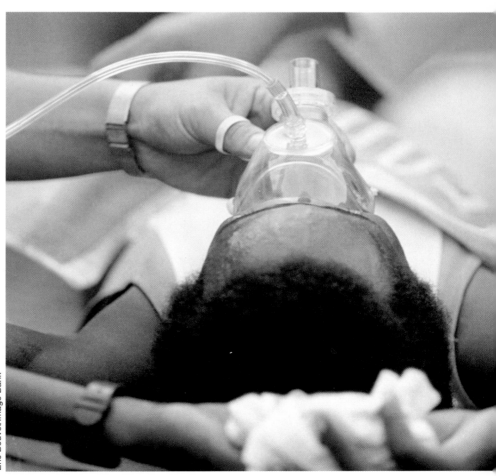

Eric Bouvet/Image Bank

1293

Oxygen deficiency

There are two main groups of people likely to suffer from a shortage of oxygen in the blood: those with a lung disease (such as pulmonary embolus or blood clot, or pneumonia) and those with heart complaints that mean the lungs are kept short of blood (for example, congestive heart failure). A lack of oxygen shows up as a shade of blueness around the lips and tongue, a condition called cyanosis.

Hemoglobin is the red pigment in blood that takes up oxygen in the lungs and carries it to the tissues where it is

The path oxygen takes through the body

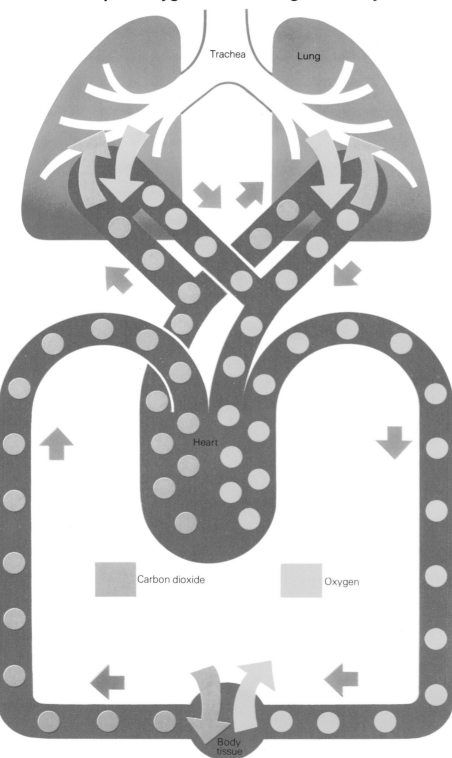

Trachea

Lung

Heart

Carbon dioxide

Oxygen

Body tissue

John Hutchinson

Ron Sutherland

released. Saturated hemoglobin is hemoglobin that is full of oxygen; it is red. Hemoglobin with insufficient oxygen looks purple. Hence an excess of low-oxygen hemoglobin leads to the blue look of cyanosis.

Associated conditions

Almost any type of lung condition can lead to there being a low level of oxygen in the bloodstream. Chronic bronchitis is perhaps the most common of these complaints (see Bronchitis), and it is often combined with emphysema, a disease where the lung tissue is destroyed to such an extent that fewer air sacs than normal are available for the exchange of oxygen between blood and tissues (see Emphysema, and Lung and lung disease).

A lack of oxygen is also associated with acute attacks of asthma (see Asthma). The condition is prevalent during severe spasms among asthmatics, which may also lead to chronic bronchitis.

Pneumonia may also lead to cyanosis, and it may be necessary to give oxygen to people who have suffered from a heart attack, because the flow of blood—and therefore the delivery of oxygen to the body's tissues—will have been drastically reduced by the attack.

Oxygen from the lungs is transported around the body in the blood. The cells exchange oxygen for carbon dioxide, which is returned to the lungs and exhaled.

pressure. This is called hyperbaric (high-pressure) oxygen. The treatment has a small but valuable place in modern medicine. It is used to treat carbon monoxide poisoning, or when people are distressed from inhaling acrid smoke, or in cases of gas gangrene (see Gangrene).

High concentration

If a person on a ventilator (artificial respiration machine) breathes a high concentration of oxygen—more than 60 percent—for a prolonged period of time, he or she can develop a lung injury. Another potential problem with oxygen therapy is its effect on patients with chronic obstructive pulmonary disorders (COPD) such as emphysema, or chronic bronchitis (see Pulmonary disorders). For some reason, when patients with COPD are given oxygen their breathing can slow or stop. Because of such problems, the level of oxygen that is administered to a patient in a hospital is always very carefully controlled and monitored.

Sea air is thought to be especially invigorating because it contains a higher proportion of ozone, a form of oxygen (see Ozone).

Giving extra oxygen

An oxygen mask is the most common way for oxygen to be administered to a patient. The type of mask that is used in hospitals allows doctors to regulate the percentage of oxygen in the air that the patient breathes. The aim is to raise the amount of oxygen in the bloodstream until it reaches normal levels. The level of oxygen in the blood can be monitored by taking samples of arterial blood.

Some people find wearing an oxygen mask over their face very uncomfortable, so they may be given oxygen through nasal cannulas instead. These are simply tubes that run under the nostrils, and through which the extra oxygen can be inhaled by the patient as needed. A tube can also be inserted directly into the windpipe (a medical process known as transtracheal oxygen).

Babies and small children can be put inside an oxygen tent. If the baby has been born prematurely, the oxygen can be fed directly into the incubator. Great care is needed when giving oxygen to premature babies, because too much can lead to a disease that causes blindness (see Premature babies).

Oxygen chambers

Low levels of oxygen in the body's tissues may be treated by putting the patient into a small chamber with oxygen that is more concentrated than usual, and which is also supplied at a higher than normal

Jessica Ehlers/Bruce Coleman Ltd.

The oxygen cycle

Green plants are the main source of oxygen for all animals, including humans. In plants a chemical reaction called photosynthesis is initiated by sunlight. Carbon dioxide and water absorbed by the plant form starch in the leaves and release oxygen.
Oxygen is breathed in by animals and carbon dioxide is exhaled and used by plants, forming a continuous cycle of interdependence. Animals, including humans, eat plants and the starch is broken down into sugars that release energy when they react with oxygen.

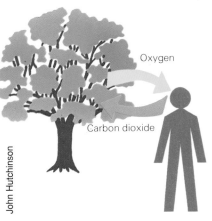

Oxygen

Carbon dioxide

John Hutchinson

Ozone layer

Q Why is ozone sometimes called a pollutant?

A Ozone is a highly reactive chemical. In the atmosphere it protects us from the sun's radiation, but if it forms at ground level it can damage lung tissue. Exposure to ozone can also trigger asthma and other respiratory problems. Ozone pollution on the ground happens when sunlight reacts with hydrocarbons and nitrogen oxides in automobile fumes. It tends to form in summer and is the main ingredient in smog.

Q Why are dark-skinned people less likely to get skin cancer?

A Skin color comes from a brown pigment called melanin, a protein which occurs in the epidermis (the outer layer of skin). Melanin is produced in epidermal cells called melanocytes. In people with dark skin, melanocytes are more active, basically because such people originate from warm climates, and their skins have developed a natural protection against the sun's harmful rays. Lighter skin becomes tanned when exposed to sunlight to protect itself from harmful rays, but this does not fully protect the skin. So dark skin is much less at risk from melanoma (skin cancer) than pale skin.

Q Will ozone depletion affect agriculture?

A Plant studies show that although higher UV radiation harms plants, some may not be affected and may even thrive on it. Plants of the same species may also react differently. When soybeans were exposed to extra UV radiation (an ozone loss of 16 percent), one variety's growth declined by 25 percent, while another's was unaffected. If the ozone layer thins by only 10 percent, crops could be damaged. Even a smaller reduction might affect agriculture because farmers could be forced to replace crops that are good but sensitive to UV radiation with less sensitive, and possibly less productive, crops.

Our use of environmental chemicals has badly damaged the ozone layer, which is our only protection from the sun's harmful rays. Scientists fear increases in skin cancer and disastrous climate changes. Can anything be done?

Sinclair Stammers/Science Photo Library

INDICATES COL

PREPARATION: Ensure
dry. Sand surface
Waterproof Abrasive Paper. Ma
area with newspaper and
Coat any bare metal or
with it. CarPlan Primer and allow to

SPRAYING: SHAKE CAN FOR M
MINUTES. Test spray on similar surf
to be sprayed to

The CFCs that power aerosols are probably destroying the ozone layer—our only protection from the sun's ultraviolet rays. A worldwide treaty now limits CFC production.

Ozone (O_3) is a rare, poisonous type of oxygen, produced by the action of electrical discharges (such as lightning) on oxygen molecules. The gas is found naturally in the Earth's stratosphere and forms a shield around the Earth called the ozone layer. This layer acts as a barrier between us and harmful ultraviolet (UV) radiation from the sun. Currently there is worldwide concern that our use of environmental chemicals, particularly chlorofluorocarbons (CFCs) found in aerosols, is damaging the ozone layer, potentially leading to global warming.

The ozone layer lies between about 9 and 30 miles above the Earth's surface, and absorbs damaging UV radiation from the sun. Ozone is created when powerful UV rays split molecules of oxygen (O_2) into two atoms. A single oxygen atom (O) then combines with a molecule of oxygen (O_2) to form ozone (O_3).

However, ozone breaks down if it meets a single oxygen atom (O). Here, the ozone molecule and oxygen atom combine to form two molecules of oxygen ($2O_2$). This breakdown of ozone happens slowly in the stratosphere and there is always a net surplus of the gas, but the total amount of ozone is very small. Even

at its most concentrated, there are only 8 molecules of ozone to 1 million molecules of other gases.

The ozone layer varies naturally from region to region and from season to season. Most of the ozone is created above the tropics, but then weather systems push it toward the North and the South Poles. So the highest levels of ozone occur at the poles and the lowest at the tropics. The amount of ozone peaks in the spring (September in the Southern Hemisphere) and reaches a low point in the fall.

Levels of ozone also vary naturally from year to year, with higher amounts recorded when there is increased sunspot activity, or dark spots, on the sun itself.

The stratosphere lies above the troposphere, which is the lowest layer of atmosphere and the part in which we live. The troposphere contains most of the water vapor in the air, so this is where most clouds form. Between the troposphere and the stratosphere lies a boundary called the tropopause. This boundary

Hole in the ozone layer (shown in white) over Antarctica. The UV is shown in purple. Altitudes are shown by a Boeing 727 (7 miles), Concorde (9 miles), and ER-2 research plane (11 miles).

Michael Gilbert/Science Photo Library

lies about 10 miles above sea level at the equator but is just 5 miles above the poles. The ozone layer occurs just above the tropopause and varies in height in the same way, lying lowest at the poles and highest at the equator.

Ozone hole

In the mid-1980s, researchers made a startling discovery: a hole had appeared in the ozone layer above Antarctica. This hole was recorded from late August to late November, as the Southern Hemisphere moved from winter to spring. Since then, the hole has continued to appear every southern spring.

The evidence for the hole came from scientists in Antarctica who were using ground-based instruments to measure ozone, and from NASA researchers. NASA started monitoring ozone in November 1978, when it launched the Total Ozone Mapping Spectrometer (TOMS) instrument on board the Nimbus 7 spacecraft. Today balloons, aircraft, satellites, and the space shuttle missions are used to measure ozone levels worldwide.

These measurements show clearly that the ozone layer has thinned all around the Earth. After allowing for natural variations, ozone declined by about 3 percent per decade between 1978 and 1991. The decline increases with latitude; above the United States, Europe, and Australia, it is 4 percent. Although scientists actually failed to find any drop in ozone over the tropics at this time, more recent measurements have shown that ozone is now decreasing there as well. The ozone over the Arctic also shows unusually high losses in spring.

However, the most dramatic changes have been found over Antarctica. Every southern spring, about 95 percent of the ozone in the lower stratosphere is destroyed. Higher up, above 15 miles, about half the ozone disappears. Ozone destruction at the poles increases when there is a stronger polar vortex (air spiraling above the poles), lower temperatures, and more stratospheric clouds.

After some weeks, the depleted ozone layer above the Antarctic breaks up and is carried away by winds. As a result, the ozone can temporarily thin at higher latitudes. This effect has been observed as far north as Australia. After a few months, though, the ozone is regenerated.

The discovery of the ozone hole rang alarm bells about the amount of UVB, the band of ultraviolet radiation with wavelengths between 280 and 320 nanome-

ters, getting through to the Earth's surface. For if there was less ozone, less UVB would be absorbed in the stratosphere. And scientists feared that increased UVB radiation would cause biological damage to human beings, triggering more skin cancers, eye cataracts, and suppressing the body's immune system. Extra UVB radiation might also harm trees and plants or microscopic marine life. Some scientists think that the ozone hole might also have a serious affect on the climate worldwide. All this has spurred researchers to find out more about the ozone layer, and many governments to take steps to stop its destruction.

Increased radiation?

UV radiation from the sun can be separated into three bands: UVA, UVB, and UVC. The ozone layer filters out UVC, which is the most active and therefore the most dangerous. For significant amounts of UVC to get through to the Earth's surface, the ozone loss would have to be enormous. The ozone layer also absorbs some UVB, the next most harmful band of radiation. So, any thinning of ozone would allow more UVB through. UVA, which is not absorbed by ozone, was thought to be harmless but now it seems that it may also be involved in causing skin cancer.

Q Does extra UV radiation harm marine life?

A Radiation from the sun can penetrate tens of yards into clear seawater. Some scientists are worried that increased UV radiation will harm microscopic plants (phytoplankton) and animals (zooplankton) which live near the surface of oceans. The food chain in the sea starts with plankton, so if they are harmed, then all living organisms in the oceans (and some on land) would find food scarcer. Recent studies on phytoplankton in the seas around Antarctica suggest that the organisms photosynthesize less when directly below the hole in the ozone layer. But the domino effect that ozone depletion might have on other marine life is not known.

Q Is sunburn dangerous?

A People receive as much as 70 percent of their lifetime's exposure to sunlight in the first 18 years of their life (see Sunburn). Epidemiological studies indicate that between one to three episodes of acute sunburn in early childhood predisposes the individual to melanoma (skin cancer). So it is important to protect skin from overexposure to UV radiation.

Q How can I protect myself from UV radiation?

T he American Academy of Dermatology and the Skin Cancer Foundation recommend a number of steps to help reduce the risk of sunburn and skin cancer. Both adults and children should avoid the sun as much as possible between 10:00 A.M. and 3:00 P.M. when it is strongest. Use sunscreen with a factor of at least SPF15 on all areas of the body that are exposed to the sun. Reapply every two hours, even on cloudy days, after swimming or sweating. Wear clothes that cover sensitive areas of the body. Hats should have wide brims to shade both the face and the neck. Avoid exposure to UV radiation from sunlamps. Sunscreen should be applied frequently on children aged six months or older; babies under six months, should be kept out of the sun entirely.

Sue Ford/Science Photo Library

The milky aspect typical of cataracts can be seen in this male patient's eyes. Aging is the most common cause, although radiation is now an increasing cause in all age groups.

Levels of UVB vary naturally from region to region. UVB is strongest near the equator and weakest at the poles. On average, the level of UVB radiation at the equator is a thousand times greater than at the poles. UVB also increases with altitude and is affected by cloud cover.

Scientists report that there was no significant increase in UVB in American cities between 1974 and 1985. However, this was probably because pollution on the ground absorbed it. By contrast, UV radiation in the Antarctic has at times increased by a factor of two to three.

Effects on health

Predicting the health effects of decreased ozone is not an exact science because there are so many factors involved, including the actions people may take to protect themselves (see Sunburn).

Scientists estimate that a 1 percent loss of ozone produces an increase of between 1 and 2 percent in UVB. This in turn leads to a 2–4 percent increase in the number of cases of two types of skin cancer: basal cell carcinoma and squamous cell carcinoma (see Skin and skin diseases).

In the US, 600,000 cases of these carcinomas are diagnosed each year. UVB radiation is blamed for more than 90 percent of these cancers. When UVB radiation is absorbed by skin cells, it can break bonds in the cells' DNA. Most of this damage is repaired by proteins made inside the cells. But if the damage is not fixed, then the faulty DNA can trigger cancer (see Cancer).

Studies have shown that, like UVB levels, basal cell carcinoma and squamous (scaly) cell carcinoma correlate with latitude. Light-skinned people living closer to the equator are more likely to get these cancers.

Both skin cancers appear as red nodules or blotches, and occur where the skin is most exposed to the sun—the face, neck, hands, arms. Because both cancers are more common in people who work outside, long-term exposure to sunlight seems to be one cause. Both cancers are simple to treat if detected early.

A more dangerous form of cancer, melanoma, can develop rapidly from a harmless-looking mole to a life-threatening disease (see Melanoma). Each year in the US, about 17,000 men and 12,000 women are diagnosed with melanoma. Usually the cancer appears on men's trunks and women's legs.

Studies suggest that people who develop melanoma have in the past received, intermittently, high doses of UV radiation that caused acute burning. Other studies suggest that the risk of melanoma increases if people were overexposed to UV radiation during childhood. Some scientists suspect that exposure to UVA, which is not absorbed by ozone, is also a factor in causing melanomas.

Evidence linking melanoma to UV radiation has come from studies of a rare disorder that is caused by a defect in a gene for repairing damaged DNA. In this disease, called xeroderma pigmentosum, the faulty gene is unable to make the enzyme needed to fix DNA damaged by UV radiation. Research shows that people who have the faulty gene are a thousand times more likely to develop melanoma than people who are carrying healthy copies of the gene.

The incidence of melanoma in the US has been increasing since the 1940s. But this increase is probably not linked to ozone loss as levels of UVB radiation in the country have not increased significantly. Also, melanomas are slow to develop, taking up to 20 years to show. So, even if an individual is exposed to extra UVB radiation as in Antarctica, any effect may take years to appear. The rise in melanoma cases is most likely caused by both the huge increase in recent years in the number of people taking vacations in the sun and the production of CFCs (discussed below).

Further evidence suggests that UV radiation suppresses the body's immunity so that the skin's immune system cannot attack forming cancer cells. There is a continuing fierce debate about whether this dampened immunity also increases the risk of catching an infectious disease. Increased UVB radiation may also cause an increase in cataracts. There is medical evidence that in some mountainous countries where UVB levels are naturally high, such as in Tibet and Bolivia, there is a high incidence of cataracts (see Cataracts).

Ozone eaters

Scientists first raised concerns about the damage to the ozone layer in the early 1970s. The US, Britain, and France wanted to build a commercial fleet of supersonic aircraft and this provoked a debate about whether the aircraft's exhaust gases (nitric oxide) would speed up the destruction of ozone. The discussion prompted intensive scientific research which centered on the stratosphere.

By the mid-1970s, US researchers had proved that stable synthetic chemicals and gases released into the Earth's atmosphere might be eating away at the ozone layer. Examples of such chemicals are chlorofluorocarbons, or CFCs, a group of gases that contain chlorine, fluorine, and carbon. Halons (or bromofluorocarbons, found in fire extinguishers), which contain bromine, fluorine, and carbon, also cause ozone loss.

CFCs are used to propel aerosols from spray cans and in the cooling coils of refrigerators and air conditioners. They are also produced in the manufacture of industrial solvents and styrofoam. CFCs were developed in the United States in 1928, but it was only after 1950 that they were used in large quantities. Industrialized countries use 80 percent of CFCs, but developing countries are rapidly using more of the chemicals.

A scientist launches a weather balloon in Antarctica. The data it sends back from the stratosphere will be used to evaluate the state of the ozone layer.

CFCs are very stable compounds. Once they escape from, say, an aerosol can or old refrigerator, they enter the atmosphere and slowly diffuse upward. After many years they reach the stratosphere. This part of the atmosphere is constantly bombarded with powerful UV radiation, some of which severs the weak carbon-chlorine bonds in CFC molecules. It is this released chlorine atom that breaks down the ozone. Just one chlorine atom can catalyze the breakdown of 100,000 ozone molecules. That is why CFCs are such powerful destroyers of ozone.

Repairing the hole

The discovery of the ozone hole inspired an international effort to phase out the chemicals causing the damage. In 1987, most of the nations that were using CFCs adopted the Montreal Protocol, a treaty committing them to reduce the emission of CFCs by 50 percent by the year 2000.

In 1990, an amendment to the treaty called for all manufacture of CFCs, carbon tetrachloride (found in solvents), and halons to stop by 2000. In 1992, the timetable for phasing out ozone-eating chemicals (which differs for developing countries) was brought forward by four years. By January 1993, 95 percent of countries that were using ozone-depleting chemicals had signed the Montreal Protocol. However, the benefits of these agreements will not be seen for several years because CFCs are so long-lived.

Bringing on substitutes

Scientists have developed substitutes for CFCs. Some of these are halocarbons, such as HCFC-22, which can replace CFC-12 in refrigeration and air-conditioning systems. In the electronics industry, water-based cleaners are increasingly replacing CFCs. Another innovation is nonpressurized or pump spray bottles, which replace spray cans that use CFCs as propellants.

International efforts to prevent the ozone layer from being destroyed further have had some effect. In May 1996, researchers from the National Oceanic and Atmospheric Administration reported that they had seen a reduction in ozone-depleting chemicals in the Earth's atmosphere. This decline in atmospheric chlorine derived from CFCs and other halocarbons should be repeated in the stratosphere within four years, as the gases in the lower atmosphere slowly diffuse up into the middle stratosphere.

When the concentrations of ozone-depleting chemicals that are in the stratosphere fall, the impact on the springtime Arctic ozone thinning should be seen immediately. However, it will be much longer before the hole that is over Antarctica can repair itself. In the past eight years, because so much chlorine and bromine have built up, the ozone is completely destroyed each spring. The Antarctic ozone hole will probably not close before the year 2050.

Joyce Photographics/Science Photo Library

Pacemaker

Q My mother is going to have a pacemaker put in. Will there be a large bump on the surface of her skin?

A Modern pacing boxes are about the size of a matchbox, and although this is fairly small, a bump is usually unavoidable. Pacing boxes are usually fitted on the front of the chest, about 2 in (5 cm) below the middle of the collarbone. If your mother is of average weight, most of the bump may be lost in the breast tissue.

Q If my pacemaker fails, will my heart stop beating?

A Only a minority of patients with pacemakers are so dependent on them that their hearts would stop completely if their pacemaker ceased working. Most patients would simply have the symptoms of very slow pulse rate: dizziness, blackouts, or lethargy on exertion. The object of the design is to prevent sudden pacemaker failure from occurring. However, there is a tiny risk of pacing box failure if there is a sudden shift of pacing wire, this sometimes occurs soon after the pacing system has been put in, if at all. You should attend a pacemaker clinic regularly, and they will check the electrical function of your unit. Eventually the batteries run down, but the clinic will have plenty of warning. It is a simple procedure to replace the pacing box.

Q If I needed to have a pacemaker fitted in an emergency, how quickly could it be put in?

A Many doctors have enough experience to put a temporary pacing wire into the heart without X rays to help them, in which case it could be a matter of two or three minutes to get some sort of pacing activity. In a real emergency, it is possible to get a heart working again by passing a wire directly into it through the chest wall by means of a long needle or by delivering pulses of electricity via electrodes attached to the skin. Usually, though, there is time to get the patient to X-ray facilities.

One of the most dramatic advances in medical technology has been the development of pacemakers for the heart. It has saved many patients from death or disablement.

People rely on the regular beating of their hearts in order to stay alive. This regular heartbeat depends upon the heart's own natural pacemaker, the sinoatrial node. The sinoatrial node initiates impulses that spread through the heart via a system of specialized electrical conducting tissues. The entire electrical timing system is called the conducting system of the heart (see Heart).

Who needs a pacemaker

Unfortunately, the heart's natural pacing system can sometimes fail to work properly. This can occur as a result of ischemic heart disease (a hardening or blocking of the coronary arteries). A heart attack may also lead to conducting system difficulties, and this requires urgent surgery to insert a pacemaker (see Heart attack). Often these pacemakers are only temporary, since the heart may recover its ability to control its own timing. If and when this occurs, the temporary pacemaker will be removed.

The majority of patients who require a permanent pacemaker are those whose conducting system has broken down completely. There is no obvious cause for this. It is almost as though the conducting system has worn out. The condition is more common in elderly people. Most patients who need pacemakers are over the age of 65 (see Aging).

When the heart stops conducting electrical impulses properly, the heart rate slows down; this is called heart block, or arrhythmia. The condition may be variable (have different manifestations or degrees of severity), leading to sudden attacks of fainting and unconsciousness. The heart may even stop completely; without emergency treatment death may result. Patients may also suffer from a continuously slow pulse rate. This may be ideal for keeping patients well while they rest, but it leads to severely disabling lethargy and breathlessness upon exertion.

How a pacemaker works

The basic principle in all the various types of pacemaker is exactly the same. Two parts make up the pacing system. First, there is some electronic means of producing regular electrical impulses that are of the correct strength and duration to cause the ventricles (the main pumping chambers of the heart), to beat.

This impulse is conducted to the heart by a wire, called a pacing lead, whose tip is implanted somewhere in the substance of the ventricles. Provided the impulses are strong enough, and there is good electrical connection between the wire and the muscle of the ventricle, a heartbeat will result from each impulse.

To coordinate the timing of the heartbeat, an impulse generator, or pacing box, sends electrical impulses to the heart via the pacing wire. This enables it to know when there has been a heartbeat, so that it does not send another impulse until the heart is ready. This is called demand pacing and is almost always the system used, because it allows the heart specialist to program the pacemaker.

The pacing box is then set at a given rate, for example, 60 beats per minute. This means that the box will produce an impulse every second unless it senses that the heart has produced a beat on its own. If the heart does produce a beat, then the pacing box will wait for another second before it produces its next impulse and so on (see Pulse).

This chest X ray shows the two main components of a pacemaker in place: the pacing box and the lead to the heart.

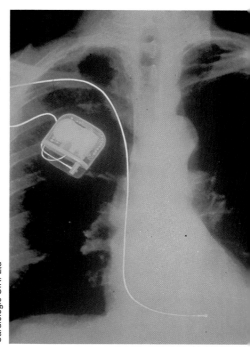

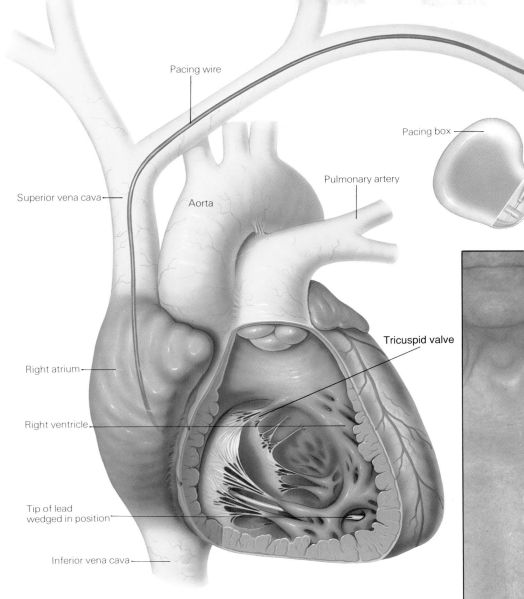

Pacing wire

Pacing box

Superior vena cava

Aorta

Pulmonary artery

Tricuspid valve

Right atrium

Right ventricle

Tip of lead
wedged in position

Inferior vena cava

Mike Courteney/Telectronics

The pacemaker, which contains the power source and circuitry to produce the electrical impulse, is implanted in the chest wall. The lead, which carries the impulse, is threaded through the pulmonary vein and the electrode is wedged into the right ventricle (above). This marvel of miniaturization is not disfiguring (right).

Camera Press

Putting in a pacemaker

Two types of systems are used. The first is temporary: a pacing wire is passed through the skin, via a special needle, into a large vein, usually around the shoulder. It is then passed into the right atrium, through the tricuspid valve, and into the tip of the right ventricle, where it makes contact with the heart muscle. The position of the wire is followed on an X ray so that it can be guided to the right place. If it is fixed to the skin, it is unlikely to become dislodged. The other end of the wire is attached to a pacing box that remains outside the patient's body.

For a permanent system the same principle is used. Once the wire is connected to the pacing box, and then the electrical

The West German chancellor, Helmut Schmidt, had a pacemaker fitted in 1981.

connection between the wire and heart is assured, the pacing box is sewn into a special pocket under the skin of the chest. Although the pacing box is only the size of a matchbox, it has enough battery power to produce impulses for years (more than 10 in some cases). Some pacemakers have an electrode in the right atrium that fires before the electrode in the right ventricle.

Pacing has saved many patients' lives. It has also prevented disabling symptoms such as recurrent blackouts. These problems mainly occur in the elderly, and the effect of pacing can be beneficial to their well-being, but age is no bar to having a pacemaker put in. A variation on the pacemaker is the automatic implanted defibrillator, which delivers a large jolt of electricity to restart the heart if the ventricles are fibrillating (quivering).

Pain

Q Why is it that severe pain can make a person faint?

A The parts of the brain that receive and analyze painful stimuli from inside or outside the body have close connections with the parts that have overall control of blood circulation, the heartbeat, and the condition of the peripheral blood vessels. Even small degrees of pain cause some change in pulse rate and/or blood pressure. However, if the pain is severe, the circulation can be swamped by these influences: the blood vessels dilate and the blood pressure drops enough to lead to unconsciousness. This process is the same for any severe unpleasant stimulus, though people vary as to what degree of pain causes such fainting.

Q I have been told that acupuncture works only psychologically to relieve pain. Is this true?

A There is no doubt that psychological factors are very important in any method of pain relief, because of the considerable psychological component in our appreciation of pain. However, it is likely that there is also a genuine physiological mechanism at work in some methods of acupuncture.

Q Is it true that some people do genuinely feel pain more easily than others?

A Yes. The threshold above which a person interprets stimulus as painful varies hugely both for psychological and physical reasons. For example, different people require different amounts of painkillers or local anesthetics for pain caused by identical stimuli.

Q Can chronic pain cause a person to become emotionally disturbed?

A Severe depression can certainly be the result of suffering from prolonged pain. Often the personality seems to be changed as the pain takes over the person's whole life. Fortunately, however, such severe pain is not very common.

Pain is familiar to most people in daily life. It is important to recognize that it is the body's alarm system, which alerts and teaches us to avoid harm and to seek attention for painful illnesses.

Pain can come in many forms. We may describe it as sharp, dull, aching, gripping, and throbbing, to name just a few. Minor degrees of pain are part of the repertoire of sensory contact with the outside world and with the workings of the body. Through the experience of pain we learn to avoid the unpleasant elements in the world, though hopefully it is the prospect of pain that warns us against an action once we have experienced it.

In disease, more severe and distressing pain generally arises from the persistent presence of some harmful stimulus in a part of the body, or occasionally, the malfunction, due to some kind of damage, of the nerve fibers that carry and analyze painful stimuli within the nervous system (see Nervous system).

A large section of the nervous system participates in the sensations of pain, from the peripheral nerves to the most sophisticated thinking areas of the cerebral cortex. There are many different types of pain. Each depends on the variety of stimuli by which it is caused, and the way in which the stimuli are analyzed by the nervous networks in the spinal cord and brain. Cultural and social factors also play an enormous role in determining the mind's response to the perception of pain.

The purpose of pain

Ironically, the ability to feel pain is vital to our well-being. This can be seen from situations in which the whole, or parts of, the body lose their ability to discern this sensation. In leprosy, for example, the nerves to the hands and feet are damaged so that pain is no longer felt there; as a result, sufferers damage their hands and feet continually without feeling any pain (see Numbness).

Similarly, a few people are born unable to feel pain at all, and they must be carefully protected from injuring themselves. Such injuries would cause physical damage to anyone who did not heed the warning messages conveyed by the pain system. People do not go around touching boiling hot saucepans because the very few times they have done so, the pain has firmly reminded them of the tissue damage that can occur.

Pain can be especially distressing to a child, even a trivial injury can trigger tears. A kiss and a hug can be highly effective treatment.

Ron Sutherland

1302

The pathways of pain

Thalamus

Cerebral cortex

Fast conducting pathway of pain to the brain

Midbrain

Slower, analytical pathway of pain to the brain

Medulla where detailed analysis of pain begins

Cervical spinal cord

Message sent to remove hand from painful stimulus

Elaine Keenan

Ron Sutherland

Pain from the internal organs warns a person in the same way of the presence of a disease. For example, indigestion that follows overeating warns a person to be less greedy with the next meal.

Unfortunately the paradox is that while the most distressing aspect of a disease may be the pain, it is that pain, its character, and its position, that enables doctors to detect the cause of the complaint and prescribe treatment. When a person has abdominal pain, it is dangerous to cover it up with painkillers immediately, since this may mask the development of painful symptoms that may herald the presence of a serious disorder. But once the doctor is sure of a diagnosis, the symptom can be treated as he or she thinks is necessary.

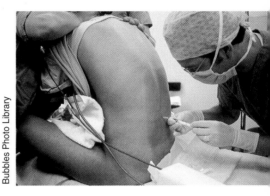

Bubbles Photo Library

When labor pains are at their worst, they can be eased by an anesthetic injected into the epidural space in the lower back. The diagram shows the pathways of pain. The picture (below left) depicts dull pain—a persistent earache; (below right) a sharp pain is caused by contact with a hot iron.

How pain occurs

Painful stimuli inside and outside the body excite otherwise unspecialized nerve endings in the skin and elsewhere. These nerve endings are attached to nerves of two different types: one is fast-conducting and conveys its information rapidly to the spinal cord (see Reflexes); the other also takes its information to the spinal cord, but more slowly. This helps to distinguish between two types of pain: the immediately felt, (and therefore reacted to) pricking pain, or dull, aching pain.

These nerve endings make many contacts with the network of fibers in the spinal cord, which are responsible for the initial analysis of the sensations and pain in particular. A second nerve fiber then takes this more organized information upward to the brain. Again this happens by two different pathways: one makes fairly directly for the thalamus (the main sensory relay station deep in the brain), and the other takes a more meandering

Alan Hutchinson Library

Q Can a husband really feel the physical pain of his wife's childbirth?

A Probably not. But if a husband is very close to his wife, his brain may synthesize some of the distress (if any) of childbirth, although this is unusual. Of course, not feeling any pain does not mean that the husband does not care.

Q Surely when someone loses the sensation of pain in a leg due to a disorder of the nerve this is a good thing?

A No. In such a situation the warning value of pain is lost and that person will not notice minor injuries, which may then progress to ulcers that can cause serious damage to the limb. Pain is a helpful sign that gives warning signals of actual or potential damage to the tissues.

Q Is there any truth in the theory that twins, although they may be separated by many miles, can feel the pain of each other's injuries?

A No, there is no real evidence that this happens and no theoretical way in which it could.

Q I have seen TV programs showing some religious initiates walking over beds of red hot coals with no shoes on. Do such people feel any pain?

A At the time, probably not. The situation is similar to the soldier who may feel no pain, even from very severe injuries, that he or she has received in a battle. If the mind is sufficiently diverted, either by the induction of a religious trance or by the fear and excitement of a battle, the brain does not pay sufficient attention for the painful sensations to reach consciousness, even though messages may be reaching the spinal cord about the unpleasant events occurring. The other point is that there is considerable cultural pressure on religious initiates to hide their pain from the world— even if it penetrates their personal pain threshold, their minds erect a barrier against feeling it.

course, making many connections with centers in the brain stem before it also arrives at the thalamus. This enables the cortex (the part of the brain where pain is actually perceived) to obtain fast reports of the painful situation, plus more slowly arriving, but more heavily analyzed, information by the slow pathway (see Brain).

The thalamus, which analyzes this information for presentation to the cerebral cortex, has rich connections with the areas of the brain that are concerned with the maintenance of emotional tone and the areas concerned with arousal. So before the perceiving brain receives any information, and especially painful stimuli, it is heavily tinged by the emotional state and affected by levels of arousal.

The final arbiter as to whether pain is perceived is the cerebral cortex. It seems that large areas of this part of the brain participate in this complex perception. The frontal lobes, especially those parts of them concerned with the analysis of emotions (the parts of the frontal lobes that connect with the limbic system) seem to be important for the perception of painful stimuli as unpleasant. People who have lost the use of this part of their brains report that they can feel pain but are not upset by it. The parietal lobes of the brain seem to be important in the localization of the painful stimulus, but they also participate in the perception of the sensations associated with pain.

Different types of pain

Skin pain: this is usually highly localized and is either a sensation of pricking or burning or a combination of both, accord-

Some cultures make a virtue of pain: in this Thai Pusau ceremony, a celebrant has both cheeks pierced by a metal rod.

ing to whether the fast or slow conducting nerve fibers are stimulated or both.

Internal pain: this is more variable (has different qualities, e.g., sharp or dull pain) although it tends to be poorly localized. It is perceived as deeper and often of a duller quality than skin pain. The stimulation of combinations of different sensory fibers may produce a variety of stabbing, pressing, or constricting pains, which can be felt coming from one's internal organs.

Referred pain: pain that comes from any internal organs may seem to be coming from areas of the body some distance from the actual position of that organ. This is because the nerves from these organs are received, and their messages analyzed, by parts of the spinal cord that also deal with those areas to which the pain seems to be referred. Thus pain coming from the heart is felt in the center of the chest and also in the left arm and in the jaw; the messages of pain spill over from their spinal analyzing centers into neighboring zones.

Thus by careful questioning of a person with a pain, doctors can usually get a clear idea of the organ involved. Not all organs refer their pains to distant sites; however, when they do, they always do so in characteristic distributions.

Pain from the nervous system: damage to the peripheral nerves themselves may be the cause of pain instead of the stimulation of these nerves by harmful external stimuli. Thus pressure on the nerve (the median nerve) in the wrist may commonly cause pain and tingling in the hand, which may spread up the arm to other parts of the body, again because of the connections in the spinal cord.

Slipped disks in the spine can cause direct pressure on the sensory nerves as they enter the spinal cord and, since the nerve being pressed carries impulses from the back of the leg, the pain is felt by the sufferer as traveling down the back of the leg (see Slipped disk).

Damage to the spinal cord itself, from pressure that is due to tumors or inflammations such as multiple sclerosis, also causes pain, which may be sent to the part of the body whose sensations are analyzed by the segment of the cord that has been affected.

Damage to other parts of the central nervous system may also cause pain. In particular, damage to the thalamus due to minor strokes may cause very unpleasant sensations and pain, since the nerves that organize the incoming stimuli become disorganized and interpret ordinary sensations as painful (see Stroke).

Phantom pains: whenever an arm or a leg has been amputated, the nerves remain in the stump. If they are stimulated by the swelling or scarring of the remainder of the limb, the brain actually registers the pain as if it was coming from the lost leg or arm. After a while the brain usually reorganizes its perceptions so that any pain is actually felt in the stump alone; however, initially the site of the pain is perceived according to where the nerves originated.

Psychological aspects of pain

Because large areas of the nervous system participate in feelings and responses to painful stimuli, it is not surprising that the state of a person's mind is an important factor in his or her perception of pain. This state of mind is strongly influenced by the situation in which the pain occurs, and the cultural and social background against which certain attitudes to pain have developed.

In the heat of a battle, a soldier may feel no pain even though he or she has suffered substantial injuries, because his or her mind can be distracted by the battle itself. Later, however, when the soldier has calmed down, the pain may become severe, although the injury has remained unchanged.

During yoga, the mind may be so diverted away from the painful stimuli by the deep contemplation of other things, that what seem to be feats of endurance, such as lying on beds of nails and walking over hot coals, can be achieved (see Yoga). It is likely that such people are not actually feeling the pain in the same way as they normally would, but rather that they are enduring it; they have managed to divert their minds from the unpleasant significance of the stimuli that are still undoubtedly reaching their brains.

The psychological effect on a person of any type of prolonged pain may be quite pronounced. Severe pain can begin a vicious cycle whereby the mental ability of the sufferer to cope with pain is progressively eroded. As a result, this can often appear to change a person's personality. It makes him or her pay attention to the pain to a greater degree than normal, leading them to perceive it as more severe. It is wrong to consider pain as being only in the mind, because all pain is really a psychological process to some extent, and it is dependent on the circumstances that initially caused it.

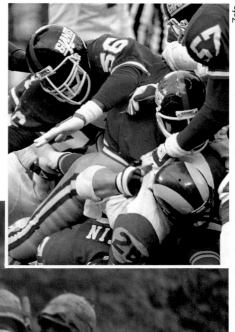

Wounded soldiers can experience a delayed reaction to pain: only when they are in a safe place will its full intensity be felt.

The threat of injury, and the pain that is associated with it, is a fact of life in a contact sport like football.

Pain management

Q Is it possible for surgery to deaden pain?

A Surgery can relieve pain but doctors use this method only as a last resort because it can destroy other sensations or create new pain elsewhere in the body. What is more, the old pain may come back after some months. The most common surgical technique for pain relief involves cutting the nerve fibers on one or both sides of the spinal cord. This procedure, called cordotomy, affects the sense of temperature as well as pain because nerve fibers for both sensations travel together along the spinal cord to the brain.

Q How do you control severe pain without medication?

A Patients in the advanced stages of cancer experience severe and widespread pain. One method of controlling it relies on electrodes implanted in the brain. The electrodes are attached to areas that are rich in cells that produce endorphins, the body's natural painkillers. The patient alters the frequency and voltage of the electrical stimulation until the pain disappears. The technique brings excellent pain relief to some patients, while leaving their other senses unaffected. Researchers are studying whether patients who undergo repeated brain stimulation develop tolerance to the stimulation, so that their pain returns.

Q How does acupuncture work?

A The acupuncturist inserts the tips of fine needles at specific points in the body. These points are some distance from the area on which they must act. A needle in the thumb, for example, reduces pain in the abdomen. After insertion, the needles are rotated to stimulate nerve signals that stop the pain. The reason why is unclear. It may be that the stimulation of sensory fibers boosts the production of endorphins and blocks the transmission of pain messages to the brain. Or it may be a placebo, the patient's expectation of pain relief alone is enough to ease the pain.

The perception of pain is influenced by the mind and the body. Pain management aims to help sufferers to tackle pain by considering both its physical and mental aspects.

One in three Americans is affected by some degree of chronic pain, according to the American Chronic Pain Association. Millions suffer so badly that they cannot sleep, work, exercise, or concentrate. People suffering from chronic pain (persistent or recurring pain) include those with cancer, multiple sclerosis, and arthritis. Doctors distinguish chronic pain from acute pain. Acute pain is intense but relatively brief, and it affects patients with short-term injuries, like broken bones.

Feeling pain

Pain warns us that something is wrong with the body. You feel pain when an injury or disease stimulates special sensory nerve endings called nociceptors, and triggers pain messages to travel from the site of the injury to the brain. Nociceptors are found in the skin and other places like the tendons. Although the cause of pain may begin in another part of the body, the sensation of pain occurs in the brain.

Pain comes in many forms, but how an individual reacts to it does not depend on the pain alone. The person's perception of pain is influenced by how he or she has been brought up to handle pain (social and cultural factors) as well as on their state of mind. For instance, a ballplayer may be so caught up in a game that he carries on playing, not realizing that he has torn a ligament. But someone who is feeling worried or depressed may experience pain more intensely. So pain relief should aim to resolve both the physiological and psychological elements of pain (see Pain).

Treatment

There are various ways of treating pain, including medication, applying cold

Acetaminophen, ibuprofen, and aspirin (below) can be bought without prescription in drugstores. Powerful narcotic analgesics are available only with a prescription.

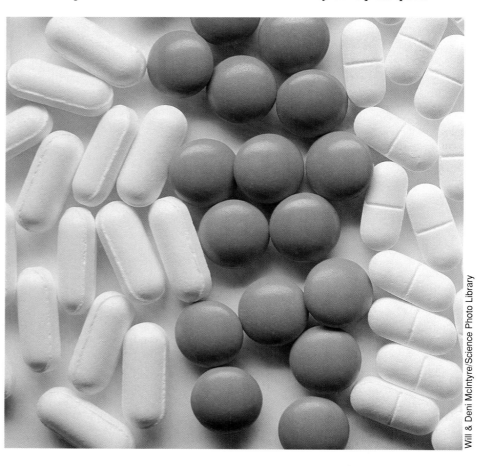

water (for burns and bruises) or massage and heat (for aches), and electrical stimulation. Some of the less common methods include biofeedback, psychotherapy, acupuncture, hypnosis (see Hypnosis), meditation, relaxation, and exercise.

Medication

A drug that relieves pain is called an analgesic. The most powerful ones are opioid analgesics, such as morphine, heroin, and codeine, which are derived from opium and synthetic chemicals related to opium. Opioids are narcotics, drugs that act on the brain to cause numbness and stupor (see Narcotics).

Opium is made from the dried juice of the opium poppy and was used to ease pain as early as 6,000 years ago by the Sumerians. Opiates mimic the effects of endorphins, a group of painkilling proteins that occur naturally in the brain. Like the endorphins, the opiates block the activation of pain neurons.

Narcotics can be addictive. What is more, the patient can build up a tolerance to the drug, and as a result larger and larger doses are needed to deaden the pain. Opiates can also cause a number of unpleasant side effects such as respiratory depression, nausea, and constipation. Therefore powerful opiates are only prescribed for severe pain, such as that experienced after surgery or with diseases such as cancer.

For moderate pain, such as that experienced with headaches, muscle strain, or bruises, patients can take nonnarcotic drugs such as aspirin. Although these are less powerful pain relievers than opiates, they are not addictive.

Aspirin is a member of a group of drugs called nonsteroidal anti-inflammatory drugs (NSAIDs), that are used to decrease inflammation, fever, and pain. They are extremely effective at high doses. Tissue can become inflamed (red, hot, swollen, and painful) following an injury or infection. NSAIDs work at the site of the inflammation, preventing the body from producing certain prostaglandins, chemicals that trigger pain and inflammation (see Prostaglandins).

In some people NSAIDs can produce serious side effects. They can irritate the lining of the stomach and cause ulcers. The drugs can also lead to nausea and vomiting and are toxic to the kidneys (see Kidneys and kidney diseases). Acetaminophen is good for treating mild pain and lowering temperature, but it does not reduce inflammation. Because acetaminophen does not irritate the stomach lining, it can be taken for abdominal pain or where there is a history of ulcers (see Ulcers). However, acetaminophen is a serious liver poison if too many tablets are

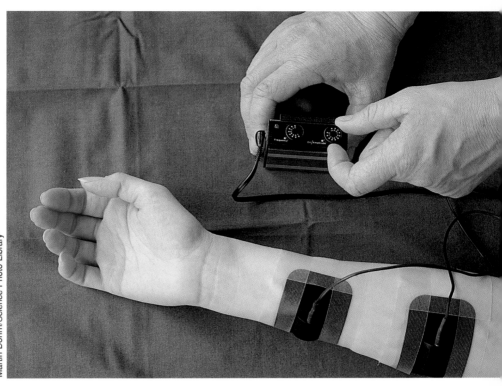

Martin Dohrn/Science Photo Library

Electrical stimulation using a TENS machine has many applications in analgesia, particularly for patients with chronic pain. It is both cheaper and safer than using drugs.

taken in a short period of time. As few as 20 tablets can cause severe liver damage (see Liver and liver diseases).

Electrical treatment

Some types of pain can be treated by electrical stimulation. Patients with chronic pain sometimes find effective pain relief with a TENS machine, a device that sends out small electrical impulses through the skin to nerve endings. TENS stands for transcutaneous electrical nerve stimulation. The patient adjusts the frequency and voltage of the electrical stimulation until the pain goes. The electrical activity of the TENS machine probably works by blocking pain signals on their way to the brain and by stimulating the release of endorphins. Some women in labor find that a TENS machine is good for controlling their pain (see Birth).

Behavior therapy

If people have felt pain for a long time, they often anticipate it and become tense. Biofeedback training is a type of behavior therapy that aims to control pain by changing the person's learned responses to it. Using biofeedback, patients have successfully treated migraine headaches, muscle tension, and high blood pressure. The technique does not work for everyone.

In biofeedback training, the patient is hooked up to machines that monitor the heartbeat and blood pressure, test how tense the neck muscles are, and so on. The patient can get this information by

looking at the monitor or by listening to it. A louder sound could mean there has been an increase in heart rate. Scientists do not fully understand how people use biofeedback to control their bodies, but patients say that imagery, for instance, thinking of a hot bath, may help them to relax their muscles (see Biofeedback).

Pain clinics

For people whose pain has taken over their lives, the answer may be to visit a pain clinic. There are more than 800 pain clinics in the United States. The clinics vary in their approach, but usually a team of specialists first looks at the patient's medical records and arranges further tests if required. A patient admitted to the clinic will then be guided through a personal treatment program.

The program may include exercises or a special diet. Other treatments may involve receiving electrical stimulation and nonnarcotic drugs. The patient's thoughts, feelings, and actions can affect the pain, so there may be individual or group psychotherapy sessions to help the patient to control these things (see Therapy).

The ultimate aim of pain clinics is to reduce the patient's reliance on pain medication so that he or she can start leading a normal life again.

Painkillers

Q Is it true that taking low doses of aspirin is good for the heart and circulation?

A Yes. Aspirin taken in very low doses helps to prevent heart attacks. The beneficial effects of aspirin were proved by long-term studies using doctors as patients.

Q Is aspirin safe for everyone to take?

A Aspirin should not be taken by anyone with a history of stomach trouble (particularly ulcers), nor should it be given to children under 12, because it can produce severe side effects, such as Reye's syndrome, when there is a viral illness present.

Q Does acupuncture really work as a painkiller?

A It certainly does work, although we are not yet sure why. In China, dentists can drill and fill teeth on people who have been anesthetized by acupuncture, which is a good test of its effectiveness. It is possible that the physical effects are aided by a placebo effect; i.e., the patient believes the treatment will work and so it does.

Q I'm pregnant—should I use painkillers for headaches?

A Because pregnant women ingest so many drugs during their pregnancy in the normal course of things—caffeine in tea and coffee; nicotine in cigarette smoke; and alcohol—it is often difficult to blame a particular drug for a particular abnormality, especially when a problem can arise from a combination rather than an individual drug. We do not know for sure the effects of many over-the-counter painkillers.

Any substance that is taken by a pregnant woman will pass to the fetus, especially during the first three months. After that, some drugs will be screened out by the placenta, but not all of them. As a general rule, drugs (even mild painkillers) should be avoided during the first three months of pregnancy. Acetominophen is probably the safest.

Most people take painkilling drugs at some time or other. How do they work and should we use them every time the stress of modern living causes discomfort?

The medical term for a pain-relieving drug is an *analgesic*. Doctors usually divide painkilling drugs into two categories: narcotic and nonnarcotic (see Drugs).

Narcotic and nonnarcotics

Narcotics, such as morphine and heroin, which are derived from opium, together with their synthetic relations, such as pethedine and methadone, act principally on the brain and often produce drug dependence (see Narcotics). Nonnarcotic drugs, such as aspirin, are rarely addictive and act directly on the site of the pain.

Narcotic drugs are usually used in highly controlled conditions, such as the hospital environment, to give relief for pain in internal organs. The nonnarcotic drugs are used to control pain felt in the joints, muscles, bones, and skin.

Pain-relieving drugs were once only obtained from natural sources. Morphine, for example, comes from the opium poppy. Purified opium preparations are still sometimes used, but most drugs that are for medical use are now usually prepared synthetically.

Most common painkillers

The best known painkillers are aspirin, acetaminophen, codeine, and morphine. Nonnarcotic drugs such as the first two are readily available over the counter and are commonly used to relieve headaches or pains such as premenstrual stomach cramps. The painkillers that are purchased from drugstores are all different combinations of aspirin, acetaminophen, and codeine, sometimes with the addition of a stimulant such as caffeine. They have different effects on the body.

Aspirin

Aspirin is probably the best known and most widely used drug (see Aspirin and analgesics). Not only does it relieve pain, it also reduces fevers and has an anti-inflammatory effect on the joints. This is why doctors often prescribe aspirin for influenza, not necessarily to kill any pain that the patient may be feeling (which is often more discomfort than pain), but in order to reduce the temperature and to help ease the aching joints experienced in such an illness. Aspirin is prescribed to ease rheumatism, often over extended periods, for its excellent antiinflammatory property (see Inflammation).

Dangers of aspirin

However, aspirin can be extremely dangerous to some people in certain circumstances. It is an irritant and can cause stomach pain with nausea and vomiting. But much more important, if it is swallowed whole, an aspirin tablet will not just irritate the stomach lining but may even cause bleeding.

For this reason, aspirin should never be taken on an empty stomach without a drink of water. Aspirin can be extremely dangerous to elderly people on poor diets, especially if they are low in iron, and to patients who are weak and recovering from an illness.

It is even possible to develop superficial stomach ulcers from aspirin use without realizing it (see Ulcers); this in turn can lead to blood loss and anemia (see Anemia). Some people are allergic to aspirin. Since aspirin is present in many commercial drugs, often under its chemical name, *acetylsalicylic acid*, it is always important to read the list of ingredients on any medicine you buy.

Acetaminophen

If for any reason a patient should not take aspirin, acetaminophen is often prescribed as a good alternative. Acetaminophen is also a mild pain reliever and can reduce the temperature, although it has no effect on inflammation and thus is of little use for treating rheumatism. It does not irritate the stomach lining and so may be taken for abdominal pain. However, it can damage the liver and should not be taken in high doses over long periods or with other drugs, with alcohol, or by someone who drinks alcohol heavily (see Liver and liver diseases).

Codeine

Codeine is an opium-derived drug, often used as part of antidiarrhea and cough suppressant medications. In addition to being a mild pain reliever, codeine slows down the action of the intestine and suppresses the cough center in the brain. Codeine is rarely used on its own, but it is frequently combined with other drugs, most commonly with aspirin and acetaminophen. As well as increasing their effects it also adds a mild pain-relieving action on the brain; on the other hand, aspirin and acetaminophen affect the site of the pain itself.

Common painkillers

	Uses	Dangers	Long-term use	Contraindications
Aspirin	Mild painkiller; brings down temperature and reduces inflammation. Good for headaches, discomfort from colds and influenza, or simple pains like backache	Irritates stomach lining; can cause ulcers and bleeding. Can cause severe side effects in young children with a viral illness	Non-addictive, but do not take regularly without doctor's advice	Should not be taken by people with stomach problems. Do not take on an empty stomach or without water. Do not give to children under 12
Acetaminophen	Mild painkiller. Used similarly to aspirin; can also be used for stomach aches	Can cause liver damage if taken in high doses for a long time	Use of large doses can cause liver damage. Use with caution with alcoholics	Should not be given to patients suffering from liver problems
Codeine	Painkiller available on prescription; contains acetaminophen and morphine-derived dextropropoxyphene. Stronger than the above	Can cause constipation, nausea, vomiting	Can be addictive and cause kidney damage	Should not be given to patients suffering from liver or kidney problems
NSAIDs (Naproxen, Ibuprofen)	Similar to aspirin	Stomach irritation, less severe than aspirin	Not addictive	Use with caution in patients with stomach problems or aspirin allergy

There are several preparations on the market that contain various amounts of aspirin, acetaminophen, and codeine. Other preparations come in various combinations with caffeine.

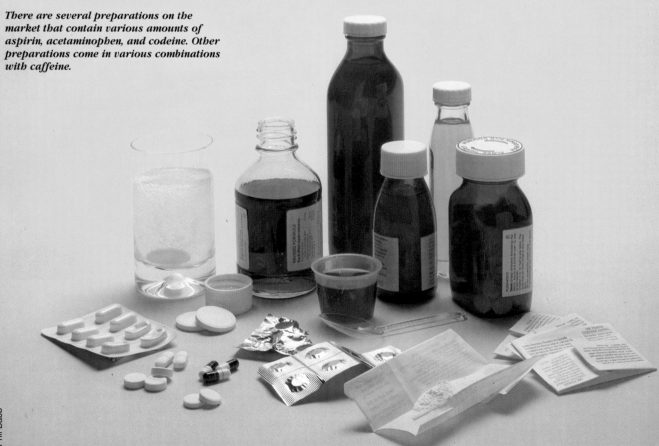

Phil Babb

Q I occasionally get blinding headaches that make me feel sick. Two aspirins have no effect. Should I take more?

A A blinding headache with nausea is a good description of a migraine. It is often difficult to tell the difference, but the classic symptoms of a migraine are a headache on one side of the head accompanied by nausea and vomiting. There are often visual disturbances and slurred speech. Migraines may respond to aspirin or acetaminophen, but they often do not. Other drugs can help if they are taken as soon as possible after the migraine starts, but a doctor should be consulted first (see Migraine).

Q In the case of an overdose, is it enough to make the person vomit to get rid of the painkilling drugs?

A Immediate action is often necessary, but in the case of an overdose, never try to take care of the patient on your own—always call an ambulance. You may be able to void the drugs before they are absorbed, but after some painkillers have entered the bloodstream (and this can be very quickly) the damage can be widespread and only amenable to medical help. If the person is unconscious, do not induce vomiting, because the vomit may be inhaled into the lungs. Acetaminophen, for example, can cause liver damage that kills several days after the overdose. The sufferer can show very few signs of damage for many hours before lapsing into a coma.

Q Is it safe for me to take acetaminophen as a painkiller? I am an ex-alcoholic and have some liver damage.

A No. Acetaminophen (Tylenol) should never be used as a painkiller if you have any sort of liver damage. A very small amount can be fatal. Because your liver is damaged it cannot perform its function of detoxification properly. Therefore the acetaminophen cannot be cleared from the system and fatal poisoning can result.

Phil Babb

Morphine

Morphine is made from opium. If it is taken repeatedly, it becomes addictive and, as a result, the painkilling effect lessens as the patient gradually builds up a tolerance to the drug. Despite this serious problem narcotics are still the

Raspberry tea is sometimes claimed to be beneficial for relieving the pain associated with childbirth and menstruation.

most effective painkiller available to the doctor, and they are used to treat almost every kind of disease.

Function of pain

Pain should be looked on a little like a burglar alarm. It would be foolish and harmful to switch off the alarm and then leave the burglars rampaging through the house: so in most cases the cause of the pain, rather than the symptom, should be sought after and cured.

Just as many burglar alarms are set off because of some passing interference, so some people will sometimes experience pain for either temporary and passing reasons that do not really require a doctor's attention. In these cases the right painkiller is both necessary and beneficial. However, it is not advisable to continue taking over-the-counter painkillers for longer than two or three days. Always read the instructions very carefully. If the pain persists medical advice should be sought at the earliest opportunity.

── TAKE CARE ──

Points to watch with painkillers

Ron Sutherland

- All analgesics cause a certain amount of drowsiness. It is wise to be careful if driving or handling machinery while taking them
- Analgesics can be harmful if they are taken over a long period of time. If you are in constant pain consult a doctor
- Be careful about taking painkillers if you are already on other drugs
- All pills, including analgesics, should be kept in childproof containers and locked in a medicine chest; children are very curious about pills
- Do not take painkillers with alcohol
- Always take painkillers with water and if possible, with or after food
- Check with a pharmacist if you are unsure about children's doses

Palate

Q Will a premature baby always have a cleft palate?

A In a normal baby the proper knitting together of the bones that form the palate takes place early during the fetus's life in the uterus. Being born prematurely will make no difference at all to the structure of a baby's mouth. So if a baby is destined to have a cleft palate it will have one whether or not it is born before its due date.

Q I am 36 and pregnant with my first baby. Does this mean that my baby is more likely to be born with a cleft palate?

A Surveys have shown that there is a relationship between the age of a mother and the likelihood of a baby having a cleft palate. But the figures show that the link is not very strong. About one in 750 babies is born with a cleft palate, and the number rises to one in 20 if someone in the mother's immediate family has the problem. If you have any concerns about this, talk to your doctor.

Q My daughter speaks with a lisp. Could it indicate that there is something wrong with the shape of her palate?

A No. A lisp usually results from the faulty movement of the tongue inside the mouth. Although the palate, particularly the hard palate, does play a part in the formation of the sounds of speech, it is a passive role compared with the active influence of the tongue, mouth, and lips. A lisp can be corrected by teaching the correct movements to make. It may be useful to talk to her doctor or her teacher, either of whom should be able to put you in touch with a speech therapist.

Q Is there such a thing as a falling palate?

A *Falling palate* is a term used to describe an abnormal enlargement of the uvula, which hangs down from the back of the soft palate. An enlarged uvula may cause constant coughing, and it is usually treated by surgery.

As an integral part of the mouth, the palate helps to break up food. It also plays a crucial role in subtly changing the shape of the mouth to create an enormous variety in the sounds and character of speech.

The *palate* is the technical word for the roof of the mouth. It is divided into two parts: the hard palate, toward the front of the mouth, and the soft palate at the back. The palette is involved in many of the functions of the mouth: eating, tasting, swallowing, breathing, and speaking. The palate can be injured, but the most common problem is faulty develop-

For a child the feel of food is as important as its taste in determining whether or not it is enjoyable. This sense of texture is picked up by nerves in the palate.

Jerry Harpur

Q **My baby has suddenly developed white patches inside his mouth, with some on his palate. What should I do?**

A It sounds like your baby has a yeast infection. This is caused by a fungus and needs treatment, so take your baby to a doctor as soon as possible. The usual treatment is to give either a topical or ingestible antifungal medication.

Q **Why is it that eating salty food makes my palate dry?**

A The sensation of a dry palate is part of the body's natural reaction to thirst. Salty food makes you feel thirsty because it temporarily upsets the body's internal water balance, drawing water out of the blood and into the tissues. The brain monitors this water level and also responds to the sensation of a dry palate. As a result, you are driven to search for a drink and thus put the blood and body tissues back into their proper equilibrium.

Q **Why is my palate so sensitive to the texture of certain foods? Sometimes the sensation makes me feel physically sick.**

A Like other parts of the body, the palate is endowed with a rich supply of nerves. When we eat, some of the nerves of the palate send signals to the brain about the nature of the food that is in the mouth. If these nerves send back the message "unpleasant," then the natural reaction of the brain is "reject." One of the most common rejection mechanisms is vomiting, which explains why food that is unpleasant to you produces the strong, physical sensation that it does.

Q **Does a cleft palate always have to be corrected?**

A Almost always. The only notable exception is if the split or cleft in the palate is very slight and affects only the area of the uvula at the back of the palate.

ment, which can lead to the birth of a baby with a split or cleft palate.

Structure

The hard palate is created by the links between the maxillae, the bones of the upper jaw, and the palatine bones on either side of the face that connect with them. The soft palate has no such bony base. Instead it is underlaid with tough fibers and with muscles that allow it to move. At the back of the mouth, behind the tongue, the soft palate splits into two, and the gaps are occupied by the tonsils. Just in front of this divide hangs a fleshy projection called the uvula.

Covering both the hard and soft palates, and forming the lining of the mouth, is a layer of mucous membrane that contains mucus-secreting glands (see Mucus). This membrane is subject to an enormous amount of wear and tear, so it has to be tough and be capable of renewing itself every minute. The membrane on the hard palate is stuck very tightly to the bony structure beneath to prevent it

The photograph below shows the normal palate of an adult (rugae and raphe can be seen more clearly in the insert). The rugae are the horizontal ridges; the raphe is the bone that runs from the mouth to the uvula.

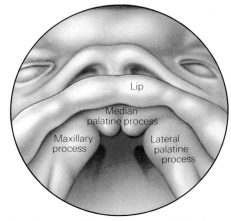

Development of the palate normally begins when the fetus is about five weeks old; by eight weeks each of the parts has formed.

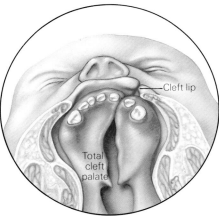

Incomplete development of both the hard and the soft palate; this type of cleft may be accompanied by a cleft lip.

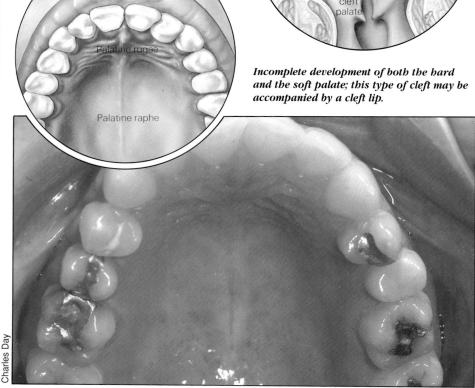

Charles Day

Normal and abnormal development of the palate

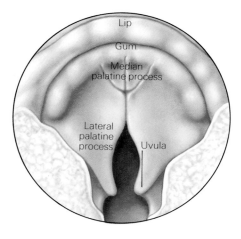

A week later the horizontal processes have grown and fusion of the two sides has begun; in another week it will be complete.

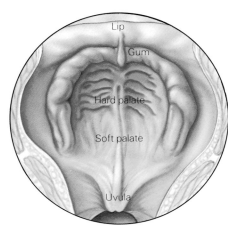

The palate at birth, showing the prominent ridges of the hard palate; these become less pronounced with age.

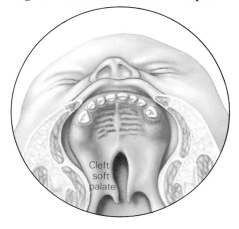

A cleft that affects the whole of the soft palate occurs symmetrically along the midline from the hard palate to the uvula.

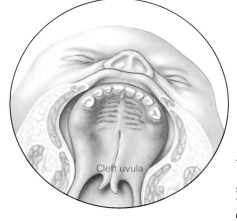

A cleft uvula; this is not a serious condition, and unlike other types of cleft palate, it does not usually require surgical treatment.

Frank Kennard

from becoming dislodged by the movements of the tongue. The ridge of bone that runs along the middle of the palate, and to which the membrane is attached, is called the raphe.

Ridges of tissue filled with fibers extend from the raphe. The ridges, which can be felt with the tongue, are most prominent in childhood. The mucous membrane that covers the soft palate extends backward to join with the lining of the back of the nose. To aid lubrication of the throat during swallowing, it is more richly supplied with mucous glands than the lining of the hard palate.

What the palate does

The soft palate contains a few taste buds, which supplement the more numerous ones of the tongue. When we eat, the hard palate acts as the mortar onto which the pestle of the tongue pushes food to soften and mash it.

When food is ready to be swallowed, the muscles of the soft palate contract and pull this part of the palate upward. This action not only helps push the food toward the esophagus but also blocks off the airway at the back of the nose. By helping to keep breathing separate from the eating process, the movements of the soft palate help to prevent choking.

The texture of food is sensed by nerves in the palate's mucous membrane. Any food that has an unpleasant texture is appropriately described as unpalatable. In extreme cases unpalatable food may make you feel sick because it causes "reject" messages to be sent to the brain, which trigger a vomiting reflex.

During normal, quiet breathing the soft palate is held in a relaxed position to allow the free passage of air in and out of the lungs via the nose. When we speak, air is taken in through the mouth and molded by the tongue and lips as we exhale. The palate is very involved in the process of speech. Movement of the soft palate creates subtle differences in the shape of the mouth's acoustic chamber, and the hard palate acts as the sounding board for the tongue and gives basic sounds the shape of speech (see Speech).

Development

The palate begins to develop as early as the fifth week of life in the womb. At this stage the face is molded in gristly cartilage; later it hardens into true bone. The palate does not develop from a single bone. Instead a pair of horizontal projections grow from the rudimentary upper jaw, under the eyes, to meet in the center of the skull. At the same time another projection grows down between the eyes to create the nose. The three pieces of cartilage finally fuse, and the fusion creates the palate. This process of growth and fusion demands precise timing and is synchronized with the formation of the outer tissues of the face, including the skin. For a perfect result, each part of the process must take place at the right time and at exactly the right rate (see Fetus).

Problems and treatment

The most serious and common defect of the palate comes from poor synchronization during the growth and fusion of the bones. The result is a split or cleft palate. A baby born with a cleft palate has a gap, usually Y-shaped, in the roof of the mouth. A cleft palate is often associated with a harelip. This second deformity is a puckering of the lip due to the faulty synchronization of cartilage growth with skin growth. Both cleft palate and harelip are believed to result from defects that are hereditary.

Plastic surgery has made a cleft palate less serious than it used to be, but the necessary operations demand great skill and careful timing. A baby with a cleft palate needs special help to eat properly.

Sometimes the hard palate may be excessively concave in shape, which will impair breathing. This problem is often associated with enlarged tonsils and tends to improve once the tonsils are removed surgically. Abnormalities of the soft palate can cause snoring and respiratory problems during sleep.

Any accident that involves a burn in the mouth, or an injury that leads to bleeding, should be treated by sucking on an ice cube. If there is bleeding from a palate injured in an accident, lie the victim on his or her side to prevent him or her from choking on blood.

Pancreas

Q I have been told that the pancreas is so important that if it is removed or destroyed, the patient's life is in danger. Is this true?

A It is true that the pancreas is one of the body's most important organs. However, it can be removed by surgery and its function replaced in various ways. The first of the problems that has to be dealt with is diabetes, since the pancreas is the only source of insulin in the body. This is done relatively easily with insulin injections.

The pancreas is also very important in the digestion of food, and when it is removed the patient is usually treated with an extract of pancreatic digestive enzymes from animal sources, which is added to food. The drug cimetidine is used to stop the stomach from producing acids, thus preventing the breakdown of pancreatic enzymes.

Q Can you injure your pancreas in an accident?

A Yes, injuries to the pancreas most commonly occur as a result of car accidents, where the upper part of the abdomen is struck with force during the crash. It can be quite difficult to tell if the pancreas is involved, and surgery is always performed if a pancreatic injury is suspected. If an injury is left untreated, the digestive juices of the pancreas leak into the abdomen.

Q Does a person who has a diseased pancreas always get diabetes?

A No; there are many pancreatic problems that do not cause diabetes. But when there is an inflammation of the whole of the pancreas as there is in pancreatitis, the insulin-producing cells in the islets are almost bound to be involved, leading to a diabetic tendency that is often less marked than might be expected from the extent of damage. A disease called hemochromatosis, in which the liver and pancreas are damaged by an overload of iron in the body, frequently leads to diabetes.

Insulin, which is vital to life, and most of the enzymes that make digestion possible are all secreted by the pancreas, one of the body's most important glands.

The pancreas, one of the largest glands in the body, is really two glands in one, almost all of which deal with secretion. It is an endocrine gland that secretes hormones (see Hormones), of which insulin (see Insulin) is the most important. It is also an exocrine gland (see Glands), one that secretes directly into the gut (or another body cavity) rather than into the blood.

The pancreas lies across the upper part of the abdomen in front of the spine and on top of the aorta and the vena cava (the body's main artery and vein). The duodenum is wrapped around the head of the pancreas; the rest consists of the body and tail stretched over the spine to the left. The basic structures in the pancreas are the acini, collections of secreting cells around the blind end of a small duct. Each duct joins with ducts from other acini until all of them eventually connect with the main duct that runs down the center of the pancreas.

Among the acini are small groups of cells called the islets of Langerhans: these serve the endocrine organ function of the pancreas, secreting the insulin for the control of the body's sugar level.

What the pancreas does

Exocrine pancreas: the pancreas produces essential alkali in the form of sodium bicarbonate to neutralize the heavily acidic contents of the stomach as they enter the duodenum. The pancreas also produces many important enzymes that help to break food down into basic chemical constituents; these are then absorbed by the intestinal wall (see Enzymes).

That most of the main enzymes for the digestion of protein are produced by the pancreas creates a problem; the pancreas itself, like the rest of the body, is basically a protein-based structure. Therefore there is a risk that it might digest itself, but this is avoided by the main protein-digesting enzyme, trypsin, being secreted in an inactive form called trypsinogen, which changes to the active form once the pancreatic juices reach the duodenum. The pancreas also produces amylase and lipase, enzymes that break down starch and fats respectively.

The digestive juices are powerful and cannot be released into the intestine safely unless food is present for them to act upon. Therefore a sophisticated control system acts on pancreatic secretions. The vagus nerve—the main nerve of the parasympathetic system (see Autonomic nervous system)—stimulates the first small secretion as a result of the thought, taste, or smell of food. Further secretion is stimulated by distension of the stomach, but most of the secretion takes place when the food finally reaches the duodenum. As this happens, cells in the wall of the duodenum release two separate hormones into the bloodstream, secretin and pancreozymin, which travel in the blood to the pancreas and speed up secretion.

Endocrine pancreas: Insulin is a substance that is produced by the pancreas in the islets of Langerhans, which lowers blood glucose levels (see Glucose). These islets also produce a hormone called glucagon, which has the effect of raising, rather than lowering, the level of sugar in the blood.

What can go wrong?

Three rare diseases can cause trouble with pancreatic digestive activity. The first is acute pancreatitis, which can cause sudden abdominal pain and collapse. The second is chronic pancreatitis, characterized by recurrent attacks of pain and failure of the pancreas to produce adequate amounts of digestive juice. The third is the inherited disease cystic fibrosis (see Cystic fibrosis), in which many glands, including the pancreas, do not produce proper secretions.

Inadequate secretion of digestive juice causes malabsorption (see Digestive system); a common cause is chronic pancreatitis, accompanied by severe pain in the abdomen, sometimes so severe to require removal of the pancreas. The condition is often associated with alcohol consumption (see Alcoholism). Acute pancreatitis can also be associated with alcohol but may occur without an apparent cause.

Finally, cancer can infect the pancreas (see Cancer). This is difficult to treat because it is usually advanced before the cause of its vague pains are apparent. Surgery may be necessary, but it is only carried out in cases where the cancer has not spread.

If the pancreas has to be removed, the body can still function. Insulin injections can be taken (see Diabetes), digestive enzymes can be sprinkled on food, or the stomach can be prevented from producing acids with certain drugs.

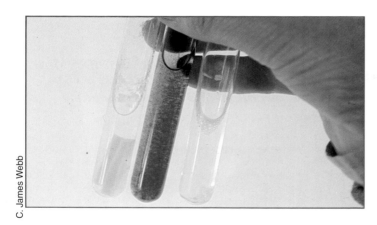

C. James Webb

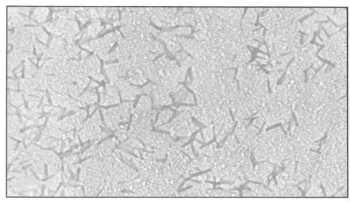

Nordisk-UK

The enzyme amylase breaks down starch. Left to right: amylase, colored starch solution added; color gone, hence starch broken down by the enzyme.

Insulin crystals, an extremely important pancreatic hormone, keep the level of blood sugar down. An insulin deficiency results in the disease called diabetes.

Dual role of the pancreas

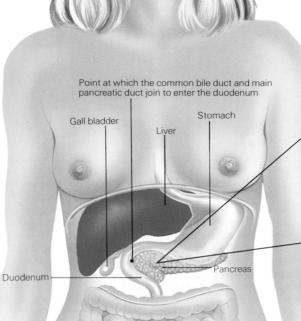

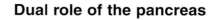

Point at which the common bile duct and main pancreatic duct join to enter the duodenum

Gall bladder

Liver

Stomach

Duodenum

Pancreas

Elaine Keenan

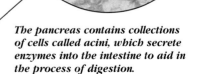

The pancreas contains collections of cells called acini, which secrete enzymes into the intestine to aid in the process of digestion.

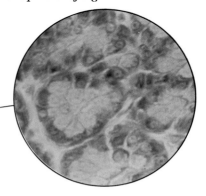

The islets of Langerhans produce the pancreatic hormones insulin and glucagon, which help balance the body's sugar level.

Science Photo Library

Pap smear

Q I recently started to bleed from my vagina after love-making. I had a Pap smear six months ago, so should I worry?

A Any woman who is bleeding in this way should see her doctor immediately to exclude the rare possibility of cancer of the cervix, or of a precancerous state. Bleeding after sexual intercourse is likely to be caused by a less serious condition, such as cervical polyps. Your gynecologist should be able to put your mind at rest.

Q Are Pap smears taken when a woman starts taking oral contraceptives because you are more likely to get cancer of the cervix if you take the Pill?

A No. Current evidence does not suggest that cervical cancer is likely to be caused by the Pill. It is simply convenient for most women to have a Pap smear done on their visit to the gynecologist's office. Pap smears may also be done at other facilities, and by many family physicians and internists.

Q At my postnatal visit I was told that I had an erosion on the neck of the womb. Is this likely to develop into cancer?

A No. It is fairly common for women to develop an erosion shortly after having a baby. The central canal through the cervix is lined with deep red glandular tissue which can pouch outward, making the part of the cervix protruding into the vagina look dark red and rough. This erosion gradually disappears, and is rarely caused by abnormal cell changes. Nevertheless, it is wise to have routine Pap smears.

Q I have had a hysterectomy, do I still need Pap smears?

A Usually the cervix is removed in a hysterectomy, so it is unnecessary to have further Pap smears since their purpose is to detect abnormal cells in the cervix. Sometimes, though, the cervix is not removed, or some abnormal cells may remain in the vagina. In either case your gynecologist will advise you on what course to follow.

Most cases of cancer of the cervix, the neck of the uterus, could be avoided if all women had regular Pap tests. This simple procedure detects precancerous conditions early enough for effective treatment.

Hank Morgan/Science Photo Library

Slides of Pap smears taken from female patients are prepared for microscopic examination. Only ten percent of such specimens will indicate abnormalities.

The earliest precancerous cell change in the cervix is called mild dysplasia (see Cervix and cervical smears). This cell change can return to normal without any treatment or it may develop into severe dysplasia, or carcinoma in situ. Here, the cells lining the cervix have some characteristics of cancer cells. Although the cells may remain unchanged for a long time, they can progress to microinvasive cancer. This means the abnormalities of the lining of the cervix have broken through to some of the underlying tissue. True invasive cancer of the cervix occurs when these abnormalities have totally invaded the underlying tissue.

All the abnormal cell changes preceding invasive cancer may be cured by removing the abnormal tissue in a minor operation. Many treatments are available, some of which do not need anesthesia.

How a Pap smear is done

Pap smears are usually performed by gynecologists or nurses as part of a vaginal examination. The cervix is at the top of the vagina, and it can be examined using a speculum that is gently introduced into the vagina. The speculum is usually metal or plastic and is shaped like a duck's bill. The two blades are about

4 in (10 cm) long and 1 in (2.5 cm) wide. When the upper and lower blades are opened the cervix can be viewed.

The Pap smear should be done before a bimanual examination so that the diagnostic cells are not inadvertently removed. The speculum may be rinsed in water or saline, or lubricated with K-Y jelly to ease its entry into the vagina.

A sample of cells is then taken from the junction between the canal through the cervix and the part of the cervix forming the top of the vagina. This area is most likely to develop the more common type of cervical cancer. The sample is removed with a wooden spatula, spread onto a glass slide, and placed immediately in a fixative medium. The slide is later stained and examined under a microscope.

Patients should relax during this examination as any tightening of the vaginal muscles will cause discomfort and make it difficult to insert the speculum. Some women may find the test embarrassing, but its importance as a preventive measure far outweighs the inconvenience.

Why have a Pap smear?

Women with precancerous changes of the cervix seldom develop any signs or symptoms. Gynecologists cannot tell if there is any abnormality just by looking at the cervix. Therefore it is vital for women to have regular Pap smears in order to prevent any cancer from developing. The earlier an abnormal condition is found, the easier it is to treat.

Pap smears can sometimes help in the diagnosis of other conditions. For example, cells from cancer of the ovary or cancer of the lining of the uterus (endometrial cancer) can occasionally be shown up by a Pap smear.

The tests are also used to detect vaginal infections which cause a discharge. This method is not totally accurate, but it may be used in centers where it is impossible to do formal studies of the bacteria present in the vagina. Infections that may be diagnosed in this way include herpes, thrush, and trichomonas vaginalis (see Vaginal discharge).

Having a Pap smear

Pap smears are done at a number of places, such as doctors' offices, hospitals, and gynecologic facilities. In the US, a woman should have her first Pap smear at 18, or after her first act of intercourse, whichever comes first. The greatest risk factor for cervical cancer is a woman's sexual history, so all sexually active women have a Pap smear each year in the US, and every other year in Canada.

About 10 percent of tests are unsatisfactory or unreliable. So if a woman has bloodstained discharge between periods, or bleeding from the vagina during or after intercourse, she should see her gynecologist as such irregularities may, rarely, be due to cancer of the cervix, and this must be ruled out.

If a Pap smear shows abnormalities it may be repeated sooner than usual. But it is unwise to have two tests done within a month as the first may remove all the abnormal cells, and the second may then be incorrectly read as negative since the abnormal cells will not have regrown. If there is a vaginal infection such as yeast or trichomonas, the test results will be slightly abnormal. The doctor will then treat the infection and repeat the test.

Treatment of an abnormality

Treatment can vary. If the changes are due to mild dysplasia, most doctors repeat the Pap smear every six months to check if the cells have returned to normal or progressed to severe dysplasia.

If severe dysplasia is detected, the area of abnormal cells is removed. Women who want children have as little surgery as possible to avoid damaging the cervix.

Sometimes the woman is seen in the outpatients clinic where the cervix can be viewed under a special microscope called a colposcope. The abnormal cells may be removed with a laser (see Lasers) or by freezing (see Freezing) or burning them off. In some hospitals a ring or cone biopsy is done under general anesthesia. Here, the entire area of cells where cancer is likely to develop (around the vaginal opening of the cervical canal) is removed.

Such minor operations cure the precancerous condition, but these women must have Pap smears for the rest of their lives to insure the disease does not return. Similar treatment is used for older women who have completed their families. If they have other gynecologic problems, such as heavy periods, a hysterectomy may be performed (see Gynecology).

Women with invasive cancer of the cervix may need radiotherapy to destroy the cancerous cells. A hysterectomy (see Hysterectomy) is usually recommended. Some 85 percent of cases that are caught early do not recur after treatment.

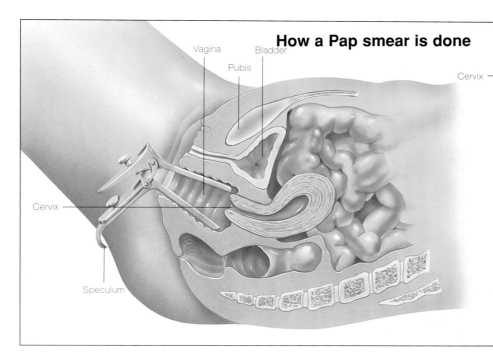

How a Pap smear is done

Vagina · Bladder · Pubis · Cervix · Speculum

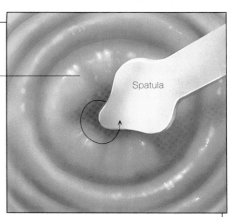

Cervix · Spatula

A Pap smear need cause no discomfort or distress. First a speculum is gently inserted into the vagina to enable the gynecologist to view the cervix. The sample of cells is taken by rotating a wooden or plastic spatula 360° within the cervix.

Chris Forsey

Paralysis

There are many different types of paralysis, ranging from a weakness in one muscle to an inability to move at all. However, what causes the paralysis can often be corrected and the outlook can be optimistic.

Q My cousin has been paralyzed in both legs for some time. Is there any hope of recovery for him?

A It depends on the cause. If his paralysis followed an injury, there is less hope than if he was suffering from a disease that caused paralysis. However, even if the motor nerves have been badly damaged, there is often some degree of recovery, which may even allow him to walk again and lead an almost normal life.

Q My father had a stroke and is paralyzed down the right side of his body. Does this mean that the stroke has damaged that side of his brain?

A No. Since the nerves to the muscles cross over at the bottom of the brain stem, a stroke that caused damage to one side of the brain will show itself in paralysis of the other side of the body. So your father has suffered damage to the left half of his brain, opposite to his right paralyzed side.

Q Does the victim of a stroke always recover from the resulting paralysis?

A There is always some recovery after a stroke, provided that the patient survived the acute stage. However, recovery depends on the extent of the brain damage and whether any other body functions have been affected. Despite this, most people show considerable powers of recovery.

Q Why do paralyzed people develop bedsores so easily, and can these be prevented?

A Even when we are asleep, we continually move around to prevent any part of our bodies from resting in the same place for too long, because the skin cannot cope with the pressure of body weight for long. Seriously paralyzed people cannot relieve this pressure and need to be turned from side to side regularly to prevent bedsores. This is one reason why badly paralyzed people are difficult to take care of at home.

One of the most important abilities that allows people to operate as independent beings is the ability to move about and manipulate objects with different parts of the body. In addition to the muscles that are needed for these obvious external movements, we need other muscles to breathe, eat, and speak (see Muscles).

Paralysis involves the temporary or permanent loss of some or all of these muscular activities, and it can be a serious threat to a person's independence. In paralysis the complex motor system that governs movements can be attacked on many levels by different diseases and injuries. It is also very important where the motor system is attacked and by what.

Children with muscular dystrophy (see Muscular dystrophy) meet to take part in outdoor activities. This inherited degenerative muscle disorder has no cure. However, specially adapted wheelchairs give body support and mobility—both essential in keeping the sufferer as active as possible.

What is paralysis?

Paralysis is the loss of normal functioning of the muscles to a part of the body. When this happens a person feels a weakness when he or she tries to use that part of the body. It is obvious when paralysis affects the arm or leg muscles: walking will be difficult or the grip will lose its strength. If, however, the muscles affected are the ones that make speech possible, then paralysis may show itself in slurred or incoherent speech. Or, if the eye muscles are affected, double vision may be experienced. The common factor in all these symptoms is that some or all of the muscles are not working properly.

How does paralysis occur?

The muscles are made up of tiny fibers that are grouped together in bundles. These bundles are each connected to the fiber of a single motor nerve cell, or motor neuron, in the spinal cord. These motor neurons are closely connected with many other nerve networks in the

Science Photo Library

spinal cord, and also with the fibers of the nerves that descend from the brain (see Spinal cord, and Brain).

Paralysis can happen as a result of damage to, or malfunction of, any part of this chain of command. Which component is damaged will have a great bearing on the character and distribution of the weakness that is experienced.

The muscles

When paralysis is caused by a disease of the muscles, the effect is usually felt on both sides of the body, and it generally affects the shoulder and hip muscles most strongly.

Diseases that affect the muscles and cause paralysis may be present from birth, like muscular dystrophy (see Muscular dystrophy); or the cells of the muscles may become inflamed. This disease is called myositis. When these diseases strike, in addition to weakness the muscles often waste away, making the affected part of the body look thin. Walking may be difficult because the hip

muscles are involved, and if the disease is severe enough, the leg muscles may become totally paralyzed. Paralysis of the shoulder muscles will make shaving and hair-brushing more difficult, even if the hands retain their ability to grip things. The diseases of the muscles that cause a degree of paralysis vary enormously in their severity, and often the paralysis is only partial. In myositis, weakness may be accompanied by pain, since the inflammation causes the muscles to swell.

The muscle-nerve junction

The connection between the surface of the muscle fibers and the nerve fibers that come to them is not direct; however, there is a very short gap across which tiny quantities of chemical transmitters jump when the nerve is activated. In a disease called myasthenia gravis, the receptor on the muscle fibers onto which the transmitter jumps is damaged and a weakness ensues. This paralysis is progressive: the muscle gets weaker the more it is used but recovers with rest.

The muscles that may be hit by this progressive paralysis vary, but often in addition to the shoulder and hip muscles, those governing the voice, swallowing, and breathing may be involved. Breathing, for example, may become very difficult, so that artificial help is needed. When the throat muscles are affected, a drink may be regurgitated or go down the wrong way into the lungs and cause the patient to choke.

Damage to the motor nerves

Weakness and paralysis of some groups of muscles can occur as a result of damage to the nerves that serve those muscles. For example, in some people the ulnar nerve, which passes down the arm, is rather exposed close to the elbow and may be damaged if the elbow is jarred continually. This jarring will lead to paral-

Someone confined to a wheelchair will have to make adjustments to his or her life; however, they need not be too restrictive. Indulging in a passion for sports is one way of overcoming a disability.

Specific causes and areas of paralysis

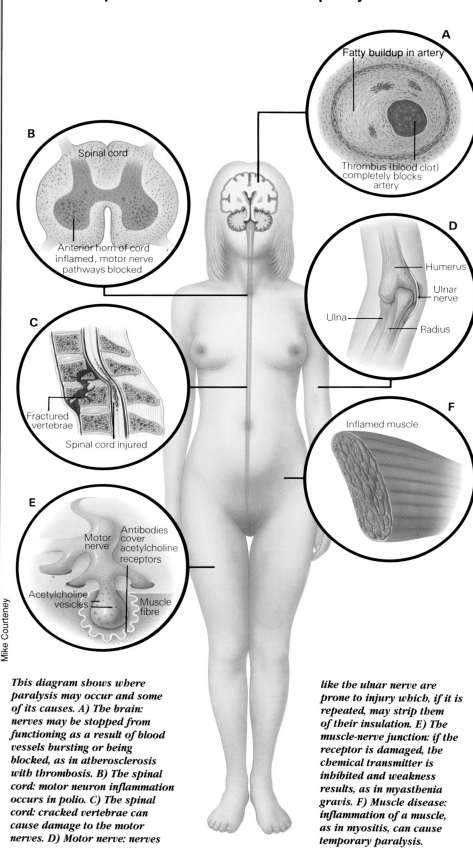

Mike Courteney

This diagram shows where paralysis may occur and some of its causes. A) The brain: nerves may be stopped from functioning as a result of blood vessels bursting or being blocked, as in atherosclerosis with thrombosis. B) The spinal cord: motor neuron inflammation occurs in polio. C) The spinal cord: cracked vertebrae can cause damage to the motor nerves. D) Motor nerve: nerves like the ulnar nerve are prone to injury which, if it is repeated, may strip them of their insulation. E) The muscle-nerve junction: if the receptor is damaged, the chemical transmitter is inhibited and weakness results, as in myasthenia gravis. F) Muscle disease: inflammation of a muscle, as in myositis, can cause temporary paralysis.

Workstations

These workstations are the type of innovation that makes life that much easier for anyone confined to a wheelchair.

The structure of these stations allow the person in the wheelchair to pull themselves out of the chair to a standing position by bracing the heels and knees against the supports shown. The backrest is then closed to give support. The person can then position the worktable in front of them.

This particular model is made of metal, and has metal tubular framing. It has a nonslip aluminum footboard, and transport wheels. The backrest has a safety lock, and the pelvic support unit is adjustable for comfort. The chest support is also adjustable.

A unit like this lets anyone with a disability lead a more active live. Standing with mechanical support results in good psychological benefits as well, for even though they are not standing of their own accord, they are at least standing up.

There are many types of standing units. For information on those available in your state, contact the local disability organization in your town and they will be able to put you in touch with suppliers.

Nottingham Rehab (Manufacturers)

ysis in the muscles of the hand. The grip will become weaker, because the thumb cannot be brought across to meet the fingers when trying to grasp something in the hand.

Individual motor nerves may be damaged by slipped disks in the spine: as the nerves emerge from the spinal cord, the slipped disks may put pressure on them (see Slipped disk). Here the paralysis affects only part of the leg or arm, and unless the damage is severe or prolonged, relief of the pressure on the motor nerve will remove the paralysis.

The spinal cord

Damage to the spinal cord usually involves damage to the nerve fibers that carry the brain's instructions down both sides of the body. The area of the spinal cord that has been damaged will determine what parts of the body are paralyzed. Both legs may be paralyzed (paraplegia) or all four limbs may be affected if the damage is in the neck (quadraplegia). The spinal cord may be damaged in an accident in which the backbone or neck are broken or displaced;

there may be blood vessel damage due to clots or hemorrhage; or there may be inflammation as in multiple sclerosis. If the cause of the paralysis can be removed, there may be almost immediate relief. One example of this is a depressed fragment of bone that presses on the spinal cord.

Diseases of the spinal cord can cause paralysis. For example, polio, which used to be common, is a viral infection of the spinal cord. It starts with paralysis of an arm or a leg and may go on to involve the entire body (see Poliomyelitis).

The brain

The nerve fibers that run from the brain to the spinal cord carry instructions to the muscles. The fibers cross over from one side to the other at the bottom of the brain stem as it meets the spinal cord. Damage to the nerves above this crossover point will cause weakness in the opposite side of the body. A common cause of this type of paralysis is a stroke, which is due to a lack of blood to parts of the brain (see Stroke). If the part of the brain that is supplied by a blocked or burst blood vessel includes the

motor nerves, then the opposite side of the body is paralyzed. Strokes usually cause this paralysis suddenly, and the brain recovers well. Paralysis caused by a brain tumor develops slowly.

The outlook following paralysis

The cause of the paralysis will determine the recovery time. Some diseases that cause paralysis will go away on their own (see Guillain-Barré syndrome). Similarly, most people who are admitted to the hospital totally paralyzed on one side because of a stroke can also walk out of the hospital, albeit with a limp. Multiple sclerosis can wax and wane, or be progressive. However, treatment is always necessary to maintain the health of the affected limbs. Physical therapy and careful nursing are absolutely vital. During convalescence, occupational therapists will help the paralyzed person to make the most of any remaining abilities so that some independence is retained. Recent research suggests that it may be possible to get the spinal cord to regenerate somewhat after injury.

Paraplegia

Q Now that I am confined to a wheelchair, should I change my diet?

A Yes, you should be eating much less than before. Because you are a lot less active now, you will not be able to burn up calories in the same way. So you are likely to put on weight, which is not easy to lose when you are confined to a wheelchair.

Q My husband puts on a brave face despite the fact that he is a paraplegic, but I know he hasn't come to terms with it. How long will it take?

A You shouldn't expect him to adjust quickly, and you should remember that different people adjust at different speeds. However, he will come to terms with it, even if it takes a year.

Q My husband has just been diagnosed as a paraplegic. I'm too embarrassed to ask the hospital doctors this, but are his sexual feelings dead, too?

A No. His sexual feelings are not dead, and you may be able to have a sexual relationship. Indeed, this will be important in his rehabilitation. However, his sexual performance may be impaired, depending on how much of his spinal cord is affected. Some paraplegics can have erections and even reach orgasm. However, remember that neither is vital for a rewarding sex life.

Q Apparently bedsores are a major problem in paraplegia. How can I prevent them?

A Sometimes called pressure sores, bedsores result from blood being prevented, by body weight, from properly circulating. This causes the skin and underlying tissue to die and leads to gangrene. The cure is simple: lift the body regularly so that the pressure is relieved and the blood can flow freely. In the wheelchair, you should lift yourself off your buttocks every 15 minutes for at least 20 seconds. If you are bedridden, you need to turn around every four hours.

No one should underestimate the extreme difficulty of this type of paralysis; however, it is important to remember that we all possess a marvelous human characteristic that enables us to come to terms with it: adaptability.

British Sports Association for the Disabled

To be told that you have lost the use of your legs, that your trunk is paralyzed, and that you are confined to a wheelchair for the rest of your life may seem like a death sentence. Following such a blow, many would feel that it is not worth living, yet with the support of relatives and friends, most people do go on to live happy lives.

Causes
The spinal cord is a cylinder of nerve tissue with 31 pairs of nerves connected to its length. Each of these nerves carry sensory information to and from particular parts of the body including the legs and the intestines. If this central highway of the nervous system is damaged, the associated parts of the body may be put out of action (see Spinal cord).

Paraplegia is a result of either direct damage to the nerves in the spinal cord or brain, or of a disease, typically of the nervous system, which spreads to or involves the spinal cord. The condition is often caused by automobile and sports accidents, or gunshot wounds to the spine; the incidence is highest in young men between 19 and 35 years old.

Coping in the hospital
"Why me?" is the unanswerable question that is most often asked; it is usually accompanied by emotional outbursts of crying, swearing, or aggression.

Close relatives usually bear the brunt of the abuse, as do medical staff. However, the paraplegic is just lashing out at his or her own paralysis. Although this can be extremely distressing for the relations, they should be reassured that this is the healthiest reaction to paralysis. It often signals a better recovery than resignation.

Aggressive outbursts are usually followed by depression, particularly since some of the routine of a disabled person's life feels humiliating. For example, the patient

One of the most important aspects of this paraplegic's rehabilitation is warmth, support, and encouragement from her family and friends (right). Paraplegics who enjoy sports (below) can join the Special Olympics, which organizes international competitions along the lines of the Olympic Games.

Will McIntyre/Science Photo Library

spends a lot of time naked to facilitate washing, and there has to be urine collection, and other undignified treatment.

How others can help

Relatives and friends will be having a hard time, too. Their initial reaction will be shock and disbelief, and they will also need help in coming to terms with the crisis. They should spend as much time as they can encouraging the patient. They should not, however, be overprotective since this only highlights the paraplegic's awareness of his or her own helplessness. It is sensible to ask the hospital social worker at this stage for help with domestic and financial worries. When the patient starts to ask about the future, relatives and friends can then put him or her at ease.

Going home again

Even if the patient seems to have adjusted well in the hospital, going home can

be a setback; the hospital routine is comforting, and the trained staff can cope with the problems of the paraplegic.

The quickest adjustment to the new circumstances are made by those who keep themselves occupied when they return home, possibly by retraining for a job.

Relationships

When one partner becomes disabled, a huge strain is put on close relationships. Many couples overcome this and become closer than before, although some couples inevitably break up. Some paraplegics meet new partners after they have become disabled.

The paraplegic usually needs much more care from a partner than an able-bodied person. However, both can eventually develop a new daily routine.

Sex is often as important to a disabled person as it is to an able-bodied person. While most male paraplegics are unable to maintain an erection or to ejaculate, this does not rule out other sorts of sexual contact. Both male and female paraplegics have claimed that sensitivity in other areas increases when part of the body is paralyzed, and a form of orgasm may be experienced.

Most female paraplegics will continue to ovulate and have periods, and this means that with special management, they can bear children. A spinal specialist should be consulted before pregnancy is decided upon.

It is more difficult for the couple to produce their own children when the man is a paraplegic. However, in some cases a spinal specialist may be able to stimulate the prostate gland to ejaculate by electrotherapy. Sperm produced in this way

can sometimes be used to artificially inseminate the woman. If a couple cannot have their own children, it may be possible for them to adopt.

Urinary problems

An able-bodied person receives warning signals when the bladder is full and can empty it more or less at will. A paraplegic receives no such signals and instead must rely on a urine collecting system.

For a male this is usually a type of condom fitted to the penis, which drains into a bag that is changed every 24 hours. Unfortunately, there can be no such solution for a female paraplegic, who has to rely on regular visits to the lavatory, plastic underwear, and absorbent pads.

Wheelchairs

A wheelchair is the paraplegic's most important aid, and it has to be chosen carefully. Any paraplegic who can afford to buy a spare chair should do so because they do malfunction from time to time. Wheelchairs should be kept in perfect working order. The more severely disabled should use a powered wheelchair.

Going back to work

Fortunately, some paraplegics can continue working in their old professions after they have been confined to a wheelchair. For others further education and training will be necessary.

In the gloomy early days it is easy to feel that getting a job is impossible. But there are a surprisingly wide range of jobs for paraplegics, and the Americans with Disabilities Act prohibits discrimination against the disabled. For those who cannot find a job, and even for those who can, hobbies and recreational activities will play an important part. Opportunities to take part in sedentary (sitting down) activities are plentiful, and for those who like sports, there is even a paraplegics sports movement.

Adapting the home

Everyone recognizes the need to adapt a paraplegic's home for ease of living, and grants are available to help those who cannot afford to do so.

If it is possible, the house or apartment should be adapted before the paraplegic comes home from the hospital. A ground floor apartment or room is ideal.

The wheelchair user should be able to leave home without help, which usually requires the construction of ramps to and from the building. Doors should be wide enough to give access; light switches should be lowered and sockets raised.

Bathrooms and bedrooms

The bathroom should be accessible directly from the bedroom, and, if there is enough space, it should have a special shower stall installed. Adequate heating is also important. Many paraplegics suffer from a dangerous loss of body heat (see Hypothermia), because their blood flow tends to be more sluggish than normal. Central heating is best, and essential in the bathroom, because direct heat from a fireplace or electric heater can burn a paraplegic's legs without him or her noticing. A paraplegic's bed needs the

most careful consideration, and the hospital will be able to give advice on the various types that are currently available.

Getting around

While invalid vehicles are the best way of getting around for most disabled people, ordinary cars can also be converted to hand controls. There are also many clubs and associations that cater exclusively for disabled drivers and passengers. It is not impossible for a disabled person to travel by public transportation—just a little more difficult.

Steve Bielschowsky

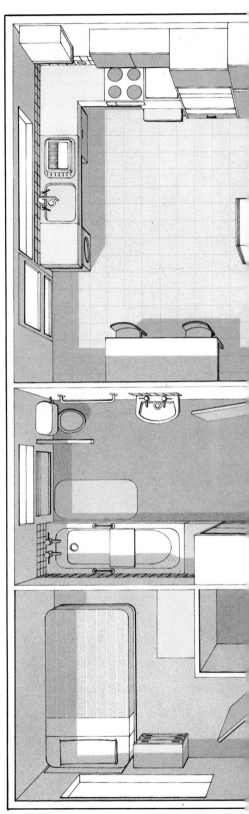

Steve Bielschowsky

The hall (above) is wide enough to accommodate a wheelchair. Carpet on the doors prevents paint from chipping when wheelchairs bump against them. In the kitchen (above right) all work surfaces are low, and there is space for a wheelchair under the sink. All the cupboards are the push-open type. In the bathroom (right) a manually operated seat allows the paraplegic to be lifted safely in and out of the water.

Nottingham Rehab (Manufacturers)

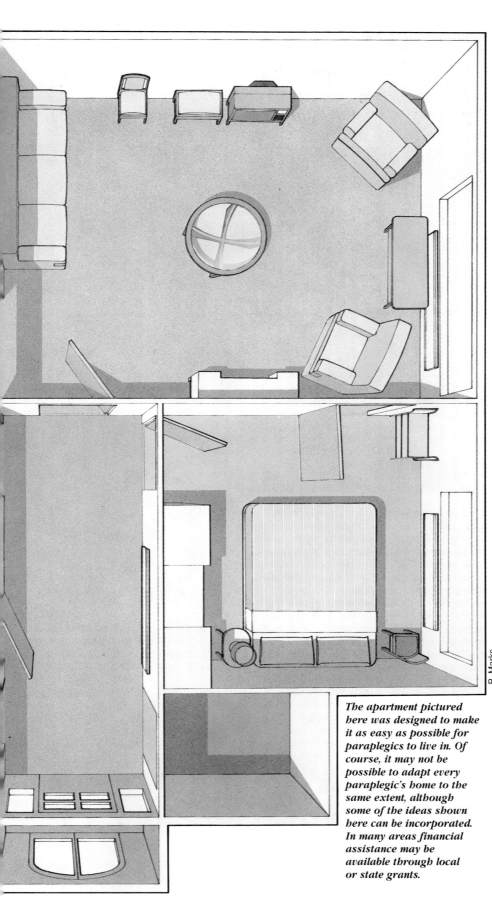

The living room is deliberately large to allow room for wheelchairs to maneuver. The window can be opened and shut by winding a handle, like those in some cars. Furniture is close to the ground, and sharp corners are kept to a minimum. Light switches, thermostat controls, and sockets for plugs have been installed at a level that is convenient for wheelchair users.

B. Marks

The apartment pictured here was designed to make it as easy as possible for paraplegics to live in. Of course, it may not be possible to adapt every paraplegic's home to the same extent, although some of the ideas shown here can be incorporated. In many areas financial assistance may be available through local or state grants.

Every room in this apartment is equipped with a red alarm cord so that help can be summoned whenever an emergency occurs. There is an intercom console in each apartment, complete with a receiver. When staff of such complexes make their rounds, they carry a handset that can be plugged into any console on the complex. If there is an emergency in any house, the staff will know about it in minutes. The staff carry equipment that also has a memory bank, so that messages can be stored.

Parasites

Q Can humans be vaccinated against diseases that are caused by parasites?

A Parasites have evolved many remarkable ways of escaping our immune defense mechanism. Diseases like malaria persist because mosquitoes develop a resistance to specific antimalarial drugs. So far, there is no sure vaccine against diseases of this kind, but scientists are working to improve prevention.

Q Are parasites especially harmful during pregnancy?

A Many parasitic diseases may increase the risk of a woman miscarrying a baby. They also increase the possibility of anemia, various vitamin deficiencies, and malnutrition. These could endanger the lives of a mother and baby.

Q Do parasites do any good in the body?

A We depend on some bacteria to help us digest food and also protect us from infection, but most parasites are not so welcome. The most harmful cause hundreds of human diseases.

Q I've heard that tapeworm eggs could help me to lose weight. Is this true?

A Years ago, some misguided people actually tried to use tapeworms to aid dieting. You would certainly lose weight if you had a tapeworm inside, but this is dangerous. Eating tapeworm eggs would fill your body with larvae and this brings about a disease known as cysticercosis. The outcome could well be fatal!

Q Does freezing food insure that parasites are killed?

A Storing food in a home freezer helps to destroy nearly all of the harmful parasites that might be present. Remember that frozen meat must be adequately thawed before cooking. This helps to insure that any of the remaining parasites will be destroyed by the cooking process.

Some kinds of viruses, bacteria, fungi, protozoa, worms, flukes, ticks, lice, bugs, flies, and leeches are the causes of hundreds of human diseases. Careful hygiene and better sanitation can help to prevent many problems.

Jerry Harpur

C. James Webb

It is natural for children to cuddle dogs, but care should be taken with hygiene. Dogs can harbor infections such as roundworm (inset) in their saliva and feces.

Parasites live in or on their hosts, depending totally on them for survival. People and animals are troubled by numerous types of parasites, which can be as small as one cell (like the malarial parasite) or be up to 65 ft (about 20 m) long, like the fish tapeworm (see Worms).

Parasites can damage hosts in different ways. Some feed directly upon tissues, such as the liver fluke (see Liver fluke), which feeds on liver cells. There is also the hookworm (see Hookworms), which lives on its host's blood.

Many parasites are more common in poorer, tropical countries. The better sanitation and living conditions found in richer countries, along with easier access to medical care and a cooler climate, all make transmission of parasitic diseases more difficult (see Public health).

Threadworms are perhaps the most common parasitic disease in countries like the United States. They live in the large intestine, and lay eggs around the anal skin during the night and cause intense itching. Poverty-stricken children are most commonly affected by these.

Fleas (see Fleas), head and body lice (see Lice), and mites are also relatively common. They differ from other parasites because they live outside the body and feed exclusively on their hosts' blood.

The parasitic lifestyle

Parasites have adapted and modified their way of life to the lifestyles of their hosts. They can overcome immune defenses, so the body can do very little to fight the parasite (see Immune system).

Parasites have voracious appetites. For example, each tiny hookworm consumes 8,000 times its own weight in human blood each day. Parasites need to produce eggs or larvae at such a colossal rate to insure that reproduction takes place and that new hosts are infected. Ascaris is a common type of parasitic worm, infesting at least one billion people around the world. It lives in the small intestine. Transmission takes place when the host eats food that has been contaminated with infected feces.

Parasites living in tissues or in the bloodstream depend on mosquitoes or other biting insects (called vectors) for transmission. Their larvae or reproductive cells are microscopic. They have to be produced in massive quantities to insure that an insect becomes infected each time it bites the host.

How parasites are spread

The eggs, cysts, or larvae of many parasites are found in the feces of human or animal hosts. In some countries, human feces are still an important source of fer-

The Robert Hunt Library

C. James Webb

Mary Fisher/Colorific!

The surrender of Singapore to Japan in February 1942 (above) and other conflicts resulted in years of captivity for some Allied servicemen. Many of those who survived Japanese prisoner-of-war camps returned with serious parasitic diseases. Workers who plant rice in watery fields in Asia (left) are prey to infestation by schistosomiasis, which is carried by larvae of the freshwater snail (inset).

tilizer and spread over the land. In poorer countries, generally, the facilities for disposal of sewage are not always adequate.

Flies and cockroaches spread eggs directly from the feces of one host to the food of another. Transmission can also take place by dirty hands. Water from wells and rivers is easily contaminated by unhygienic disposal of feces and sewage.

Soil that has been contaminated with feces often harbors larvae that are able to penetrate the bare feet of the next host. This is how hookworm is transmitted. Feces may also contain eggs or cysts that infect secondary hosts like cows or pigs (in the case of the tapeworm) and freshwater snails (in the case of bilharzia). In this way, parasites multiply and are spread further afield.

Obviously, better sanitation and more careful disposal of feces would interrupt the life cycles of all these parasites. This would help to bring the diseases that they cause under control. Better hygiene and more care when handling food is also essential to prevention (see Hygiene).

Meat infestation can be a serious problem, for richer as well as poorer nations. For example, pork can contain 1,000,000 larvae of the parasite trichinella in a fraction of an ounce (a single gram). Eating even a very small quantity of such infected meat may be very dangerous. Careful, thorough cooking is necessary to make all meats safe.

Q Can a parasite live in a human without giving a sign of its presence?

A Yes. Many intestinal worms cause no symptoms at all in well-nourished people. It is actually to a parasite's advantage not to cause too much harm, for if the host dies, so does the parasite. A check on the health of ex-soldiers who had been prisoners in Asia during World War II showed that many still had various parasitic infestations. Some of these had been present but had not given symptoms for decades.

Q I have been losing weight since returning from my travels in Pakistan. Could this weight loss be the result of some parasitic disease?

A Parasitic diseases may cause weight loss, as can many other illnesses. You should consult your doctor at once, so that he or she can perform tests and discover the cause.

Q Is it true that dogs carry parasites that can be transmitted to humans?

A Dogs can harbor around 40 different infections harmful to man, including several types of parasite. The most dangerous of the latter is a small tapeworm, which lives in the dog's intestines. Eggs are discharged with the feces. Contamination of food leads to a severe infestation with larval cysts that can develop in the liver and lungs. This problem is called hydatid disease.

Toxocariasis is another common and serious infestation that can cause blindness in young children. It is caused by a small worm that wanders around the human body. Fecal contamination of food is the source of infestation.

Q Can parasites be spread to humans through blood transfusions?

A Malaria may be spread by transfusion if medical facilities are poor. Donated blood is usually checked thoroughly for diseases before it is given in a transfusion.

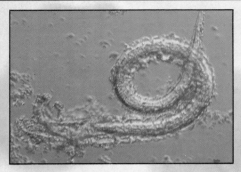

An ancylostoma larva, which causes hookworm infestation in the intestines.

The hatching of the ascaris larva, which infects the intestines and stomach.

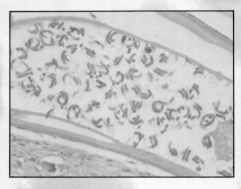

Onchocerca parasites, which cause river blindness, live in the skin nodules.

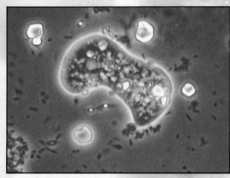

Amoebic dysentery results from Entamoeba in contaminated food and water.

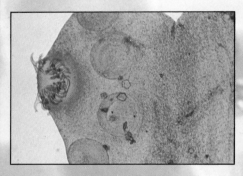

A tapeworm (taenia) attaches itself with its hooks and suckers to the intestine.

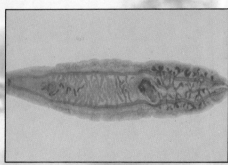

The liver fluke (clonorchis) infects the liver and bile duct.

The anopheles mosquito is an insect vector that transmits malaria through a bite (above left). Malaria parasites (plasmodium) line a mosquito's stomach (above right).

The most common parasitic diseases

Infestation	Parasite (proper name)	Parts of body where parasite lives	How transmitted	Harmful effects	How many people affected in world	Parts of world where most common
Malaria	*Plasmodium*	Bloodstream; liver	Mosquito bite	Recurrent fever; anemia; ill health; miscarriages; often causes death	Over 200 million each year	Africa; Latin America; India; Southeast Asia; Asia
Amoebic dysentery	*Entamoeba*	Large intestine	Cysts from feces are spread by flies. These contaminate both food and water	Diarrhea; dysentery; liver abscesses	Over 400 million at any one time	All parts of the world, but Africa, Latin America, Asia especially
Hookworm	*Ancylostoma, Necator*	Intestines	Eggs are passed in feces and hatch in the soil; larvae burrow into bare feet	Weight loss; anemia; malnutrition	Over 600 million	Africa; Latin America; Asia
Bilharzia (also called schistosomiasis)	*Schistosoma*	Veins around intestines and bladder	Larvae live in fresh water, and burrow through human skin; the larvae grow and develop into snails	Damage to the liver and bladder; often fatal	Over 200 million	Africa (Egypt especially); China
Filariasis	*Wuchereria; Brugia;* and others	Lymph vessels	Mosquito bites	Elephantiasis	Over 250 million	Asia; Africa; parts of South America
Ascariasis	*Ascaris*	Intestines and stomach	Eggs from feces are spread by flies and by contaminated food and water	Malnutrition with heavy infestation; obstruction of the intestine. Light infestation causes no symptoms	Over 1 billion	All parts of the world, but Africa, Asia, and Latin America especially
River blindness	*Onchocerca*	Adults live in nodules beneath the skin; larvae live in the tissues and eyes	Bites from blackflies, which tend to live in rapid-flowing rivers	Blindness; skin damage	Over 40 million	Africa; parts of South America
Guinea worm	*Dracunculus*	Beneath the skin of feet and legs	Larvae live in water fleas, which contaminate drinking water	Increased risk of foot and leg ulcers	Over 80 million	Africa; Asia
Tapeworms	*Taenia* (beef and pork tapeworms); *Diphyllobothrium* (fish tapeworm)	Intestines	Cysts and larvae are present in infested meat and fish, and these mature into adult tapeworms if meat is not properly cooked; smoked or cured meat are common sources of infestation	Malnutrition and anemia. The pork tapeworm can sometimes kill if cysts are formed in the brain. Tapeworms may not produce symptoms	Over 65 million	Many parts of the world, but especially Africa, Asia, South America, Scandinavia (fish tapeworm)
Liver fluke	*Clonorchis*	Liver and bile duct	Cysts are present in raw fish	Liver damage and obstruction	Over 20 million	Asia
Threadworms (pinworms)	*Enterobius*	Large intestine and anus	Contamination of bedding; clothing; dirty hands; fingernails	Itching; can cause secondary infection through irritation	Over 200 million	Worldwide

Another important transmission route for parasites is by insect vectors. A vector becomes infected when it bites the host. The parasite multiples within it, and the infected vector is soon able to pass the disease on to new hosts with each bite. In this way, amoebic dysentery can be spread by flies, and malaria is spread by anopheles mosquitoes (see Malaria). One way of controlling such diseases is by attacking the insect vector. Breeding grounds can be destroyed by draining mosquito-ridden swamps and using insecticides.

Effects of parasites

Parasites can cause considerable harm. But the damage to the host may not be obvious, appearing only after a long time.

Infestation with ascaris or tapeworms, which live in the intestines and feed on partly digested food, may not be noticed by a healthy host. In poorer countries, where many people do not have the food they need for good health, such parasites contribute to the widespread problem of malnutrition.

Sometimes the damage done to the host is so terrible that whole populations have chosen to move away from villages rather than remain exposed to a very debilitating disease.

The thorough cooking of pork helps to insure that any parasitic larvae contained in the meat are completely destroyed.

Parasitic disease

Prevention

If you live in or visit a country where parasitic diseases are a major problem, these rules will help you to stay healthy:

- Check that drinking water is safe to use. If you are in doubt, drink only boiled water or use purifying tablets that contain chlorine or iodine

- Never eat food that has been left in the open or exposed to flies. Eat food that has been cooked recently and thoroughly. Wash hands and maintain hygiene when handling food

- Wash all fruit and vegetables before eating. If possible, use detergent

- Avoid exposure to insects. Wear sensible clothing and use insect repellent sprays and gels containing DEET. Use mosquito nets or burn pyrethrum mosquito coils at night

- In malarial regions, take antimalarial pills. Seek your doctor's advice well before going on your trip

- Do not swim in canals or rivers, and do not walk around with bare feet

Detection

Your doctor will perform the following tests if you report feeling unwell after returning from an area where parasitic diseases are common:

- **Blood tests:** Blood is first examined under the microscope for signs of any of the nonspecific changes found in parasitic infestations, e.g., disordered white blood cell counts and anemia. Blood is then checked carefully. Malarial parasites, trypanosomes (which cause sleeping sickness), and the larvae of some filarial worms can all be seen under the microscope

- **Stool tests:** A fresh stool sample is examined under the microscope for the eggs, cysts, and larvae of parasites. Almost all of the parasites produce eggs with a characteristic size and shape. Finding and recognizing them requires skill. Several stool samples may be necessary if the infestation is not a heavy one

- **Urine tests:** The urine may contain eggs in diseases such as bilharzia. These may be detected by using a technique of centrifugation or filtration. The resulting sediment is then examined under a microscope

Roger Payling

Treatment

Drugs are available to treat most parasitic diseases, and treatment is often a simple matter. However, where the host suffers damage over a period of many years, treatment to kill the parasite may come too late. Drugs cannot undo the liver damage that occurs in schistosomiasis or the deformity caused by elephantiasis.

Drug treatment is not always practical for dealing with large communities. Some drugs are too toxic for use on a large scale and have to be carefully supervised. Whatever the treatment, it is vital to focus on prevention, too, so that reinfection becomes less likely.

Outlook

Many parasitic diseases have proved difficult to eradicate completely. Preventive programs can be costly. The poorer countries, that have the widest problems with parasites often have the fewest resources to deal with the problems.

There have been advances in recent decades. As basic hygiene, sanitation, and health improve throughout much of the world, the parasitic diseases of poverty are becoming less inevitable.

Parathyroid glands

Q I heard that years ago when the thyroid was removed during surgery, the parathyroids were often accidentally removed too. What happened in cases like these?

A The results of the surgery were disastrous. The patient would develop a very low level of calcium in the blood, and this led first to tetany (an uncontrolled muscular spasm that occurred particularly in the hands and feet) and eventually to the loss of respiration, unless the problem was corrected. Fortunately, once the condition was recognized, it was easy to treat by giving the patient vitamin D. These days the parathyroids may be removed deliberately in cases of cancer in the thyroid region. However, this is done to replace the parathyroid activity with vitamin D in order to release calcium into the bloodstream.

Q My mother has an overactive thyroid gland. Is there any chance that her parathyroids will be affected?

A No. Although the thyroid and parathyroid glands are close together the disease processes that affect each are quite separate, and so her parathyroids should be fine. Incidentally, it is possible to develop a raised level of calcium in the blood simply as a result of a severely overactive thyroid gland.

Q When my father recently underwent surgery on his parathyroids, he was injected with blue dye. What was the reason for this?

A The parathyroid glands are very small organs, and it is not surprising that they are extremely difficult for a surgeon to find during surgery. For some unknown reason the parathyroid glands are able to absorb a dye called Evan's Blue. This coloring allows the surgeon to see them more easily, so that they are distinguished from the rest of the tissues. Many surgeons now use this technique to help with the operation.

The tiny parathyroids are among the most important glands in the body. They produce a hormone called PTH, which is vital for maintaining the delicately balanced quantities of calcium in the bloodstream.

The parathyroids are four tiny glands found behind the thyroid glands, which in turn are found just below the larynx in the throat. They play a major part in controlling the levels of calcium in the body. Calcium is a vital mineral, not only because it is the major structural element in the formation of bones and teeth, but also because it plays a central role in the workings of the muscles and nerve cells (see Calcium). The body's calcium levels have to be kept within fairly constant boundaries, otherwise the muscles stop working and fits may occur. The parathyroid glands keep the calcium levels in balance.

The absorption of calcium into the bloodstream is controlled by vitamin D (see Vitamin D), which we get from sunlight and some foods, and an important hormone produced by the parathyroids called parathyroid hormone, or PTH. If the level of calcium is too low, the parathyroids secrete an increased quantity of the hormone, which releases calcium from the bones to raise the level in the bloodstream. Conversely, if there is too much calcium, the parathyroids reduce or halt the production of PTH, thus bringing the level down (see Hormones).

The parathyroids are so small that they can be difficult to find. The upper two are

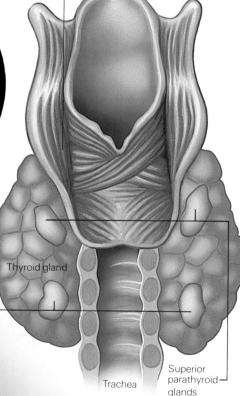

This hip X ray shows a prominent bone cyst, which was later operated upon. A parathyroid tumor was discovered and removed in the operation.

Venner Artists

Thyroid cartilage

Thyroid gland

Inferior parathyroid glands

Trachea

Superior parathyroid glands

The tiny parathyroid glands are usually situated near the thyroid gland at the back of the larynx in the throat. The upper two, the superior parathyroids, are behind the thyroid. In this illustration the inferior parathyroids are inside the thyroid.

1331

Zefa

Q How are the parathyroids affected if the diet is deficient in calcium?

A A low level of calcium in the diet will certainly tend to raise the output of parathyroid hormone from the parathyroids. In fact, it is more common for the diet to be deficient in vitamin D than in calcium. However, this, too, will result in a low blood calcium level, since vitamin D is essential for the absorption of calcium from the bones into the bloodstream.

Q My brother has kidney trouble and he had to have his parathyroids removed. Why did he have to have this done?

A The kidney contains an enzyme that is necessary to activate vitamin D. Without this enzyme, a lack of active vitamin D causes the blood calcium to fall, and the parathyroids may enlarge to compensate for this.

Q If you start having muscular spasms, does it necessarily mean that your parathyroids have failed?

A There are many different types of muscle spasm, and anything from an epileptic attack to abdominal cramps can be responsible. However, if you have tetany, which is an uncontrollable contraction of the muscles, usually starting in the hands and feet, a lack of PTH may be responsible. In fact, a more common cause of tetany is a disturbance of the blood's acid and alkaline balance.

Q Can PTH arise from any area aside from the parathyroid glands?

A Yes. It's a sobering thought that a number of different hormones can be manufactured by various types of cancer, and PTH is one of these. It can be manufactured by cancers of the lung and kidney. It is also worth noting that PTH used to be injected into patients to correct calcium levels, but that this has been discontinued because of its uncertain biological effects on the body.

situated behind the thyroid gland; the lower two, however, can actually be inside the thyroid or occasionally down inside the chest.

Like most endocrine (hormone) glands, the parathyroids can cause two main problems. They can be overactive; this leads to a high level of calcium in the blood; or they can be underactive, leading to a dangerously low level (see Endocrine system, and Glands).

Overactive parathyroids

Hyperparathyroidis, or overactive parathyroids, is a common problem. Doctors now measure the level of calcium in the

Vitamin D, which is so essential for the absorption of calcium, is found in fish oils and is synthesized from sunlight.

blood as a routine part of the biochemical screening test that is carried out on practically all hospital patients, and also on many patients by their own doctors. As a result more instances of unexpectedly high blood calcium levels have been found, whereas in the past the level of calcium in the blood was measured only when an abnormality was suspected. It is now thought that as many as one person in a thousand may show some degree of parathyroid overactivity.

The interaction between blood calcium and PTH

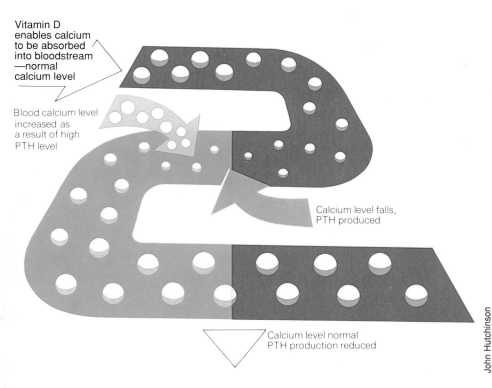

Vitamin D enables calcium to be absorbed into bloodstream —normal calcium level

Blood calcium level increased as a result of high PTH level

Calcium level falls, PTH produced

Calcium level normal PTH production reduced

John Hutchinson

This diagram shows how, as the level of calcium in the blood drops, the parathyroids increase production of PTH; once the blood calcium level returns to normal, production of PTH is reduced.

In the remainder of cases there is a tumor (see Tumors). Usually this affects only one gland, and only a tiny minority of patients will be found to have a tumor that is malignant (see cancer).

It is not certain what the best treatment is for those people with a slightly higher blood calcium level but without any symptoms. In general most younger patients are advised to have an operation, since the high level of calcium may eventually damage the kidneys. The outlook following treatment is usually very good.

Underactive parathyroids

In contrast, underactivity (hypoparathyroidism) is rare, unless, of course, the parathyroids are removed during surgery on the thyroid. People suffering from this disease are often tired. They may start having seizures and there may be signs of tetany, a muscular spasm that initially affects the hands and feet.

There can also be marked psychological problems. Many patients will have depression, but a large number show irrational overactivity. As well as all the symptoms of low blood calcium, people who have hypoparathyroidism are susceptible to candida (see Yeast) infection of the nails.

Fortunately this disease can be combated effectively by taking vitamin D by mouth. Even though a careful eye has to be kept on the calcium level, the outlook after treatment is very good.

One other condition is called pseudohypoparathyroidism. Here, the parathyroids are normal; however, the body does not respond in a normal way to the parathyroid hormone.

Symptoms

A raised blood calcium level may be caused by hyperparathyroidism. However, it is important to realize that there could be other causes. For example, one common cause of high levels of blood calcium is a cancer that leads to secondary deposits of cancer tissue in the bones. This causes the bones to be eaten away and a lot of calcium to be released into the bloodstream. An excessive intake of vitamin D can also cause a raised calcium level.

The two main symptoms of a raised calcium level are thirst and increased urination. There may also be fatigue, poor concentration, loss of appetite, and vomiting. Where overactive parathyroids are the cause of the high blood calcium, many patients develop kidney stones. In this disease the urine contains a lot of calcium which tends to settle in the kidneys (see Kidneys and kidney diseases).

People with overactive parathyroids also seem to suffer from indigestion. In about 10 percent of cases the amount of calcium that is released from the bones as a result of the high level of PTH is so great that the bones themselves begin to show signs of strain—there may be bone pain, some loss of height, and even spontaneous fractures. X rays show a characteristic picture of cysts in the bones, particularly the hands. The combination of bone problems, kidney stones, and indigestion has led to the old saying among doctors that the disease causes problems with "bones, stones, and abdominal groans."

Treatment

The only effective treatment for the disease is surgical removal of the overactive gland. In most cases all the glands are bigger than normal (hypertrophied), and the standard surgical procedure is to identify all four glands and then to remove three-and-a-half of them. The remaining half-gland provides enough PTH to keep the calcium level under control.

What can go wrong?

Symptoms	Causes	Treatment
Overactive parathyroids (hyperparathyroidism) Thirst; increased urination. Pain in the stomach; kidney stones; general feeling of ill health	Benign tumor of one or more glands. Hyperplasia (enlargement) of the glands, often due to kidney disease	Surgical removal of the affected gland or glands. The outlook is good, but in kidney disease it depends on the kidney problem
Underactive parathyroids (hypoparathyroidism) Tetany; uncontrollable muscle spasms. Tiredness, irritability, depression, psychosis	Idiopathic (this means cause unknown). There may be yeast infection of the nails. Surgical removal of the glands	Vitamin D by mouth is very effective, but the level of calcium in the blood has to be monitored carefully

Parkinson's disease

Q Can Parkinson's disease be caused by alcoholism?

A No. Although alcoholism does cause damage to other parts of the brain, it does not seem to attack the cells that are linked with this illness.

Q Is it true that although Parkinson's disease does not affect the intellect, some psychiatric illnesses have similar symptoms?

A It is true that the mind is not affected until the disease becomes very advanced, when slight mental deterioration is not uncommon. But no mental illness has symptoms like those of Parkinson's disease.

Q I am in my 30s and sometimes my hand shakes almost uncontrollably when I reach for my coffee mug. Is this Parkinson's disease?

A No. The trembling of the hands so characteristic of the disease is at its worst when sufferers are doing nothing. Reaching for a cup of coffee would end the shaking if you had Parkinson's disease.

Q My father was disabled by Parkinson's disease. Does this mean I will be too?

A There does not seem to be a clear-cut link with heredity, so just because your father had the condition does not mean you will be more at risk. Even in the unlikely event that you do contract the disease, current therapies should insure that you will not be as disabled as he was.

Q My mother is being treated for Parkinson's disease, and sometimes her hands do curious twisting movements. Is this part of the symptom pattern?

A No. It is probably a side effect of L-dopa, the drug your mother is most likely taking. If the movements trouble her they can be stopped by adjusting the treatment she is receiving.

Parkinson's disease is a common illness of older people. It causes the limbs to shake and makes simple movement difficult. Modern medication has done much to prolong the active years and slow the progression of disability.

Catherine Pouedras/Eurelios/Science Photo Library

The old names for Parkinson's disease, paralysis agitans or shaking palsy, describe one of its most common symptoms. A person who suffers from this disease (named after an 18th century English physician, James Parkinson) experiences a shaking or tremor of the limbs (especially the hands), stiff limbs, and difficulty in carrying out certain types of movement (see Tremors). In advanced stages there are associated troubles with control of circulation and perspiration.

It is a common disease of middle-aged and elderly people, but treatment can, to a great extent, postpone the onset of any disability for many years.

Causes

In most cases the disease is caused by premature aging of deep-seated brain cells in an area called the basal ganglia. These cells normally form a complex control system that coordinates the muscle activity that allows us to perform specific types of movement freely and unconsciously. This sort of muscle activity is involved in the swinging of our arms when we walk, in facial expression, and in the positioning of limbs before we stand up or walk (see Coordination).

Difficulties occur when the brain cells that allow the body to perform these tasks die off prematurely (see Brain).

A shuffling, unbalanced walk, rigid posture, and slow tremor are typical symptoms of Parkinson's disease, and many sufferers cannot walk unaided.

Symptoms

The symptoms usually develop very slowly and are often assumed to be part of the normal process of aging. At the beginning they seem to occur on one side of the body only. Ultimately, however, both sides are usually affected.

The most noticeable symptom is the trembling of the hands, which shake in a pill-rolling tremor as if the person is rolling something between his or her fingers and thumb. It is most evident when the arms are inactive, and the shaking usually stops as soon as movement begins, for example, when reaching for a cup.

The muscles of people afflicted with the disease become unusually stiff. In the early stages it causes aching shoulders and discomfort first thing in the morning, after hours of rest (see Stiffness). The face is also less mobile than usual, causing a deadpan expression.

Walking is also very difficult. After a hesitant start a person with Parkinson's disease moves forward quickly in a shuffling manner. He or she takes small steps and leans forward in a stoop. This difficulty in walking can sometimes lead to severe falls if the usual automatic reaction of using the hands to break the fall is also impaired, as is often the case.

To begin with, the intellect is not affected, but after some years the patient may gradually lose the ability to perform higher mental tasks. In this advanced stage of the disease every physical movement becomes increasingly difficult.

The disease is accompanied by a drop in blood pressure when the patient stands up, which results in fainting, and by slurred and distorted speech, caused by muscle damage.

Treatment and outlook

The usual treatment is the drug L-dopa, which is given in tablet form. It replenishes the brain's supply of dopamine, the chemical transmitter produced by cells in the basal ganglia, and it alleviates many symptoms of the disease. Transplantation of dopamine-secreting fetal adrenal gland tissue into the brain has helped in some cases, but this surgical treatment is still in the experimental stage (see Glands).

Although degeneration of the brain cells cannot be reversed, medication, regular exercise, and proper nourishment will allow the patient to lead a full life for at least 10 years from the onset of the disease. After this period it becomes more difficult to control the symptoms, but new dopamine-mimicking agents are now available that are able to extend even further the years of useful activity.

Progressive symptoms

- Limbs become stiff, causing aching joints
- Face becomes immobile
- Limbs stiffen further, making it difficult to initiate movements
- Gait becomes small-stepped and stooping
- Reduction in sweating or increased occurrence of greasy face, due to abnormal activity of sweat glands
- Feelings of faintness accompany standing
- Walking now difficult because of stiffness
- Hands tremble almost constantly when inactive
- Fingers increasingly affected by slight tremor

Rex Features

After much speculation, it has now been confirmed that former Olympic and world heavyweight boxing champion Muhammed Ali has Parkinson's disease.

The position of the basal ganglia

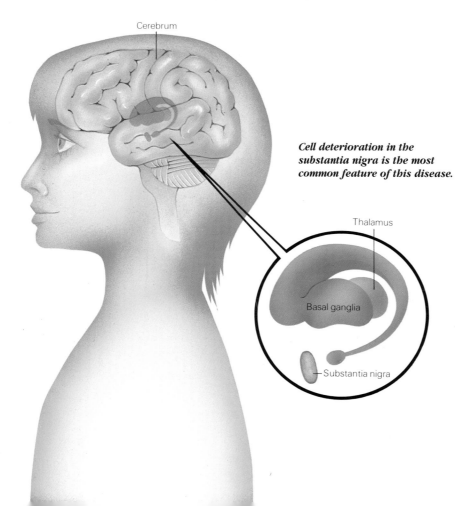

Cerebrum

Cell deterioration in the substantia nigra is the most common feature of this disease.

Thalamus

Basal ganglia

Substantia nigra

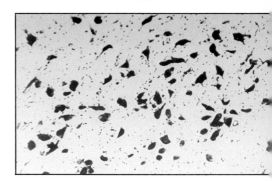

Sandoz Products Ltd./MediCine Ltd.

Dopamine produced by cells (top) in the basal ganglia is severely lacking in patients with Parkinson's disease (above).

Pathology

Q Recently I had a mole removed for cosmetic reasons, and my doctor sent it to a pathologist. Does she suspect cancer?

A No. Virtually anything that is removed from the body is examined by a pathologist under a microscope. This is to guard against the million in one chance that a spot or lump may be cancerous.

Q A friend of mine died quite suddenly at the age of 43 and an autopsy was done. Was foul play suspected?

A An autopsy hardly ever implies that foul play is suspected. Two types of autopsy are usually carried out. The first type is performed when the doctor has no idea of the cause of death. The second type is performed when doctors feel it would further their knowledge of a disease. Consent of a relative is usually required.

Q Is being a pathologist a dangerous occupation?

A Yes, it can be. All doctors run the risk of catching diseases from patients, but certain branches of pathology are especially risky. This is most true of microbiologists, who handle dangerous, highly infectious material in their daily work. Each year, there are cases of serious infections in doctors and laboratory personnel, and deaths do occur.

Q When I was pregnant, I had to give blood samples. I felt fine, so why was this done?

A Although pregnant women often feel well, they are susceptible to certain disorders. The most common is anemia, so this blood test is done routinely. Often a test is performed to see if the mother has been exposed to German measles (rubella). If she hasn't and she is infected during pregnancy, it can be very harmful to the baby. By carrying out screening tests, problems can be anticipated and treated. Blood tests such as alpha fetoprotein (AFP) can help in diagnosing birth defects.

People think of a pathologist either as someone dissecting a corpse in the morgue or working in the medical examiner's office to unravel homicides and violent deaths. In reality the scope of pathology is far wider than this.

Every patient in the hospital and many who go to a doctor's office make use of pathology services. The treatment clinician is responsible for the care and treatment of patients, but the final, definitive diagnosis often rests with the pathologist.

Pathology is the medical specialty that deals with the causes and changes produced in the body by disease. Because the field is now so wide it is subdivided into seven main areas: histopathology, forensic pathology, hematology, chemical pathology, microbiology, cytology, and immunology. Each attempts to give a definite answer to what is often an educated clinical guess.

For instance, although appendicitis is one of the most common emergencies needing surgery, it can be a very difficult diagnosis to make. The surgeon therefore needs the pathologist to assess if the appendix was really inflamed after it had been removed. If the inflammation is someplace else in the abdomen, different treatment may be required.

Pathologists are doctors who, in addition to the same four-year training as every other doctor, spend one year working in clinical medicine (that is, with patients) and a further five years training in pathology. Early on in the training, the pathologist specializes in one particular branch as the work of each branch is very different.

The different specialties
Histopathology: This is what many people mean when they use the term *pathology*. This department does autopsy work, examining tissues removed during surgery.

There are two reasons for carrying out an autopsy. Deaths that occur in suspicious circumstances are automatically referred to the medical examiner, as are those that occur soon after surgery, or following

A

Pathologists take samples of blood, tissues, and organs for examination under a microscope. In (A) a breast section is shown to be noncancerous. In (B) a section of the kidney is examined for abnormalities. The Pap smear in (C) shows cancer of the cervix: note the debris and elongated orange cell. The slide (D) shows skin from the scalp, with growing hair follicles. In (E) and (F), blood smears are shown. The first is normal; the second has excessive white blood cells.

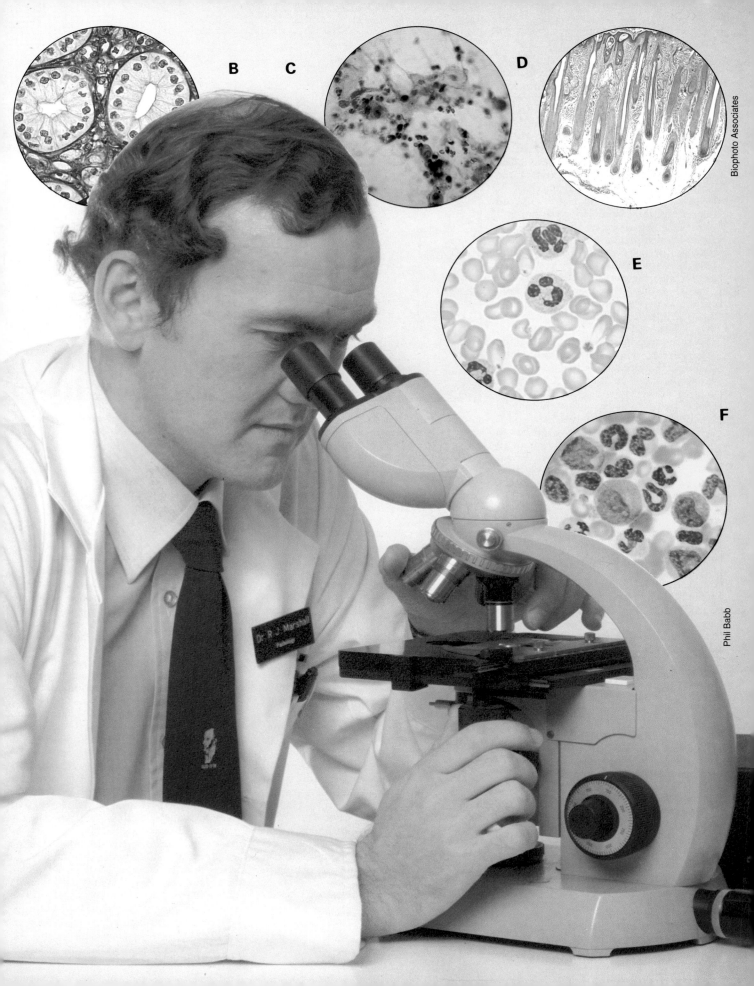

B

C

D

E

F

Biophoto Associates

Phil Babb

Dr. R. J. Marshall

PATHOLOGY

trauma or caused by alcohol. The medical examiner decides if an autopsy is needed.

Another occasion when an autopsy is requested is when a doctor feels that the treatment of the disease was correct, however, for educational purposes may wish to explore the extent of the disease, or whether another disease was present. The doctor then asks the permission of the closest relative to perform an autopsy.

Such examinations often turn up the unexpected. One study showed that in a third to a half of cases, the patient had either been misdiagnosed or there was significant disease present in addition to the one diagnosed. Thus autopsy results can further the progress of medical science.

Most of this department's work concerns specimens removed by a surgeon in the operating room. Virtually everything that is removed is sent for examination. This is because the histopathologist is the only person who can give a definite diagnosis by examining a specimen under a microscope (see Biopsy). A harmless-looking mole may turn out to be a skin cancer, and because of pathology, a potentially life-saving diagnosis.

When a specimen is received, it has to be left to fix in a preservative for about 12 hours, depending on its size, and is then embedded in wax. This takes 24 hours. It is fixed in a wax block because a special machine cuts fine slivers (about one-millionth of an inch thick) and this can only be done from a fairly rigid substance like wax. These thin sections are then stained different colors with chemicals and examined under a microscope.

For urgent specimens a frozen section can be done. This is what happens in a suspected case of breast cancer. The patient is warned that she may have cancer and gives consent for removal of the breast if it is confirmed. The surgeon just removes the suspicious lump and sends it immediately to histopathology where a small piece is taken off, deep frozen, cut very thin, stained, and examined under the

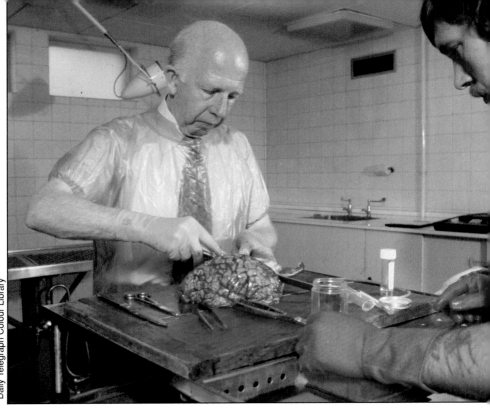

Daily Telegraph Colour Library

microscope. If it is benign, the patient is left with a small scar on the breast. If it is cancerous, the surgeon removes enough tissue to include the whole cancer.

Though it is quick, this procedure is not used for all specimens as it gives less than perfect results. If there is any doubt at all, the pathologist recommends halting surgery until the routinely prepared specimen can be examined two days later.

Cytology: This department is closely linked with histopathology. However, the cytologist looks at the individual cells that make up the human body. Pap smears are examined in an attempt to detect cancer in its earliest stages. Smears are quite painless and simply involve scraping the outside of the cervix (where the womb joins the upper part of the vagina) and smearing the tissue onto a glass slide. If the smear looks cancerous, a gynecologist takes a larger specimen and sends it to the histopathologist. If cancer is confirmed and is still at an early stage, surgery is carried out to remove the cancerous part of the cervix, and the patient is often cured (see Pap smear).

The cytologist looks at a variety of other cells for potential cancer; for instance, cells from a lung cancer may be found in sputum, and those from bladder cancer in the urine (see Cancer).

Forensic pathology: This department deals with the effects that violence, criminal or otherwise, has on the human body. Forensics is morbidly fascinating to everyone, but only in the last 70 years or so has it acquired respectability as an independent branch of pathology. Most people are aware of some of the forensic

Medical examiners perform autopsies on people who have died in suspicious circumstances to obtain vital clues.

techniques used from watching certain television programs. For example, one can judge the time of death from the temperature of the corpse and the degree of rigor mortis (stiffening of the muscles that occurs after death, but then disappears).

Pathologists can give dramatic assistance to the police. In one example, a man lured women to his farm, killed them, and dissolved their bodies in sulfuric acid. A forensic pathologist at the scene picked up an object and instantly recognized it as a human gallstone. The police soon found the false teeth of the victim, from which she was identified. Needless to say, forensic pathology requires a strong stomach.

Hematology: This department investigates blood disorders (see Blood). About half the volume of blood consists of cells and half of plasma, a fluid containing many different chemicals (see Plasma). Hematology is mainly concerned with the cells, namely the red blood cells that carry oxygen, the white blood cells that fight infection, and the platelets that make the blood clot. Nearly everyone who goes to the hospital has a routine hematology screen, in which the three cell types are counted by a machine.

Extra information can be found if blood film on a glass slide is examined under a microscope. If the red blood cells are small and pale, it suggests anemia due to iron deficiency. If they are large and reduced in number, this suggests pernicious anemia (see Pernicious anemia). A

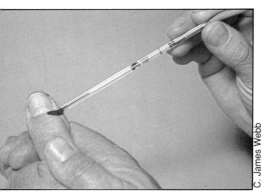

C. James Webb

A blood sample is drawn off into a pipette ready for laboratory tests.

reduced number of platelets could mean that the patient has a tendency to bleed a lot. Abnormal white blood cells could mean blood cancer, while the presence of immature red and white blood cells may suggest cancer elsewhere in the body. Other specialized tests exist, such as measuring the amount of iron in the body or carrying out very detailed clotting tests.

Another specialized test performed by the hematologist is examination of bone marrow, where the blood cells are manufactured (see Marrow and transplants). To collect the specimen, a needle is pushed through the bone, marrow is withdrawn, and quickly spread on a slide. This test is used to confirm a diagnosis, in particular, of leukemia (see Leukemia).

The hematology department also looks after blood transfusions. Anyone who requires a blood donation has first to give a small sample so that the blood group can be cross-matched. Giving the wrong blood to a patient can cause death, and it is the job of skilled technicians to insure this never happens (see Blood donor).

Chemical pathology: This department measures a wide range of chemicals in blood, urine, feces, stomach fluid, and so on. Common tests include measuring the amount of oxygen or salt in the blood, however, the possibilities are almost endless. Many hormones can be measured.

Some drugs in the blood can be measured to insure that the patient is receiving the correct amount. Some drugs are often used in overdoses. It is vital to test the blood level as this will determine how vigorously the patient should be treated. The treatment for certain overdoses is in itself dangerous and only justified if the patient's life is in danger (see Overdoses).

Diabetics make a great deal of use of this department. In diabetes there is a deficiency of the hormone insulin which removes sugar from the blood so that it can be taken up by the cells and supply them with fuel. Normally diabetics can test their own sugar level at home by measuring the

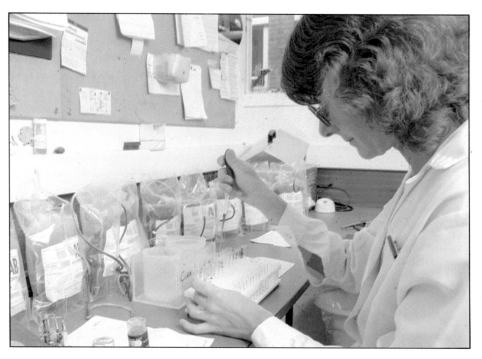

sugar in their blood, but if the condition gets out of control, then more accurate measurements are needed in the hospital (see Diabetics).

Microbiology: This department identifies which kind of microorganism is causing a particular infection. Microbiology departments usually study the relatively small group of pathogenic (disease-causing) microorganisms. These include: bacteria, which cause many disorders including pneumonia and typhoid; viruses, which cause many infections including AIDS, influenza, and the common cold; protozoa, which cause diseases such as malaria and amoebic dysentry; and fungi, which cause disorders such as thrush.

Identifying microorganisms is another skilled job. A specimen is taken as cleanly as possible, without touching anything else to avoid contamination. It is then smeared over a growth plate containing a special jelly substance, which is kept at body temperature. In about 24 hours the bacteria grow enough to be identified. Antibiotics kill only a particular range of microorganisms, so identification is vital to insure effective treatment.

There is definite risk to workers in this department. Although strict safety precautions are taken, several cases of infections acquired from samples occur each year.

Immunology: This department looks at how diseases progress and the role of the body's immune system. As a result of research into AIDS and cancer, many discoveries have been made in this area in the last 10–15 years (see AIDS and Cancer). Immunotherapy, where drugs are used to enhance the immune system, is

In the hematology laboratory, technicians use a variety of methods to test blood for the presence and type of disease.

also increasingly successful. Progress in immunology has also undoubtedly helped fight cancer in many cases.

The future

Vigorous research is going on in all departments of pathology. One area is a cure for some forms of leukemia. Hematologists and immunologists are working to solve the problem of the body's rejection of bone marrow tissue (a current form of treatment). It has been discovered that the body can reject cancerous cells, and if this rejection can be boosted, it may be a new weapon in the fight against leukemia and other diseases. Genetic analysis of tissues is another rapidly developing area of both medical and forensic pathology.

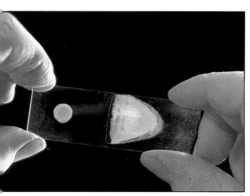

A blood sample is spread across a slide for examination under the microscope.

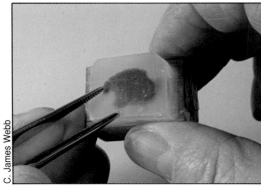

Tissue from the liver is embedded in wax, then sliced and stained for testing.

Pediatrics

The branch of medicine concerned with the health and illnesses of children is called pediatrics. From the time a child is born the utmost is done to prevent, alleviate, and cure disease.

Q I am due to give birth soon, and feel slightly anxious about the first few weeks of caring for my baby. Is there anyone I can talk to about this before leaving the hospital?

A Yes. An ideal opportunity to discuss any worries, no matter how trivial they seem, is when the pediatrician examines your baby before you leave the hospital. He or she can answer any questions you may have, and refer you to sources on which you can rely.

Q I understand that newborn babies cannot see. When will my baby be able to see me?

A Babies can see as soon as they are born, and are instinctively interested in the human face. They focus best at about 12 in (30.5 cm), roughly the distance a breast-feeding baby is from its mother's face.

Q Our son was born five weeks early and had to be nursed in an incubator for two weeks. Will he grow and develop normally?

A Yes. Premature babies usually need help with feeding at first, but once they have developed the ability to suck, they should grow as well as any other baby. There is no reason why your son should not be the same as every other child.

Q I got very angry with my three-month-old baby recently when he would not stop crying. I picked him up and shook him vigorously. I am frightened I might harm him in the future. What should I do?

A Shaking babies hard can be very harmful, especially when they are so young. The blood vessels around the brain can be damaged, causing a clot to form between the brain and skull. If you feel that you may injure your baby, you should seek expert help immediately so that you can improve your relationship with your child. You can do this through your family doctor. Remember that your problem is not an uncommon one, and you are not alone.

A pediatrician is a doctor who cares for children from the moment they are born until they reach puberty. These age limits are not fixed; the pediatrician may already have been involved during the pregnancy along with the obstetrician (the doctor concerned with pregnancy and childbirth, see Obstetrics) if a problem was anticipated. In the hospital the pediatrician works together with other specialists to care for children. He or she also works with other pediatricians at centers specializing in rare problems.

The birth of a baby
Fortunately the vast majority of babies are entirely normal at birth and start to breathe spontaneously a few seconds after delivery. However, in some cases, for instance with a forceps delivery or in a premature birth, a baby is more likely to have difficulty in breathing. Therefore there is usually a pediatrician in the delivery room at such times to help the baby. As it is not always possible to predict which babies will have problems, a pedi-

atrician is available at the hospital 24 hours a day. However, even if a baby needs some encouragement to start breathing, once this is established almost all babies have no more trouble and are returned to their mothers.

Special care baby units
About one in eight babies is admitted to a special care baby unit, usually for only a short time. This usually occurs because the baby is preterm (born more than three weeks before he or she was due) or because he or she has not grown as well as usual in the uterus. Often such babies are too weak to feed properly and need

Thanks to advances in medicine, most babies are not only born healthy but, with pediatric care, they also remain that way.

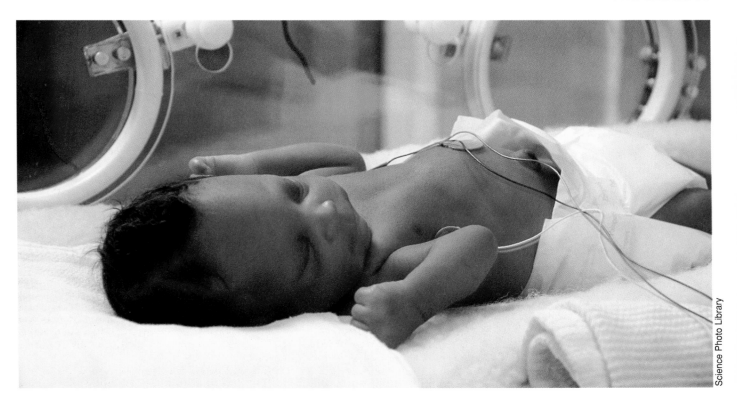

Science Photo Library

to be fed through a tube for a few days. The tube is introduced via the baby's nose or mouth into the stomach. Such babies are kept warm in incubators.

Some babies born prematurely may weigh less than 3.4 lb (1.4 kg). To help these babies survive and grow normally, a great deal of skill and complicated equipment is needed. Very tiny babies must have their breathing and heart rate monitored continuously. They may also be given fluids by way of a vein, and need to spend time on a respirator.

It is important for the parents of a premature baby to get used to the special care unit, and to spend time with their baby. Even the smallest and sickest of babies can usually be fondled through an incubator port. As the baby grows stronger, its parents can help to care for it in the hospital, in readiness for going home (see Premature babies).

Premature babies are often placed in incubators where their vital signs are monitored and they are kept warm and fed.

Children in the hospital

Most children who are admitted to the hospital are brought as emergency cases. They may have had an accident at home or on the highway, or need prompt treatment for respiratory disorders, appendicitis, or upsets. Children may also be admitted to the hospital for minor procedures such as tonsillectomy or repair of a hernia. Or they may have other problems such as difficulty with feeding or failure

Camera Press

1341

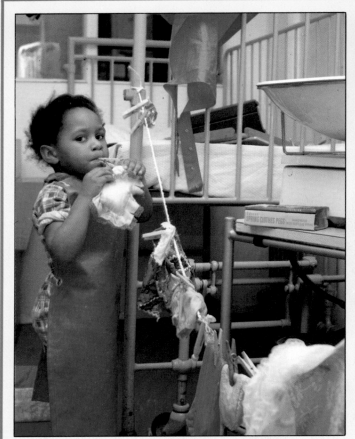

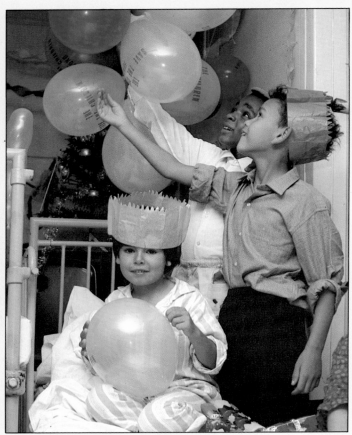

Guidelines for young children in the hospital

- Children are naturally anxious about their first visit to the hospital, so it is best to prepare them beforehand so that they know what to expect. This way fears can be dealt with, and their stay can be made more enjoyable.

- Explain to the child what the hospital is. If possible take him on a tour of the children's floor before he is admitted.

- Tell the child what is going to be done to him or her, and be honest if something will be painful. Don't be an alarmist.

- When you are packing the child's bag let him or her choose some favorite things, such as a toy or comforter.

- Try to stay with the child in the hospital if this is at all possible, otherwise visit frequently and bring along other members of the family. Children are welcome too.

- Be prepared for tears, they are a normal and healthy reaction. In most cases, the child will soon stop crying and begin to get interested in the activities on the floor. If problems persist, speak to the play therapist.

- Ask the staff on the floor any questions you have, however busy they seem. If you feel reassured you will give your child more confidence.

- Afterward don't expect the child to be entirely fit; discharge only means he or she is well enough to be home.

- Expect a difficult period following his stay in the hospital: dependence and bedwetting are common, but normally resolve within in a short while.

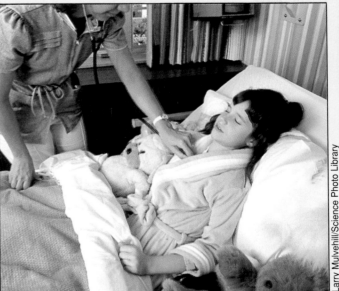

Q I am worried about my son having his whooping cough immunization, as I have heard there can be side effects. What do pediatricians advise?

A An extensive survey has been done on the link between immunization and neurologic (brain and nervous system) disease in children. This has shown that it is very rare for children to have serious complications with modern whooping cough injections. Immunization is recommended for all children unless there is a family history of neurologic illness or seizures. If you are in doubt, ask your doctor. Whooping cough is rare now thanks to immunization, but it can be a terrible disease causing permanent damage to the lungs.

Q My eight-month-old baby has a high temperature. Is it because she's teething?

A Almost every childhood complaint has been attributed to teething at some time. However, teething causes irritability and dribbling, not fever or convulsions. So, if your daughter has a fever, you should take her to your doctor right away. Meanwhile, keep her cool, give her liquid acetaminophen, and plenty of fluids.

Q I am worried about my four-month-old son's hearing. Is he too young to have it tested?

A No, he isn't. If you are in any doubt, arrange to see the pediatrician or your family doctor at once. They will probably do some preliminary tests, and then arrange for him to have a full examination by an audiometrist (hearing specialist).

Q I am concerned that my 18-month-old granddaughter doesn't eat properly, however my daughter says there's nothing wrong. Who is right?

A Many children of this age lose interest in food as they test out newly acquired skills, such as walking and talking. Their food requirements also lessen as their growth rate slows. As long as your granddaughter has lots of energy and is growing well, there is no need to worry.

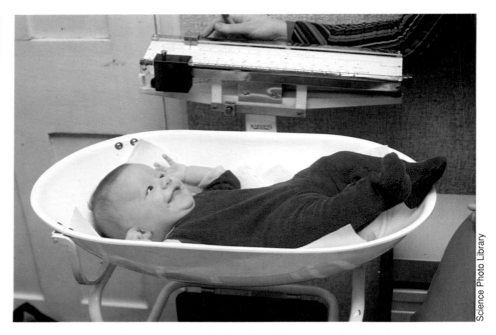

Science Photo Library

Tiny babies are weighed at frequent intervals to see if they are putting on weight and if a change of diet is needed.

to grow properly, which can be resolved by a period of observation and treatment in the hospital.

A stay in the hospital is very likely to be a child's first time away from home and family. During the last 30 years great efforts have been made to minimize the deep and lasting impression such an experience can make on a child.

Perhaps the most important change is that most children, irrespective of their condition, are admitted to pediatric floors and everything is geared to suit their particular needs.

Today children's floors are bright and cheerfully decorated, and filled with plenty of interesting things to do. It is routine for a play therapist to be present, as well as a teacher during schooltime. Children are no longer expected to lie still in bed all day, unless they are so ill that they prefer this. They are usually dressed and playing, and are hard to distinguish from healthy children.

Another important change has been in recognizing how vital it is for children, particularly the under-fives, to have their mothers or very familiar persons with them as much as possible. Mothers are encouraged to stay with their children in the hospital if possible. Also pediatric floors now have very relaxed attitudes toward visiting times and not only welcome parents, but other children and members of the family as well.

Nevertheless a hospital stay can be a disturbing experience for a child, especially as some potentially painful or uncomfortable tests and medical procedures may be inevitable. Often, fears and upsets are alleviated if children are allowed to talk about their worries. Young children may not be able to do this. However, they can be encouraged to express themselves through stories and play. Play therapists are expert at talking to children in this situation and helping them to voice their fears. It is important to identify the exact cause of their anxiety so that they can be reassured.

Child development

Children are continually growing, physically, mentally, and emotionally. It is an important part of pediatrics to observe these changes, identify problems if they occur, and advise on how best to deal with them (see Growth).

The routine surveillance of most children is carried out by pediatricians and family doctors. The time of the examinations should be spaced so that children are seen at key points of their development, especially in the first two years of their life.

The first major check on babies is in the first week of life before leaving the hospital. The primary concern here is to look for any congenital abnormalities, such as hip dislocation or heart disorders. There is a similar review at six weeks to insure that the baby is growing well, and that there are still no congenital problems. Again, the hips and heart are looked at closely. This is a good opportunity for the mother to discuss with the pediatrician any problems she may have with feeding, sleeping, and generally coping with her new baby. At about eight months the emphasis is on general devel-

Preventive pediatrics

Age of child	6 weeks	2 months	4 months	6 months	15 months	18 months	2 years	4–5 years
Immunization		Triple vaccine (diphtheria, tetanus, whooping cough); Polio	Triple vaccine; Polio	Triple vaccine; Polio	Measles, mumps, rubella; Tuberculin test	Triple vaccine; Polio		Triple vaccine (diphtheria, tetanus, whooping cough); Polio
Surveillance checks	General exam for congenital defects; growth, feeding problems			Hearing, sight, overall development (at 6–12 months)		Overall development, especially walking, language, behavior	Overall development, behavior, vision, language	Preschool assessment

opment. By this time babies should be smiling, babbling, and be aware of what is happening around them. At this stage, many are sitting up and beginning to crawl. Hearing tests and a test for strabismus (crossed eye) should be done around this age (see Hearing).

The next examination is at about 18 months when most children are walking and starting to talk. At two years, language skills, vision, and behavior are assessed; at five years readiness for school is assessed.

This method is designed to discover abnormalities as soon as they arise. However, parents should not feel they have to wait for the next appointment if they are worried, particularly about their child's vision and hearing. There are a great many specialists and resources available, and the most appropriate help must be chosen in each case. For example, a child with a physical disorder, such as a heart murmur, may be referred to a pediatric cardiologist, while severe behavioral problems may require psychiatric help at a child guidance center or at the hospital.

A child whose overall development is giving cause for concern may be referred to a local assessment center. Here a whole team of experts is able to meet and examine the child. Such experts often include pediatricians, specialists in hearing and vision, orthopedic surgeons, physical therapists, psychologists, teachers, and speech therapists. They may be able to assess a child immediately or may need to admit him or her briefly to the hospital for tests and closer observation. A plan for any further therapy can then be made.

Preventive medicine is important too, and includes immunization of children. These are done as a matter of routine at the doctor's office. These are very important and should not be missed. As well as major checkups, babies may attend frequently for weighing when they are small. These visits are usually arranged individually with the doctor's office.

Preschool assessment
Before a child starts school a program of regular physical examinations is arranged. Nowadays, most babies are born healthy and with pediatric care, remain so.

A child's health and development are closely monitored. Many tests can be used, such as the apnea monitoring system (left), which checks for irregularities in breathing, as well as physical examinations (below).

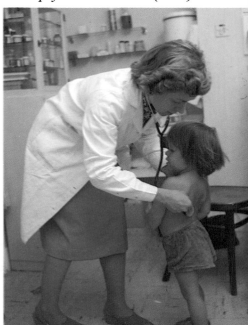

Tim Hazael/Boc Group/Science Photo Library

Pelvic inflammatory disease

Q Do sexually transmitted diseases cause PID, and what are the symptoms?

A Yes, chlamydia accounts for half of all cases of PID. But up to 75 percent of women with the disease and 50 percent of men have no symptoms, and it can lie dormant for many years. Symptoms include a discharge from the vagina or penis, and pain during urination for men. Gonorrhea is similar to, but less common than, chlamydia.

Q What happens in a laparoscopy?

A While a patient is under anesthetic, a small cut is made just below the navel and a tube is inserted. Through this the surgeon looks at the organs and takes samples of cells and fluid. Another small cut may be made above the groin to allow a probe to manipulate the organs. It is low-risk surgery.

Q How does PID affect a woman's fertility?

A Scar tissue in any of the reproductive organs can inhibit conception, but it is usually the tubes that are a problem. These can be repaired surgically, but it is a very skilled operation that has only a 50 percent success rate. In vitro fertilization (IVF) bypasses the tubes, but it is costly and time-consuming, with a success rate of only 10–15 percent.

Q What other conditions have symptoms similar to PID?

A Both ectopic pregnancy and appendicitis can cause acute pelvic pain and are emergencies that need immediate hospitalization. Other causes of pelvic pain are: cysts and fibroids; pelvic congestion (enlarged veins in the uterus); endometriosis (where fragments of the uterine lining become lodged in other parts of the pelvis); and irritable bowel syndrome. A type of intestinal inflammation called Crohn's disease leads to pain and fever. Thrush makes it easier for infections to reach the pelvic organs. Cystitis causes pain during urination.

Pelvic inflammatory disease *is a general term that is used for infections of the female reproductive organs. If it is left untreated, the consequences can be serious.*

Pelvic inflammatory disease (PID) refers to any inflammatory condition of a woman's pelvic organs, but is a term most commonly used to refer to bacterial infections of the pelvic organs. It affects the cervix (the neck of the uterus where it protrudes into the vagina), the ovaries, the uterus, the fallopian tubes, and other parts of the pelvis. It is one of the main causes of infertility in women, usually because the delicate fallopian tubes, which connect the ovaries to the uterus, become damaged by scar tissue, or adhesions that cause an obstruction.

Conventional treatment is essential at first. However, self-help and alternative remedies can stop the condition from coming back and can sometimes even repair any damage that has occurred.

Basically, the faster treatment is carried out the better. However, doctors can have difficulty in recognizing and diagnosing the disease and identifying the precise infections.

Symptoms

When PID has reached an acute stage, there may be severe pelvic pain, a high temperature, and possibly vomiting and diarrhea. If acute PID is left untreated, it can lead to death through septicemia (blood poisoning). To avoid septicemia in severe cases, a hysterectomy may be necessary (see Hysterectomy).

PID can also be:
Subacute: Similar symptoms to acute PID, but less severe.
Chronic: Constant PID of varying severity over long periods of time.
Recurrent: Periods of health that are interspersed with PID attacks. However, all varieties of the disease need to be taken seriously.

Other symptoms include:

- unusual (malodorous) vaginal discharge; very common
- lower abdominal pain, which may be on one side only, and especially one that becomes worse during sex or menstruation; during urination or defecation or when the woman moves around
- lower-back pain
- nausea or dizziness
- irregular or heavy bleeding

The doctor generally takes vaginal swabs to assess the presence of PID. However, the infection can be difficult to spot; further tests may be performed to be certain.

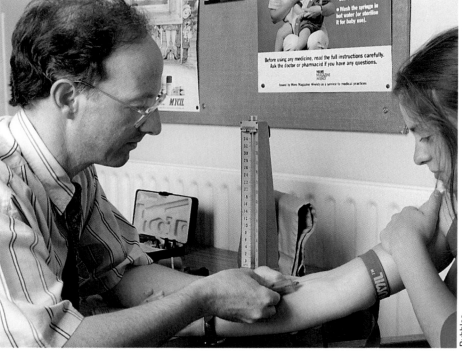

Bubbles

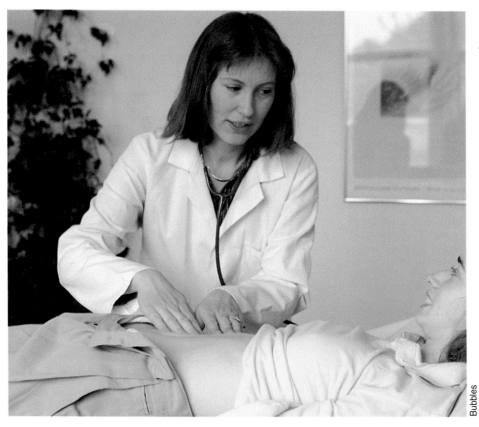

Bubbles

Tenderness and swelling of the abdomen can be a sign of PID. This is why the doctor may feel the abdomen for such symptoms during an internal pelvic examination.

can be beneficial because it stops the infection from spreading, and stops the organs from being jolted and becoming further inflamed.

Fast treatment is also vital. In one study women who received treatment within two days had no complications, whereas 30 percent of women who did not receive any treatment for a week or more had reduced fertility as a result (see Infertility).

Make sure that your partner is tested and treated for the infection as well, and do not have sexual intercourse until you are better, and have completed the course of antibiotics.

Sometimes you may be offered surgery, particularly if you have chronic symptoms. However, this does not always help, and if organs are removed it can mean you will never be able to conceive.

A fallopian tube may be removed if it is damaged because, if it is not, there will always be a risk of ectopic pregnancy. This condition occurs when a fertilized egg is unable to travel to the uterus and starts to grow in the fallopian tube instead. Ectopic pregnancy can be very dangerous for the mother (see Ectopic pregnancy).

Causes
As with all infections, PID can take hold when you are exposed to the infecting agent. Women are most susceptible when they are run down. Specific risk factors include:
- Sexually transmitted diseases (STDs) such as herpes, HIV, syphilis, gonorrhea, chlamydia, and genital warts (see Sexually transmitted diseases)
- the insertion or the removal of a contraceptive IUD
- a termination (abortion), a miscarriage, and giving birth
- abdominal surgery (for example, having the appendix out)

Tests
If you have any of the symptoms listed above, you should visit your doctor or a hospital genitourinary (GU) clinic as soon as possible.

To test for infection, the doctor takes swabs from your vagina and possibly cervix. This is not unlike having a Pap smear (see Pap smear). She or he may give you a pelvic examination by inserting two fingers into your vagina, while feeling your abdomen for any tenderness or swelling (see Internal examination).

Further tests might include: swabs from your urethra and rectum, and blood and urine tests. Less commonly, a doctor might perform an Ultrasound, endometri-

al biopsy, and in some cases, although this is quite rare, a laparoscopy is performed (see Laparoscopy).

During an ultrasound test, a transducer that transmits sound waves is passed over the abdomen so that a picture of the internal organs appears on a screen. It is completely painless and does not appear to be harmful (see Ultrasound).

An endometrial biopsy involves passing a small tube into the uterus so that a sample of tissue can be taken (see Biopsy). Although it is uncomfortable, it is not painful. Laparoscopy is the only sure way to diagnose PID, and this is usually done under a general anesthetic, although occasionally only a local anesthetic is administered (see Anesthetics).

Treatment
Treatment is with antibiotics—usually with several kinds—because different bacteria have to be fought with different drugs. This is why it is so important to identify the infections correctly.

If you have acute PID, you may be admitted into the hospital so that the antibiotics can be administered intravenously and your condition, and reaction to the drugs, more carefully monitored (see Antibiotics).

Some women require bed rest, some do not. If a woman is in extreme pain, walking may exacerbate it. Resting in bed

Self-help
Antibiotics can kill the body's beneficial bacteria as well as the harmful ones, and so upset the body's natural balance. Eating unsweetened live yogurt three times a day (preferably on an empty stomach), and taking acidophilus tablets (available from health food stores), will help put back the beneficial bacteria.

Once you have had an attack of PID you are more likely to develop it again, so it is very important to be careful about personal hygiene (see Hygiene).

To prevent PID, or any other STD, always use a barrier contraceptive such as a condom or a diaphragm, if you do not know your partner's sexual history.

Have checkups at least twice a year at the genitourinary (GU) clinic if you are having sex in any relationship(s) other than a monogamous, long-term one.

Do not have vaginal sex following anal sex, unless your partner washes first.

Ask to be tested for infection and treated if necessary if you are about to have an abortion, any treatment that opens up the cervix (having an IUD fitted, for example), or if you are pregnant.

Many women like to take vitamins (see Vitamins), however, there is no evidence of their having a beneficial effect on the immune system (see Immune system).

Pelvis

Like a large bony hoop, the pelvis forms a complete ring around the lower part of the human body. It protects the organs within, forms a framework for muscles, and is the base to which the legs are hinged.

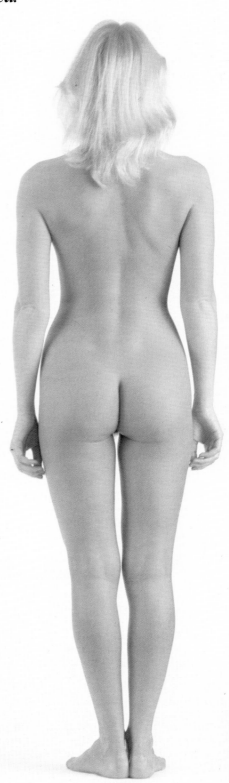

The pelvis is designed to bear the weight of the human body when it is running, walking, standing, or sitting. In women the pelvis is relatively wide to help accommodate the presence of the growing fetus during pregnancy, while at the same time partially protecting it. It is this that gives a woman's hips their characteristic shape. Pelvic problems are most usually the result of damage or deformity of the bones and the muscles and ligaments connected to them. Many such problems manifest themselves as backache and associated pains.

The bones and joints

The pelvis is constructed from a group of immensely strong bones. The back of the pelvis is made up of the sacrum, a triangular structure that forms the base of the spine, and consists of five individual bones or vertebrae fused together to form a solid structure. No movement is possible between these bones. Attached to the base of the sacrum is a small projection of bone, the rudimentary human tail or coccyx, made from four fused vertebrae. The joint between sacrum and coccyx is padded with a disk of fiber-impregnated cartilage. In young people, some movement is possible at this joint, but this disappears later in life. In young people, too, there are true joints between the bones of the coccyx, although this is more pronounced in girls (see Joints).

Joined to each side of the sacrum is a massive hipbone or ilium, whose curved top can easily be felt through the skin (see Hip). The ilium is filled with marrow and is one of the major sites of blood cell production (see Blood). The vertical sacroiliac joints between the sacrum and ilium are toughened with fibers and bound with a crisscross series of ligaments. The surfaces of the bones are slightly notched, so they fit together like a loosely connected jigsaw, giving extra stability.

About two-thirds of the way down each ilium is a deep socket, the acetabulum, which is perfectly shaped to accommodate the ball at the end of the femur or thighbone. Below this socket, the hipbone curves around toward the front of the body. This part of the pelvis is the pubis and it is supplemented by a loop of bone known as the ischium, which forms the basis of the buttock. At the front of

A woman's pelvis is wider than a man's to allow room for the growing fetus during pregnancy, and it is this that gives a woman's hips their characteristic shape.

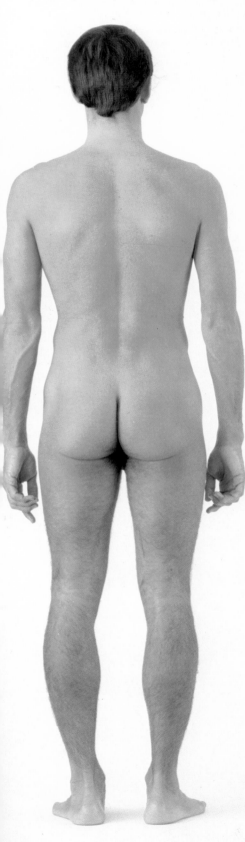

the body, the two pubic bones come together at a joint called the pubic symphysis. Padding the junction between the two bones is a disk of cartilage called the interpubic disk. More ligaments bind this joint together and also run from the top of it to the ilium to help keep the pelvis stable (see Cartilage).

Sexual differences
Of all the bones in the body those of the pelvis show the most difference between male and female, for the simple reason that the female pelvis has to provide more space inside the body to allow for the development of the fetus. The pelvis of a man is much longer and narrower than that of a woman, and because it has to bear a greater weight, consists of bone that is much less delicately molded. Thus the cavity created by a woman's pelvic bones is boat-shaped, and that of a man heart-shaped.

Because of the shape of her hipbones, and the shape and angle of placement of their sockets or acetabula, a woman stands with her feet relatively wider apart than a man, and with her legs at a different angle to her pelvis. The joints of a woman's pelvis also change during pregnancy to allow for expansion during the process of birth (see Birth).

Balance and movement
When you are standing upright, your center of gravity passes within your pelvis and the line connecting your center of gravity with the ground runs from your pelvis to your feet. As soon as you move your pelvis or feet you automatically move this line outside the supporting base of your feet. Unless you make appropriate correcting movements, you will fall over (see Balance). This means that throughout each moment of your everyday life, except when you are lying down, your pelvis bears the weight of all the upper part of your body (your head, arms, and trunk).

The human skeleton is constructed in such a way that it is possible for the body to stay upright, on two legs, without falling over. As part of this design plan, the pelvis is not absolutely vertical but positioned at a tilt. This tilt, which is more pronounced in women than in men, makes it possible for you to swing your hips and bear your weight on alternate legs as you walk. Without the tilt your hips would be too vertical and you would fall flat on your face. At every footfall the pelvis, but particularly the hip joints, act as living shock absorbers for the stress energy that passes up the legs, and in the course of a lifetime, prevents the whole skeleton crumbling from too much stress (see Skeleton).

Phil Babb

This exercise, called pelvic rotation, will help to loosen back, pelvis, and hips. Lie on your back with your arms to your sides and your knees bent. Put your feet flat on the floor or as near to the buttocks as possible. Raise your hips off the ground and rotate your pelvis 10–20 times. Rest and repeat the rotation exercise.

The pelvis muscles
The muscles of the pelvis do two very separate jobs. One is to make body movements possible, the other is to hold in the contents of the abdomen, and quite literally, prevent them from falling out of the body. The pelvic muscles of movement are the piriformis, which run under the

main muscles of the buttock, and the gluteus maximus and minimus, which join the top of the thigh bone with the front of the sacrum. Contractions of the piriformis make it possible for you to move your thigh out sideways, as you do when taking a step with your toes turned out to the sides (see Movement).

The other main muscle of movement in the pelvis is the obdurator internis. Fanned out so that it is attached at several places within the bony pelvic ring, the muscle forms two large triangular sheets that join up with a tough tendon. This, in turn, is connected to the femur (leg bone). The main job of the obdurator internis is not to move the body from place to place but to keep it stable when standing still. It is this muscle that makes the continual adjustments needed to keep the stationary body balanced.

The other group of pelvic muscles are grouped together to form an elastic sheet of tissue called the pelvic diaphragm or pelvic floor. The two main muscles in this diaphragm are the levator ani, which forms most of the lower margin of the pelvic cavity and can be felt working if you pull in at your anus (see Anus), and the coccygeus, which supports the coccyx, particularly during the act of defecation and while a baby is being born.

The layers of tissue, including ligaments and small muscles, that lie over the pelvic diaphragm, together form the perineum. In women, however, the word *perineum* is often used to describe only the tissues between the anus and the opening of the vagina (see Vagina).

Internal organs

The pelvic diaphragm does not form a complete seal over the base of the pelvis. Inevitably there must be gaps to allow for the passage of urine and feces out of the body, and in women, to make both sexual intercourse and childbirth possible. These functions, affected by muscles, give the clue to the vital body organs which the pelvis protects—in both sexes the bladder and the tube, the urethra, through which urine passes to the outside of the body, and the lower part of the gastrointestinal tract, the rectum and its exit, the anus. These exits are guarded by rings of muscle called sphincters which, in adults, can be relaxed by conscious control to allow urination and defecation.

In men, essential glands that act as lubricants for the externally placed sex organs are found within the pelvis, among them the prostate and seminal vesicles. In women, all the reproductive organs are housed within the pelvis—the ovaries, fallopian tubes, uterus (womb), and vagina. The vagina also has a sphincter muscle which contracts powerfully during intercourse (see Orgasm).

Like all parts of the body the pelvis has a supply of blood vessels and nerves, and the main ones lie near the bones. Passing in front of the pelvis are the femoral nerve and femoral blood vessel supplying the thigh. Beneath the sacroiliac joint,

The structure

The boat-shaped female pelvis provides enough space inside the body to allow for the development of the fetus and houses all the female reproductive organs. The pelvic diaphragm protects the internal organs.

Female pelvis

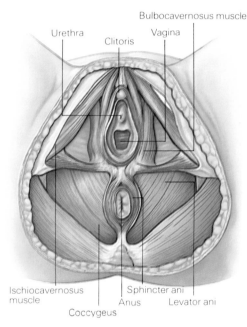

Urethra
Clitoris
Bulbocavernosus muscle
Vagina
Ischiocavernosus muscle
Sphincter ani
Anus
Levator ani
Coccygeus

Female pelvic bone

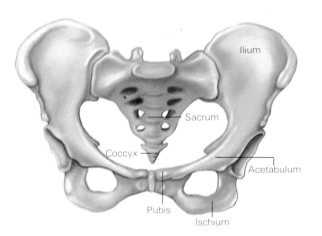

Ilium
Sacrum
Coccyx
Acetabulum
Pubis
Ischium

The pelvic muscles (female)

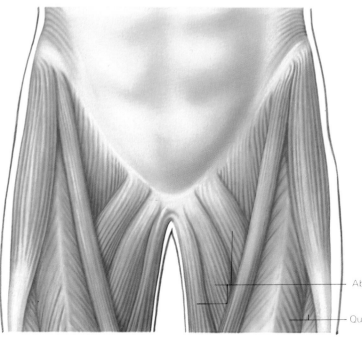

Abductors of the thigh

Quadriceps femoris

Frank Kennard

of the pelvis

The heart-shaped pelvis of a man is much longer and narrower than a woman's, and because it has to bear more weight, consists of less delicately molded bone. Glands that act as lubricants for the external sex organs are contained in the pelvis.

Male pelvis

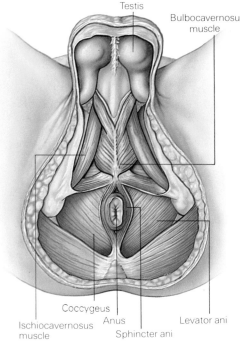

Testis

Bulbocavernosus muscle

Coccygeus

Anus

Levator ani

Ischiocavernosus muscle

Sphincter ani

Male pelvic bone

through a gap between the ilium and the sacrum, runs the sciatic nerve, which extends up the back (see Sciatica).

What can go wrong?
Each of the separate organs within the pelvis can have specific things go wrong with them, and such problems may lead to pain either in the pelvis itself or in the back, legs, or the abdomen. However, the main problems of the pelvis arise from disease of the bones that form the framework of the pelvis, or from conditions which affect the muscles that complete its base (see Lower-back pain).

In both women and men it is important that the pelvis is strong enough to support the body's weight and to take the strain of movement. The disease of rickets, which retards bone growth and may weaken bone, is caused by a lack of vitamin D and is a significant cause not only of poor pelvic development but also of pelvic weakness (see Rickets).

The tilt of the pelvis that makes our upright, two-legged stance possible also leads to problems, the most common of which is backache. This arises from many causes, including, most commonly, strain of the muscles joined to the sacrum and whose contractions help move the pelvis, and problems with the sacroiliac joints. These joints often have such problems because they have little muscular support. The softening of the ligaments that bind the joint at the end of pregnancy results in a characteristic lower-back pain which may persist after the baby is born. A similar sort of pain arises from any trouble experienced at this joint.

To avoid back pain resulting from strained pelvic muscles and ligaments, follow all the general rules: adopt a good posture with your abdomen held well in and your back straight, lift things sensibly using the muscles of your arms and legs and keeping your back straight so that you do not put excess strain on your pelvic muscles and ligaments, and sit in a chair that provides support in the correct places (see Back and backache).

Accidents that lead to pelvic injuries are uncommon, but they can happen. Falls from heights and crushing blows may break any of the bones in the pelvis. If this happens, the great risk is that the broken ends of bone may pierce one of the internal organs, particularly the bladder. For this reason, and because this sort of accident may well involve spinal injuries, the victim should never be moved. The paramedics who are called to the scene will most likely bind the person's legs and feet together just enough to restrict movement. If possible, they will try to prevent the victim from urinating. If the bladder or ureter has been ruptured the urine will leak into the internal tissues during urination and cause irritation. With sufficient bedrest and prompt treatment a fractured pelvis usually heals in a couple of months.

Ilium

Sacrum

Acetabulum

Pubis

Coccyx

Ischium

The pelvic muscles (male)

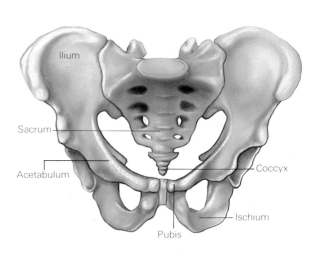

Gluteus maximus

Hamstrings

Q Why do women swing their hips more than men when they walk?

A The reason for this lies in the shape and positioning of the pelvis. In women, the pelvis is, comparatively speaking, much wider than in men and more tilted, and the bones of the thighs join the female pelvis at a different angle. This means that a woman thrusts her legs out at a wider angle as she walks and this, in turn, makes her hips swing more than a man's.

Q I had a sneezing fit the other day and felt quite weak in the pelvis afterward. Can sneezing strain your pelvis?

A Yes, sneezing, and coughing even more so, can strain the internal muscles of the pelvic region because both actions lead to a large buildup of pressure inside the abdomen, and, as they expel air at high speed from the body, demand powerful contractions of the pelvic muscles.

Q I had my first baby quite normally, but I seem to be much larger this time, although I'm only 24 weeks pregnant. Does this mean my pelvis may not be able to accommodate this birth?

A Only your obstetrician can answer this question by doing an internal pelvic examination, but often women seem much larger in their second pregnancies than in their first because their abdominal muscles are not so tight. You should discuss any worries you might have with your obstetrician.

Q Can some exercises damage your pelvis?

A As long as you are careful, you should have no problems. However, one exercise can actually damage the pelvic muscles: the one in which you lie on your back and lift both legs in the air, keeping your knees straight. If you have any hint of pelvic trouble, avoid this exercise. It can be particularly damaging for a mother who has recently given birth, and should under no circumstances be attempted as a postnatal exercise.

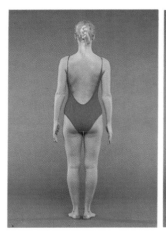 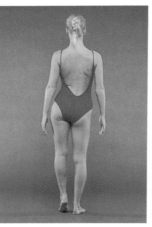 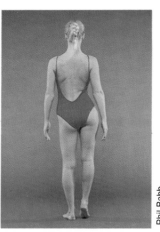

Phil Babb

The pelvic side lift: standing, lift the left side of the pelvis toward the shoulder, but keep your shoulders in a straight line. Repeat with the right side.

Apart from tears that occur during labor, the most common problem to affect the muscles of the pelvic diaphragm is weakness leading to dropping or the prolapse of the pelvic organs. This is especially the case following childbirth. One symptom of such weakness is so-called stress incontinence, that is, leakage of urine, or feces, when a person puts stress on the muscles.

The best preventive measure for this complaint is a series of exercises during pregnancy to strengthen the pelvic floor. If necessary, a repair operation can strengthen the pelvic diaphragm.

During pregnancy there is additional strain on the muscles of the back, which can lead to backache if the correct posture is not maintained while carrying the baby.

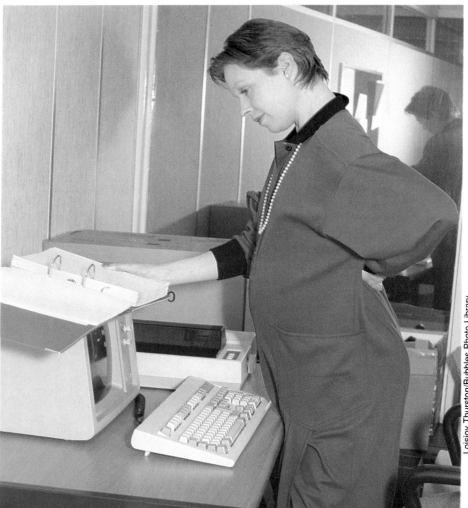

Loisjoy Thurston/Bubbles Photo Library

Penicillin

Q Can the body build up a resistance to penicillin if you take too much of it?

A The body itself does not build up a resistance to penicillin, although it will produce antibodies that attack penicillin. However, the bacteria that the penicillin attacks can become resistant, and some are capable of producing an enzyme (penicillinase) that renders penicillin inactive.

Q Whenever I take penicillin my urine smells very strong. Is this normal, or could it be a sign that something is wrong?

A This distinctive smell is quite normal. Sixty percent of an injected dose of penicillin passes through the body very quickly and is excreted in the urine, making the urine smell of penicillin.

Q I have heard that some people have died after taking penicillin. Is this true?

A This is extremely rare, but it has occurred in patients who are allergic to penicillin. The recorded cases of death were almost all due to misadministration of penicillin when it was overlooked that the patient was allergic to the drug. Generally all penicillins are safe and problems only occur when there is an error in the prescribing. To avoid such errors (which are not always fatal but will make the patient feel very ill) people who are allergic to penicillin (or any other drugs) should carry something, such as a bracelet or a tag worn around the neck, that informs others of their allergy in case of an emergency.

Q After I took penicillin I suffered from diarrhea. Is there a connection?

A This depends very much on how the penicillin was administered. If you took the penicillin orally then there could be a connection. Mild diarrhea results if the penicillin kills off some of the resident and balanced population of bacteria that are naturally present in the human gut.

The power of penicillin to destroy bacteria and combat potentially fatal infections has made it one of the most valuable drugs used in medicine today.

A discovery that was to revolutionize medicine was made in 1928 when the British bacteriologist, Sir Alexander Fleming, noticed that one of his experimental culture plates of bacteria had been contaminated by spores from a mold. Later he realized that the colonies of bacteria that were growing on the plate were beginning to die. He identified the mold as belonging to the *Penicillium* family, and he isolated the bacteria-killing substance secreted by the mold and named it *penicillin*. It was not until 10 years later, however, that clinical trials were performed, the curative properties

Penicillin is one of the most effective bacteria-killing drugs available today. Certain types of penicillin can be taken orally and are therefore very easy to use.

were established, and the commercial production of the drug began. Penicillin was the first antibiotic to be developed, and it has since become one of the most valuable drugs available for the treatment of a wide range of bacterial infections.

How penicillin is made

The original crude extracts of the fermentation of the mold contained a mixture of many different penicillins. Penicillin is still made by growing the mold on a broth in large vats, but the addition of various chemicals has allowed a number of naturally produced penicillins, such as benzylpenicillin and phenoxymethlypenicillin, to be isolated and developed independently. Several semisynthetic penicillins have also been produced; they are called semisynthetic

Zefa

Q Why is it necessary to have penicillin injections rather than to take it orally as with many other drugs?

A The way penicillin is administered depends on the type of infection and the type of penicillin prescribed. Some penicillins are destroyed by the acid juices of the stomach and are only effective if they are given by injection. Other types of penicillin can withstand the acidity of the stomach and can be taken in pill or liquid form.

Q I keep hearing about different penicillins. Why are there so many?

A The wide range of penicillins available allows the doctor to select the correct one for you. The decision is based on the nature of the infection (some bacteria have built up a tolerance to particular kinds of penicillin) and the patient's reaction to drugs.

Q I am allergic to penicillin. Does this mean that I have less defense against diseases? If I should need an antibiotic, are there any alternatives that I could take?

A Up to 10 percent of people are allergic to penicillin, and all people probably have some antibodies to penicillin but at a level that does not cause clinical allergy. There are now many other antibiotics that can be used instead of penicillin. In most, but not all, cases they do not produce an allergic response in people who are allergic to penicillin.

Q I keep getting colds and bouts of the flu. My friend told me that next time I get ill I should go to my doctor for penicillin. Will it really help?

A No. Your friend, like so many others, believes that penicillin cures all. But neither penicillin nor any other antibiotic will have any effect on viruses and will do absolutely nothing for the common cold. If penicillin is overused there is a danger that resistant strains of bacteria will develop.

Radio Times Hulton Picture Library

Sir Alexander Fleming (1881–1955) is the man who revolutionized modern medicine when he discovered penicillin.

because although the chemical structure of the penicillin has been altered, the basic structure of the drug is still produced by fermentation.

How penicillin works

Penicillin works by destroying the cell walls of the bacteria that are multiplying, causing the bacteria to literally explode from internal pressure. It is not effective, however, against resting organisms that are not making new cell walls.

The great advantage of penicillin over the antiseptics that were in use before its discovery is that it does not affect human cells; the traditional antiseptic drugs were often more toxic than the bacteria themselves were (see Bacteria).

Some of the other antibiotics, such as the tetracyclines, work quite differently; they interfere with bacterial growth. Tetracycline and penicillin prescribed together are less effective than when prescribed separately (see Antibiotics).

Uses

Penicillin can treat a wide range of bacterial infections, such as pneumonia (see Pneumonia), gonorrhea, rheumatic fever, septic wounds, and sometimes, tonsillitis.

Depending on the type of infection, the severity of the condition, and the type of penicillin prescribed, dosages may be

Beecham Group plc

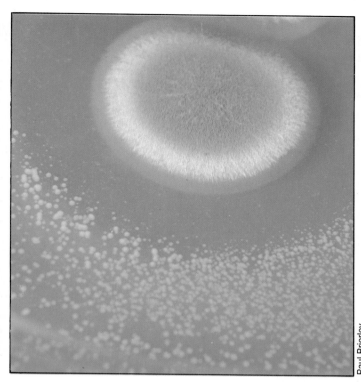

Paul Brierley

Paul Brierley

Penicillin is extracted from the mold Penicillium notatum *(above). The spores from this mold form a barrier against the spread of bacteria (above right).*

administered either orally or by injection. To be effective when it is taken orally, the penicillin must be of a type that is resistant to the acid juices of the stomach.

Penicillin is distributed throughout the body, except to the nervous tissue and bone. Concentrations can vary and sometimes it may be necessary to inject penicillin locally if high concentrations are required to treat specific infections in particular organs or parts of the body.

Dealing with possible problems

Penicillin is a very useful, effective, and safe drug if it is administered with care. In reality, there are only two dangers associated with its use: overuse, which leads to the development of resistant strains of bacteria and is the reason why penicillin should not be taken for trivial infections; and misuse when it is prescribed to patients who exhibit allergic responses.

Bacteria can become resistant to penicillin in two ways: they can develop a tolerance to the drug and become resistant; or they can produce an enzyme called penicillinase that breaks down the penicillin molecule, rendering it inactive. Some of the semisynthetic penicillins have been produced specifically to be resistant to attack by penicillinase.

For several years now the production of penicillin has been undertaken on a very large scale. Although the process is highly industrialized, the basic technique remains the same. The penicillin is extracted from mold grown in a broth in large vats.

Although this enzyme attacks the central ring of molecules that are common to all penicillins, the altered chemical structure of the semisynthetic variety (the addition of different side branches), reduces accessibility to the central ring and thus increases its resistance to attack. Penicillins are sometimes given together with inhibitors of the enzymes that break down penicillins.

About 10 percent of people have allergic reactions to penicillin. A cross-allergy can also occur, so that a person who is allergic to one kind of penicillin may also be allergic to the others. The main symptoms are itching and rashes (see Eczema), swelling of the throat and face, swollen joints, and fevers. Other adverse symptoms that occur when penicillin is taken orally include sickness, diarrhea, heartburn, and itching in and around the anus.

Unfortunately there is no simple test to show a potential allergy to penicillin, so if there is a suspicion that a patient may be allergic to the drug, it is generally advisable to prescribe another kind of antibiotic. However, if penicillin must be used, it is possible to perform some skin tests. Although these tests are not completely reliable, because the allergic reaction may actually be caused by breakdown products of penicillin in the body, or other products that are developed during the manufacturing process, they do identify those people who are likely to have a rather serious reaction to the medication, a reaction that, in some extreme cases, could be fatal.

Penis

Q I have a growth on my penis that has steadily become larger over the last three months. I'm sure that it's cancer, but I'm too terrified to go to my doctor to find out.

A Cancer of the penis is rare, and usually it is a persistent, slowly enlarging sore or ulcer, rather than an actual growth. What you describe sounds more like a genital wart. These are caused by a virus that is usually picked up during intercourse with someone who already has them. They are not dangerous, but become embarrassingly unsightly as they grow and multiply. You should certainly go to your doctor or to a clinic to confirm the diagnosis and to be treated. The wart will usually disappear quickly after the treatment has been completed.

Q I have a slight discharge from the end of my penis when I get up in the morning. Will it go away on its own, or should I go to see my doctor?

A This does not sound serious, but it would be wise to have tests done. It sounds like a mild attack of nonspecific urethritis, but you can't be certain until a sample of the discharge is looked at under a microscope. Some sexually transmitted conditions that look mild can develop with seriously permanent consequences for you and any sexual partners you may have.

Q Is there a connection between the overall size of the penis and virility, or the lack of it?

A Length of penis varies from one individual to another. The idea that a long penis makes a man a better lover is strictly a myth. Someone with a penis that is shorter than average is still very capable of giving real pleasure to his partners. It is also true that a penis's dimensions when it is in a flaccid state have no bearing on its size when it is erect. A small organ may well be larger than expected when a full erection has been achieved.

This remarkable organ performs two quite unrelated vital functions. It is an outlet for relieving bodily waste and also the man's primary sex organ.

The penis is a unique piece of engineering. No other structure, either natural or man-made, can raise itself spontaneously without assistance from a flaccid to an erect position in quite the same way. It has two distinct functions. The penis penetrates the vagina so that semen that contains sperm can pass from the man to fertilize the woman. It is also a clever apparatus in the male through which urine can pass out of the body.

Structure
The penis consists of a central tube called the urethra through which urine passes when a man urinates. This is also the track through which semen passes during sexual intercourse (see Urethra).

The urethra connects the bladder, where urine is stored, to a hole at the tip of the penis (the meatus). Semen enters the urethra during intercourse through a pair of tubes called the seminal ducts, or vas deferens, which join it shortly after it leaves the bladder. A tight ring of muscle at the opening from the bladder into the urethra keeps the passage closed. Urine only emerges when this is intended.

The penis usually hangs down in front of the scrotum, which is a wrinkled bag containing the testes in a slack or flaccid state. Penis length varies from 2.5–5 in (6–12 cm). When it is sexually stimulated, it becomes stiff and erect, usually pointing slightly upward. It is then 4–8 in (10–20 cm) long. The tip of the penis, called the glans, or helmet, is the most sensitive area. The valley behind the glans is the coronal sulcus; the main length of the penis is the body or shaft; and the area of the penis where it joins the lower abdomen is called the root.

Erection
The largest part of the penis consists of three groups of cells that are responsible for erection. These areas are supplied with a rich network of blood vessels. When a man is sexually excited, the amount of blood that flows into these areas increases enormously. Engorgement with blood makes the penis longer, thicker, and rigid. It also rises as internal pressure increases. After ejaculation and excitement subsides, blood flow diminishes and the penis returns to its flaccid state as the extra blood drains away (see Erection and ejaculation).

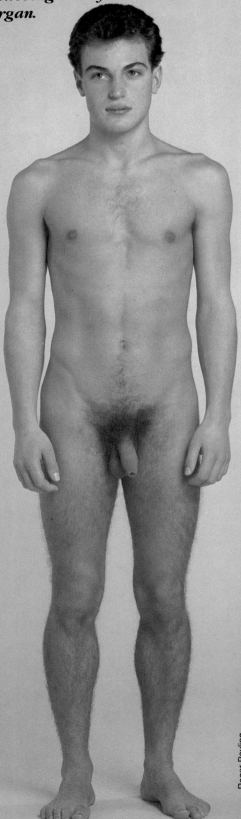

Roger Payling

The foreskin and the glans

The delicate glans is protected by a loose fold of skin called the foreskin or prepuce. As the penis becomes engorged with blood and enlarges during erection, the foreskin peels back to leave the glans exposed to the stimulation that eventually leads to orgasm (see Orgasm).

Skin on the glans and foreskin produce a greasy substance called smegma that acts as a lubricant facilitating the movement of the foreskin over the glans. It is important to wash this away regularly. Failure to do this can result in a soreness or inflammation of the foreskin and a condition called balanitis. The presence of repeated or persistent balanitis is sometimes a medical reason for performing a circumcision, if it has not been performed at birth or for religious reasons (see Circumcision).

Infections

The chief hazard to which the penis is exposed is infection, particularly sexually transmitted infections called sexually transmitted diseases (STD; see Sexually transmitted diseases). An inflammation of the urethra, when it discharges pus, is usually accompanied by discomfort or pain in passing urine. This condition is called urethritis. It can be caused by gonorrhea (see Gonorrhea), when the discharge is copious and yellow, or nonspecific conditions (see Nonspecific urethritis), where the discharge is likely to be less and more mucous in appearance. These conditions are potentially dangerous, both to the patient and his sexual partners, and they should be treated as soon as possible.

A more serious, but less common, disease that makes its initial attack on the penis is syphilis. This normally shows itself as a single ulcer near the head of the penis. It may be no more than a painless cut or fissure in the skin, and it will probably go away in a few days. Unfortunately this is only the first stage. If it is left untreated, syphilis will develop and become fatal (see Syphilis).

Another condition that may affect the penis is phimosis, where the foreskin is too tight to peel back during an erection or sticks to the glans. In paraphimosis, the foreskin forms a band around the coronal sulcus and causes the tip of the penis to swell up. Herpes genitalis causes small ulcers similar to cold sores to appear on the penis. Except for herpes genitalis, which is persistent, these conditions respond well to treatment (see Herpes).

Severe problems with impotence can be treated effectively now with surgically implantable devices.

The anatomy of the penis

Immediately below is a detailed view of the penis, showing all of its parts. The illustration (below, right) shows the male genitalia, internal and external. The section through the shaft of the penis (center) shows the three groups of tissue that are responsible for erections. (Bottom) a longitudinal section of the penis is shown. The path of the urethra is clearly visible.

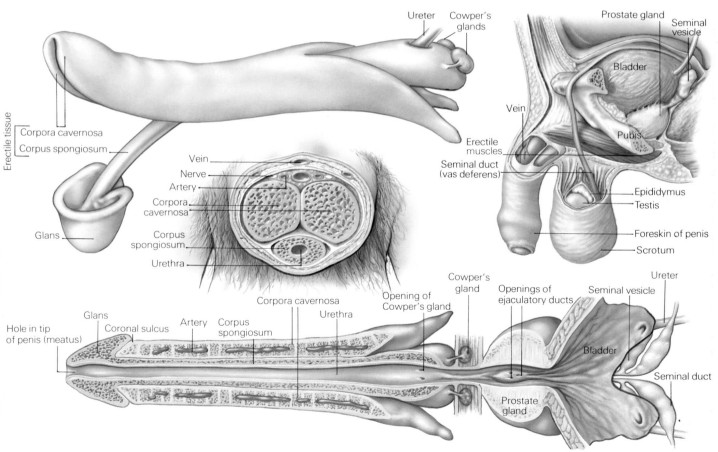

Frank Kennard

Peritoneum

Q Will surgery for peritonitis leave me with bad scars?

A Unfortunately yes. Since it is not possible before surgery to say what the cause of the peritonitis is, the surgical incision has to be placed in the middle of the abdomen, so that every part of the abdomen can be inspected. Also, there is a high probability of infection in the wound afterward, and this can lead to a scar.

Q What are my chances of getting peritonitis?

A Your chances of getting peritonitis are really very low, especially if you did not have acute appendicitis as a child or young adult. However, as you get older, if you suffer from a perforated duodenal ulcer or a ruptured diverticulum, your chances of getting peritonitis will increase.

Q I understand that appendicitis can lead to peritonitis. Why is this?

A Peritonitis occurs when an infected appendix ruptures, releasing fecal matter into the peritoneal cavity.

Q How would I know if my child had peritonitis?

A Your child would complain of severe pain in the abdomen. The pain would be constant and made worse by any movement. He or she would also feel nauseous, would probably vomit, and have a slight fever and a rigid abdomen. His or her breathing would probably be rapid and shallow.

Q Does peritonitis always need surgery?

A Yes, almost always. The main reason for surgery is to discover the cause of the peritonitis and to do something to stop it right away. Some causes of peritonitis, such as inflammation of the pancreas, can be diagnosed by a blood test and may not need an operation.

The peritoneum lines the abdominal cavity and covers all the organs inside the abdomen, allowing them to move freely. However, if it becomes inflamed, a patient can become very sick with peritonitis.

Positions of the peritoneum and omentum

Cross section (top) and longitudinal section (bottom) of the abdominal area of the body.

The diagrams indicate the two types of peritoneum: visceral and parietal.

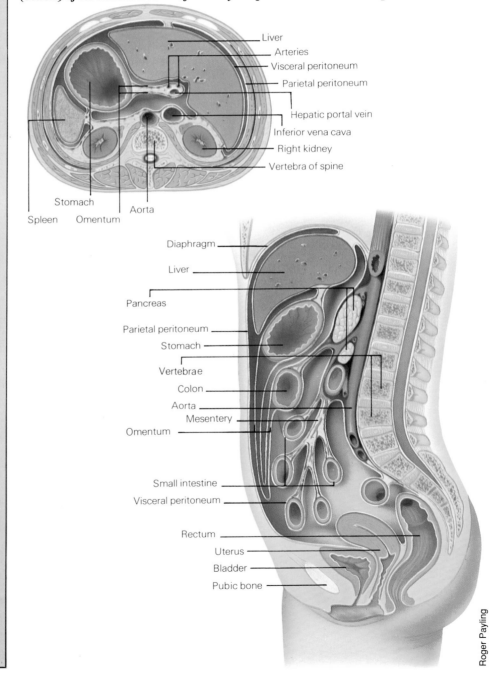

Liver
Arteries
Visceral peritoneum
Parietal peritoneum
Hepatic portal vein
Inferior vena cava
Right kidney
Vertebra of spine
Stomach
Aorta
Spleen
Omentum

Diaphragm
Liver
Pancreas
Parietal peritoneum
Stomach
Vertebrae
Colon
Aorta
Mesentery
Omentum
Small intestine
Visceral peritoneum
Rectum
Uterus
Bladder
Pubic bone

Roger Payling

The peritoneum is a thin membrane that lines the abdominal cavity and also covers all the organs contained within the abdomen. Thus, the liver, the stomach, and the intestines are covered with peritoneum, as are the spleen, gallbladder, pancreas, uterus, and appendix. Even though the peritoneum is very thin (if it was separated from the organs that it covers, it would be transparent) it is very strong, and the way it is attached inside the abdominal cavity creates various spaces where fluid could collect in the event of a leak from one of the intra-abdominal organs.

The function of the peritoneum

The main function of the peritoneum in a healthy person is to allow the various bodily organs inside the abdomen to move freely. For example, when a person eats a meal, the stomach and the intestines become mobile and the muscles in their walls contract. This allows the food that has just been eaten to be both mixed up and then propelled along on its journey through the digestive system (see Alimentary canal). During this process

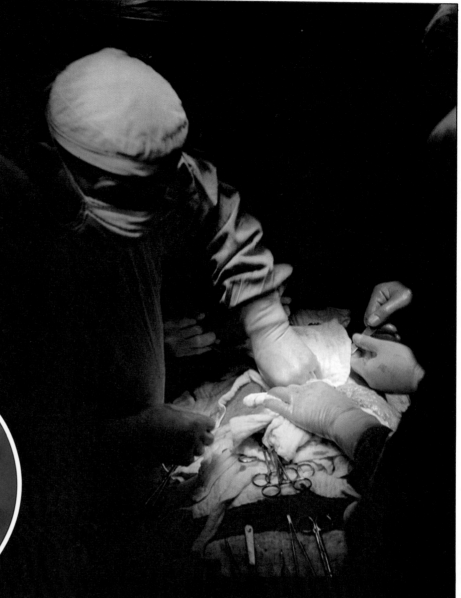

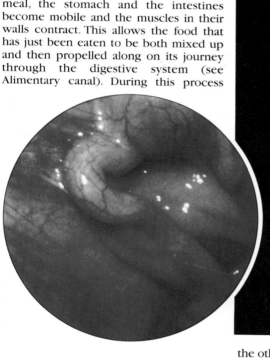

Roger Payling

Frank Kennard

The shiny material that covers this inflamed appendix is the peritoneum; if the appendix ruptures, the membrane will become infected.

both the stomach and intestines can slide over one another largely because they are both covered with peritoneum, separated by a thin layer of fluid.

The peritoneum that covers the above-mentioned organs such as the stomach, is called the visceral peritoneum. However, the peritoneum also lines the abdominal cavity, and where this occurs, the peritoneum is called the parietal peritoneum. The latter has an extremely sensitive nerve supply, so that any injury or inflammation that occurs in this layer is felt as an acute localized pain. The visceral peritoneum, on

the other hand, is not so sensitive and pain is only experienced if, say, the intestine is stretched or distended. Even then, the pain is not very localized and is felt as a dull ache, usually in the center of the abdomen. These differences in how pain is felt in the abdomen have an important bearing on the symptoms of various disorders of the intra-abdominal contents. In effect, they can often indicate from what type of illness the person is suffering.

The omentum

One structure that should be mentioned here is an extension of the peritoneum called the omentum. Shaped a little like an apron, it consists of fat with a rich blood supply and is covered with peritoneum. It hangs down from the stomach

Abdominal surgery is performed in most cases of peritonitis. After the cause of the infection has been dealt with, the abdomen is washed out with a warm saline solution.

peritoneum, outside the intestines. Its role is to act as a fat store and to help limit infections in the abdominal cavity by sticking to the affected area.

Ascites and adhesions

Two of the ways in which the peritoneum can be affected by disease are by ascites and adhesions. In ascites there is an excess amount of the lubricating fluid normally present between the parietal and visceral layers. It is caused either by an imbalance in the mechanism that controls the amount of fluid that is produced

Q Is a puncture in the peritoneum more serious in certain areas than in others?

A A puncture of just the peritoneum is usually of little consequence. Much more worrying would be a puncture of the intestines or stomach or other organs, which could cause severe peritonitis. Also, puncture of a main blood vessel in the abdomen may occur, causing hemorrhage.

Q Does peritonitis always lead to the formation of adhesions?

A Yes. However, in many cases the adhesions disappear after a short time. The initial adhesions are made of a sticky substance secreted by the peritoneum, and this may or may not be eventually converted into fibrous tissue.

Q If someone is stabbed in the abdomen, does peritonitis always result?

A No. A knife can penetrate all the muscle layers and the peritoneum, enter the abdominal cavity some considerable distance, and fail to puncture the intestine or a blood vessel. The intestine, which is covered with slippery peritoneum, often slides to one side of the knife blade.

Q I have had a duodenal ulcer for many years. How would I know if it had perforated?

A You would experience severe pain all over the abdomen, unlike the indigestion-type pain you are probably now getting. It would be so severe that you would be unable to carry on with your work.

Q I have just had peritonitis from a burst appendix. How long will it be before I am back to normal?

A It usually takes about three months from the time of the operation before you are completely back to normal, if there were no complications. After this time, there shouldn't be any restrictions on what you can do.

(such as occurs with liver disease) or it happens when the peritoneum is irritated to a minor degree over a long period of time (such as can happen with a slow-growing tumor; see Tumors). A person with ascites usually has a very distended abdomen, although often the distention is not accompanied by any sort of pain.

Normally, the various intra-abdominal organs such as the stomach and the intestines are attached by mesenteries, membranes that contain a series of branching arteries, veins, lymph vessels, and nerves. The mesentery is the lifeline of the organ to which it is attached. Otherwise the organs have a certain amount of movement. Adhesions occur where a part of one of these organs becomes stuck to the abdominal wall or another organ. This can happen after an abdominal operation or after peritonitis.

The effect of adhesions is twofold. First, the mobility of the organ involved is impaired, which may lead to obstruction of the large intestine; and second, the large intestine may twist around an adhesion, cutting off its blood supply and eventually leading to gangrene of the large intestine.

The symptoms of adhesions may vary considerably; they can range from recurrent attacks of abdominal pain to complete obstruction of the large intestine with pain, constipation, and abdominal distention. Bowel obstruction that is caused by adhesions sometimes corrects itself without surgery. However, if it continues for more than a few hours, surgery is needed to divide the adhesion and to check that the bowel has not become gangrenous (see Gangrene). Adhesions after an abdominal operation cannot be prevented, so some people tend to experience recurrent problems from adhesions.

Peritonitis

A third disease that can affect the peritoneum is peritonitis. The peritoneum becomes inflamed due to infection, irritation because of harmful substances, or injury. The main symptom is pain, which differs from other pains in that it is constant and may be very localized. The patient with peritonitis usually lies still and any movement of the abdomen is extremely painful. Even coughing and breathing may cause severe pain in the abdomen. However, patients who take narcotics or steroids may have peritonitis but feel no pain.

With abdominal pain that is due to other causes, such as an obstruction with adhesions, the patient experiences waves

Boxers risk serious injuries, including blows to the abdomen, which can damage internal organs and lead to peritonitis.

Science Photo Library

or from a kick or an automobile accident. Peritonitis can also result from infected fallopian tubes in women, and it can also be a complication of pancreatitis.

Treatment and outlook

The treatment of peritonitis will obviously depend on the underlying cause. Most causes require an operation, but there is one—pancreatitis (diagnosed by a special blood test)—where surgery is considered unnecessary and even dangerous. Because the patient has been vomiting constantly, he or she will be given fluid through an intravenous needle. If an infection is present, antibiotics will be given. A tube is usually passed into the stomach to drain off excess fluid.

Surgery will depend on the cause of peritonitis. If it is caused by appendicitis, the appendix will be removed, and if it is caused by a perforated ulcer, the perforation (hole) will be repaired. After the cause has been dealt with, the abdominal cavity is washed out with warm salt water.

Most people make a complete recovery from peritonitis, and within a few months their health is generally back to normal. Occasionally the patient can be troubled by adhesions that may require further surgery. In cases of peritonitis that involve the peritoneum in the pelvis, women can have problems with fertility, as the fallopian tubes may become blocked. However, this is not always the case (see Infertility).

of pain; when this reaches a peak, he or she may roll around in agony, changing positions frequently. It is very unusual for a patient with peritonitis to do this.

When the peritonitis has been present for some hours, the peritoneum on the outside of the intestine becomes inflamed and the normal movements of the intestines (peristalsis) cease altogether. This is known as paralytic ileus. Eventually, because nothing is passing through the alimentary canal, the stomach fills up with fluid, which will cause the patient to vomit (see Vomiting).

The spread of peritonitis can be prevented by the omentum, which has the property of being able to stick to areas of inflammation, block infection, and prevent it from spreading to the rest of the abdominal cavity.

When a doctor examines a patient for possible peritonitis, he or she looks for lack of movement of the abdominal wall, a feeling of rigidity when the abdomen is pressed on, and an absence of intestinal sounds. The patient may show signs of shock: fast pulse, low blood pressure, and pale and clammy skin (see Shock).

Causes of peritonitis

Peritonitis can be caused by various diseases including acute appendicitis (see Appendicitis). In this condition the appendix becomes inflamed and may rupture, releasing pus into the peritoneal cavity (see Pus). The initial symptoms of pain around the navel are caused by the stretching of the appendix wall, but when the pus is released, the parietal peritoneum

After having survived many hair-raising stunts, the famous escapologist Harry Houdini died of peritonitis after being punched in the stomach.

becomes inflamed; the pain becomes localized to where the pus is, often the lower right side of the abdomen.

If appendicitis is allowed to progress beyond this stage, it may either become blocked off by the omentum and loops of small intestine, leading to the formation of a lump known as an appendix mass, or it may develop into widespread peritonitis. The latter is much more common in young children, probably because the omentum is not fully developed. Peritonitis can have severe or even fatal consequences.

Another cause of peritonitis is a perforated duodenal ulcer (see Ulcers). A tiny hole is made by the ulcer through the wall of the duodenum, so that bile, pancreatic juice, and gastric juice flood out into the space between the visceral and parietal peritoneum. These digestive juices have a corrosive effect, and if the resulting peritonitis is not treated at an early stage, it becomes infected and the patient becomes very ill (possibly fatally) with bacterial peritonitis.

Among the other causes is a condition called perforated diverticulitis (see Diverticulitis); here a diverticulum, a blind-ended sac on the side of the large intestine, ruptures, with consequences similar to those of a ruptured appendix.

Peritonitis can also be caused by an injury to the stomach, such as a stabbing,

---

Symptoms of appendicitis

Early symptoms

- Colicky (gripping) pain in the stomach that comes and goes
- Loss of appetite
- Constipation
- In children, a respiratory infection may show symptoms that imitate appendicitis; these could be genuine

Later symptoms
GET MEDICAL HELP AT ONCE

- More pain in the appendix area (right lower abdomen)
- Pain may move up or down from umbilicus (belly button)
- Slightly raised temperature, e.g., 99.5°F (37.5°C)
- Slight increase in pulse rate

In children, peritonitis can follow very quickly when the appendix ruptures, usually in a matter of hours after the first onset of pain. This is also very serious in a young child, because the omentum, the abdominal policeman, is not well developed, and the infection can spread very rapidly.

Pernicious anemia

Q My mother is starting to look very pale. Could she have pernicious anemia?

A Although all types of anemia make people look very pale, people with pernicious anemia may display other characteristics and symptoms. These include prematurely gray hair and a rather striking lemon-yellow skin color. If your mother's paleness persists, have her see her doctor so that he or she can diagnose the cause and then decide on a treatment.

Q Does pernicious anemia run in families?

A Pernicious anemia is one of a number of diseases where the body's immune (defense) system has turned against some normal part of the body. In pernicious anemia the stomach lining is attacked, thus preventing absorption of vitamin B_{12}. Immune system problems do run in families, but these may vary from family member to family member.

Q My aunt is receiving injections for pernicious anemia. Will the condition correct itself, or will she have to continue treatment?

A Pernicious anemia can be successfully treated by having injections of vitamin B_{12}. These can be given every month or every three months. With these injections your aunt will be totally protected from the effects of the disease. However, the vitamin deficiency will not go away, and she will always need injections.

Q I have been told that I need a bone marrow examination for suspected pernicious anemia. Will it hurt and is it really necessary?

A The normal way of looking at the bone marrow is to extract some from the ilium (one of the pelvic bones) through a short needle. This is done under a local anesthetic. Doctors can tell from the blood film if you have pernicious anemia, but the bone marrow will confirm the diagnosis.

At one time pernicious anemia, as its name implies, was a fatal disease of unknown origin. Now it can be controlled by lifelong vitamin B_{12} injections.

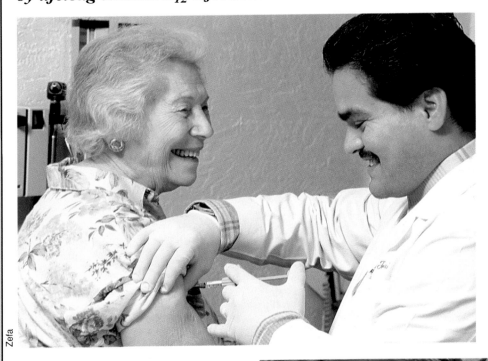

Zefa

Regular injections of vitamin B_{12} (above) keep patients with pernicious anemia healthy. People who eat a lot of raw fish (right) are particularly vulnerable to vitamin B_{12} deficiency because the fish may contain a tapeworm that absorbs the body's supply.

It would be difficult to invent a disease that causes both severe anemia (see Anemia) and disorders in the nervous system simply by attacking the lining of the stomach. Nevertheless, pernicious anemia is just such a disease.

Causes

Pernicious anemia results from the formation of antibodies by the body's own immune (defense) system to the cells that line the stomach. As a result, no intrinsic factor (the substance vitamin B_{12} depends on it for its absorption) is produced, and because of this a vitamin B_{12} deficiency occurs. The bone marrow needs both vitamin B_{12} and folic acid to make an adequate number of red blood cells; when either is deficient the number of red blood cells is reduced, and those remaining are larger and more irregular in shape than normal (megaloblastic anemia). Also a lack of vitamin B_{12} usually results in a reduction in the number of white (infection-fighting) blood cells (see Blood).

Alan Dunns

Although pernicious anemia only refers to the disease that is caused by the production of antibodies to the stomach lining, there are other reasons why the body may run short of vitamin B$_{12}$ and folic acid. The human body contains about 3 mg of vitamin B, and the average daily requirement is only one-thousandth of this. Vitamin B$_{12}$ is only found in food of animal origin, so strict vegetarians who never eat anything of animal origin may run short of this vitamin, but otherwise a dietary deficiency is rare (see Vitamin B).

People can also become deficient in vitamin B$_{12}$ if they have an operation to remove their stomachs; this may result in a shortage of intrinsic factor. Intestinal disease may also produce pernicious anemia, particularly if the ileum (the last part of the small intestine where vitamin B$_{12}$ is absorbed) is involved. An inflammation of the intestine called Crohn's disease is the most common reason for this.

Folic acid deficiency can be due to a lack of fresh vegetables in the diet. Intestinal disease causes folic acid deficiency much more commonly than it causes vitamin B$_{12}$ deficiency. Folic acid may also be lacking in pregnant women, who should take a folic acid supplement.

Symptoms and dangers
Symptoms include paleness, lethargy, tiredness, and breathlessness. Nosebleeds

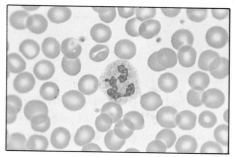

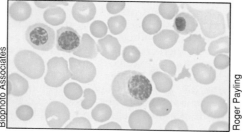

Biophoto Associates

Roger Payling

may also occur, and in severe cases, heart failure. In addition to the symptoms of anemia, patients also show other characteristic features, such as prematurely gray hair and yellow skin.

Pernicious anemia develops over a long period of time; the level of hemoglobin (the red oxygen-carrying pigment in the red blood cells) falls very slowly and the body is able to adjust to its effects. Often the hemoglobin level has to get to a very low level before it becomes apparent.

Without treatment anemia that is due to any cause may be fatal. However, death

In comparison with normal blood (top left), the red blood cells in pernicious anemia are large and irregular, and the white blood cells are more segmented (above left). Typical sufferers have prematurely gray hair and pale or yellow skin (above).

is unusual because the condition is easy to recognize, and can be treated promptly by giving the patient a blood transfusion (see Blood transfusion).

In pernicious anemia, because it affects the cells that line the stomach, there is also a loss of the normal hydrochloric acid production. Although this does not produce many symptoms, there may be a slightly increased risk of stomach cancer.

Perhaps the most serious complication of pernicious anemia is its effect on the nervous system. A lack of vitamin B$_{12}$ causes problems in the spinal cord that result in failure of those parts of the cord that carry sensation from the legs to the brain. There is a tingling in the legs, followed by a numbness, weakness, and difficulty with balance (see Spinal cord). In the later stages the arms are also affected. This complication (subacute combined degeneration of the cord) responds to treatment with vitamin B$_{12}$ injections, which are given to patients regularly.

Pernicious anemia should never be treated with folic acid, because although this corrects the anemia, it allows the neurological problems to get worse.

Treatment and outlook
With pernicious anemia the missing vitamin B$_{12}$ has to be given on a regular basis (either monthly or every three months) by injection. Since the cause of the vitamin deficiency is the stomach's failure to secrete intrinsic factor (a disorder that will never improve) the treatment lasts for life. However, patients who have regular vitamin B$_{12}$ injections should remain completely well.

Zefa

Personality

Q I've been told that the first five years of a child's life are critical in terms of the formation of personality. Is this true?

A Yes. Think of a baby as a piece of blotting paper: he or she is constantly absorbing information, and is more sensitive to his or her environment than at any time in the future. Thus a child who has been overprotected in the first five years will tend to be hesitant about making contact with other people later in life; or if a child was not given enough affection in the first two years, he or she is likely to be stunted in his or her emotional responsiveness.

Studies have revealed patterns that illustrate this. It has been shown that patterns of behavior seem to repeat themselves over generations. For example, mothers who were cared for in a sensitive and intelligent way tend to find it easier to give this sort of mothering to their children, who will, in turn, develop the same sensitivity.

The other, more disquieting, side of the coin shows that parents who physically damage their children tend to pass on the same patterns of behavior: their children might well become the same sort of parents. It seems that such parents have a lower sense of their own worth and find it hard to make their children feel valued.

Q What is meant by a criminal personality? Are there certain traits that make a person more likely to turn to crime?

A There is a school of thought that maintains that certain personality characteristics are more prevalent among hardened criminals of both sexes than among noncriminals. The criminal type tends to be antisocial, impulsive, and cares little for the feelings of other people, as might be expected. This type of person also tends to be very extrovert and unusually emotional. The sum of these qualities may add up to a criminal personality, if such a term can be defined, but remember that in personality there are no hard and fast rules.

Your personality is what makes you different from everyone else. What you inherit and what you experience are factors that influence its development.

Personality is often defined as the more or less constant pattern of behavior and way of thinking and feeling that characterizes an individual. By and large an individual's personality remains much the same throughout life: a happy-go-lucky child develops into an optimistic adult, whereas a timid youngster generally maintains his or her reserve as he or she gets older, unless powerful influences combine to alter his or her apprehensions. This is not to say that an individual cannot modify his or her personality if he or she really wants to, but the process can take considerable effort over a long period of time.

In any family it is normal for the children to have different personalities: the boisterous and outgoing child is quite normal, and so is her quiet, reflective sister.

Traits of personality

Perhaps the most easily noticed parts of personality are character traits, which are qualities that a person exhibits under certain circumstances. Honesty, meanness, perseverance, kindness, stubbornness, patience, courage, and modesty are all examples of character traits, and although a person may be said to possess a given trait, he or she will not, and is not expected to, display that trait in every situation.

A man may be scrupulously honest in all his business deals, yet may take office stationery home without a second thought. A woman may be generous to neighbors and friends, yet be unexpectedly thrifty to the point of meanness toward her own family. A child may be highly aggressive at school, yet meek and mild in his or her home. In spite of such

variabilities, however, these qualities are often regarded as part of the permanent personality if they occur regularly.

Roles

The roles we play in life are not attributes of personality in themselves, but they very much affect when and where we display various traits in our personality. A man may find that, in his role of sales manager at work, to survive he has to be aggressive, dominating, and quick to make firm decisions without consultation; at home, however, these qualities might be almost absent. His sales team would regard him as dominant in personality, whereas his wife may even think of him as submissive. The different roles he plays make each quality apparently very real parts of his personality.

Society encourages people to play roles by supporting them when they fit the stereotype for that role. A politician who sometimes said that his opposing party had done something good would soon be out of a job, whatever the facts of the matter; a mother who freely admitted that she felt no affection for her newborn child would be branded as an inhuman

The Kobal Collection

Some actors and actresses can submerge themselves totally in the parts they play to project a different personality in every film. Tom Cruise has this gift. Some TV stars, such as Oprah Winfrey, project a particular personality on screen, which may be very different from their off-screen personality.

monster, even if she later added the saving line "but of course I love her/him very much now." Sadly, counselors not infrequently have to deal with clients whose personality lies more in the role that society has given them than in traits that they possess themselves (see Therapy).

Zefa

Personality types

Since the display of a wide range of different traits is a matter of occasion and circumstances, many scientists have looked for broader classifications that describe a person better and more consistently. Perhaps the simplest classification is that developed by the English psychologist Hans Eysenck, who has reduced the variables to just three: extroversion (as opposed to introversion), emotionality (versus stability), and tough-mindedness (as against tender-mindedness). Everyone has these qualities to some extent, but the usefulness of

Q I keep on hearing the term *split personality*. Is there really such a thing?

A Yes, but it is rare. People with this condition behave in radically different ways at different times, almost as if more than one person inhabited the same body. Strictly speaking the condition is known as multiple personality. Although it is sometimes confused with schizophrenia (which means "split mind"), split personality has nothing at all to do with that condition. In schizophrenia the speech and thought processes are often split up and confused, whereas in multiple personality each personality within the same body is lucid and coherent.

Q Why do some people become so violent when they are drunk? My boyfriend seems to turn into a different person when he's had a few drinks, and I become very afraid of him.

A Aggression is a powerful element in every personality. It shows itself more in some people than in others, and most of us succeed in keeping it in check. But alcohol seems to release, or relax, these control mechanisms, and latent aggression sometimes emerges. In large quantities alcohol also clouds judgment and has a depressant action, which may put the drinker in a bad mood. These three effects combine to produce a cocktail, which can, as you say, make your boyfriend seem like a different person.

Q Do twins have the same personalities?

A Identical twins develop from the same egg, are of the same sex, and resemble each other very closely, suggesting an identical genetic program. Fraternal twins develop from two separate eggs, are not necessarily of the same sex, and may not resemble each other physically at all. It does seem to be the case that identical twins are far more similar in personality than are fraternal twins, who may be completely different from each other in personality.

The games children play often reflect their personalities. When dressing up, an extrovert child, such as the girl above, will usually choose flamboyant clothes that attract attention.

Eysenck's system is that, instead of saying a person is or is not an introvert, for example, the qualities can be estimated on a rating scale, giving an idea of how extroverted, emotional, or tough-minded a person actually is.

It is also possible to show that these qualities are related to a person's speed of learning and various other phenomena that, on the surface, seem to have little to do with personality itself. This sort of evidence implies that these three personality factors are real in themselves, rather than something observed by one person in one situation, as can happen with traits such as courage, honesty, and so on. This means that the qualities could be inbuilt, and can be likened to continuous pressures that move a person to act in a certain way. Even when there may be circumstances in which, say, the emotional person finds it better to go against his or her natural inclinations, the pressure will be there.

Inherited or acquired?

Anyone who has brought up more than one child will be aware that children from the same family can show very different personalities almost from the moment they are born. This implies that some aspects of personality are probably innate and may be determined genetically (see Genetics). Since parents can, unknowingly, bring up successive children in very different ways, researchers have studied to what extent identical twins (who develop from a single egg and therefore have an identical genetic program) raised together have similar personalities. Results show that identical twins are much more similar than fraternal twins (who develop from separate eggs) or nontwin siblings in their measures of emotionality, activity, sociability, and tough-mindedness.

This suggests that in some respects personality is a matter of inheritance, but this should not be thought of as the only factor, or even the most important factor, that determines an individual's personality. Rather, many facets of our personality are heavily influenced by our experiences in life. Personality similarities between fraternal twins, who generally have much the same upbringing but different genetic influences, show clearly the influence of upbringing. At the same time, the different ways in which we behave in various circumstances show that we can change certain aspects of our personalities if we have to (see Environment).

Abnormal personalities
One of the interesting consequences of measuring individuals' degrees of extroversion, emotionality, and so on is the discovery that many of the mental illnesses and conditions dealt with by psychiatrists are associated with extremes of one or more of the personality characteristics described by Eysenck's tests. Neurotic conditions, such as phobias, obsessions, and compulsive behavior, are generally associated with extreme emotionality (see Neuroses). In addition, people who tend to become depressed often show the same high emotionality combined with very low extroversion (in other words, with high introversion).

Hysterical people show high emotionality combined with very high levels of extroversion (see Hysteria).

Psychotic individuals, such as psychopaths and schizophrenics, differ from neurotic, depressive, or hysterical individuals in that

they are often unexceptional in their degree of emotionality and extroversion. However, they are rated as extreme for tough-mindedness, so much so that the scale for tough-mindedness is actually called the psychoticism scale. Many criminals, incidentally, rate surprisingly high on all three variables.

Those hardy souls who sail single-handed around the world must have an unusual degree of self-reliance to endure the stark loneliness of months on end at sea on their own. Sir Francis Chichester (inset) on his famous solo circumnavigation on his yacht Gypsy Moth IV.

Changing personality

To some extent, all forms of psychotherapy are concerned with modifying how a person acts, thinks, and feels. This, by definition, is changing an individual's personality. A marital or other relationship problem may, at least in part, be caused by a so-called clash of personalities, and its solution may involve getting the partners to change the way they behave, think, and feel (see Psychotherapy).

Phobias and similar problems are often treated by reducing the anxieties of the person in question (see Anxiety). If this is achieved, the patient will, on any personality questionnaire, seem less emotional—this aspect of his or her personality will have been changed.

One curious fact arises when attempting such changes. The neurosis of a shy, reserved introvert is easier to cure than a similar condition in a brash, outgoing extrovert. This also means that it is generally easier to change an introvert into something of an extrovert than it is to quiet an extrovert and give him or her the reflectiveness of an introvert.

Influences on personality

It has already been mentioned that personality is modified as a person matures, but other influences can also have effects of varying magnitude. Long periods of stress will increase emotionality and aggressiveness, and may also make the individual more reserved (see Stress). Patterns of upbringing will also have some effect on a child's personality, although it is not easy to predict what the effect might be. For example, a child may follow the pattern set by one or both parents, or may rebel completely against both. Certainly parental influence is a very important factor, particularly in the

It is sometimes suggested that personality is predetermined by the astrological sign under which a person is born. Is it possible, however, that people who believe this tend to modify their behavior in order to fit their astrological profile?

first five years of a child's life. Studies have shown that some patterns are even repeated in succeeding generations.

There is also no doubt that personality in its widest sense can be affected by the long-term effects of alcohol or drugs, by traumatic shock, and by brain injury (see Drug abuse). What is surprising, however, is just how constant the broad outlines of an individual's personality stay even when he or she is faced with powerful outside influences. The leopard does not so much change its spots under duress, it merely changes how it displays them.

CLARKSTON